HOLMAN HAMILTON

Prologue to Conflict

The Crisis and Compromise
of 1850

The Norton Library
W · W · NORTON & COMPANY · INC ·
NEW YORK

PREFACE

CRISIS AND conflict have held abundant and often tragic meaning for Americans. More frequently than not, and certainly during the Civil War Centennial, the country's concern with the past has been concentrated mainly on wars and combatants rather than on forces, situations, and men that have made wars possible or inevitable. Generals and colonels are the preferred protagonists; battles and campaigns, the settings of the action. It is part of the purpose of this study to show that a national peacetime crisis and a compromise stemming from it possessed dramatic qualities of their own, equal to—though different from—those of war itself.

Most people who know something about the give and take of 1850 correctly identify the year with the names of Clay, Calhoun, and Webster. That is fine so far as it goes. But it would be well for more students and general readers to place proper emphasis on the roles of others, notably Stephen A. Douglas, Zachary Taylor, Millard Fillmore, and William Wilson Corcoran, who were part of an impressive company of leading men who made positive or negative contributions along the path to compromise. This book contains a reevaluation of celebrated and half-forgotten figures, provides a perspective for what they did and said, and reassesses the strategy and tactics of Northerners and Southerners, Easterners and Westerners, Democrats and Whigs in that great debate of 1850.

To do this, neglected manuscripts have been consulted. Special note has been taken of the effectiveness of lobbying activities. The House of Representatives has been accorded its proper place; minimized in nearly all accounts, the House—not the Senate—saw the decisive moves in late August and early September. An effort has been made, on the one hand, to treat the events of 1850 as they were seen by people of the time by stressing contemporary views, labels familiar in 1850, and the actual words and phrases of men who knew Jefferson Davis as a United States senator and Abraham Lincoln (if at all) as an erstwhile, single-term member of the House. Finally, on the other hand, the Compromise of 1850 is viewed within the context of present day historical scholarship by bringing to bear upon it materials unknown or unperceived at the time and by seeing it as the result of the interplay of various forces—sectional, national, and economic.

Prologue to Conflict is the beneficiary of aid contributed by so many individuals and institutions that to list them all would be to make unreasonable demands upon the publisher. The author, however, takes this opportunity to express his heartfelt gratitude to historians, librarians, archivists, personal friends, kinsmen, and many other generous associates for facts, interpretations, and encouragement through the years. He acknowledges with deep devotion the inspiration of his beloved wife, Suzanne Bowerfind Hamilton. The kindnesses of colleagues at the University of Kentucky, particularly Professor Thomas D. Clark, are likewise abidingly appreciated. Thanks, too, are extended to the University of Kentucky Research Fund Committee, which financed a part of the essential travel and research.

Lexington, Kentucky   H. H.
November 20, 1963

CONTENTS

MAPS

CHAPTER I

Forty-Nine and Forty-Niners

.⟞⟞⟨⟨O⟩⟩⟝⟝.

ALL THREE hundred and sixty-five days immediately preceding 1850 are linked in the thinking of
many Americans with a single spectacular event.
Gold had been discovered in California, and the Gold Rush
of 1849 saw thousands of adventurous spirits cross the
Isthmus or round the Horn or traverse the western plains
and deserts in quest of quick riches in El Dorado.

In San Francisco and Sacramento and along the Tuol-
umne and Mokelumne rivers, men from New York and
Philadelphia mingled with Southerners and New Eng-
landers in the scramble for sudden fortunes with the magic
of pick and pan. Sprawling settlements with descriptive
names—Mormon Gulch, Yankee Jim's, Old Dry Diggings,
Hangtown, Rough and Ready, Angel's Camp—mushroomed
near the realm of Spanish languor, tolling bells, and un-
scarred space.[1] The color, bluff, and violence of the Gold
Rush have been depicted so often on screen and stage and
in books that they are familiar the world over.

It is ironic that other aspects of the goldrush year and its
successor are not nearly as well known. So dramatic are
accounts of these forty-niners and the gold fever impelling

them westward that one tends to forget other forty-niners
involved in no less memorable events. While the tens of
thousands in the West sifted gravel for the glint of gold,
hundreds of thousands "way back East" found release for
their own pent-up energies through outlets perhaps more
significant in the sweep and drift of history.

2

THE UNITED STATES in 1849 was home to nineteen and a
half million people—nineteen and a half million who were
white and free. Three and a half million more, ebony to
"high yellow," were cotton pickers, coachmen, waiters, body
servants, workers in sugar, rice, and hemp; except for not
quite a half million free Negroes, all these were slaves—the
property of citizens.[2] Negro "bucks" and "wenches," their
parents and their children, presented serious political problems which had social or economic overtones. From diverse
points of view white men argued testily about slavery's
virtues and slavery's demerits. Consciences, pocketbooks,
and partisan exigencies frequently determined opinions that
were less objective than their adherents imagined.

Antislavery attitudes, in great measure, were part of a
general wave of reform. Shakers, spiritualists, Millerites,
converts of all sorts and denominations of all shades
typified a trend away from religious orthodoxy. Social
reformers like Neal Dow of Maine directed crusades against
the demon rum. From pulpit and platform, orators struck
with invective against redlight districts and gambling hells.

[1] Joseph H. Jackson, *Anybody's Gold* (New York, 1941), 20-26,
421-22; John W. Caughey, *California* (New York, 1953), 239-58;
Julian Dana, *The Sacramento: River of Gold* (New York, 1939), 122.
[2] J.D.B. De Bow, *Statistical View of the United States . . . Being
a Compendium of the Seventh Census* (Washington, 1854), 45, 63,
82. The 1850 census figures have been presented in round numbers,
as there was no census in 1849.

Phrenology was popular and competed with vegetarianism and free love in attracting prophets and cultists. Pacifism had its fanatics, with the learned blacksmith Elihu Burritt one of its ablest champions. Communitarian experiments, modeled on Brook Farm or New Harmony, flourished for a year or a decade. This was also the gaudy day of Amelia Bloomer, when "putting pants on females" became a cartoon theme. And in 1848 a large gathering at Seneca Falls, New York, had spoken for the rights of women and particularly the right to vote.

It was an age when newspapers abounded. The personal journalist, scribbling in his sanctum, usually made little money from his enterprise but evidently derived some compensation from his forays into print. In an atmosphere where license impinged on liberty of the press and in a moral climate where each ism had its champion, it was inevitable that such fanatics as extreme antislavery men would trespass on propriety and even on patriotism. William Lloyd Garrison, bitterly determined, took the position in the Boston *Liberator* that even constitutional safeguards of slavery must not block immediate abolition.[3] Gamaliel Bailey's *National Era* in Washington was calmer than the *Liberator* and perhaps as influential. Bailey opened his drawing room at the nation's capital to antislavery people of every stripe. He seemed especially happy to print the articles and books of women like Harriet Beecher Stowe and, two years hence, would serialize the first publication of *Uncle Tom's Cabin.*[4]

Political, philanthropic, and literary interests frequently overlapped in 1849. Poets like John Greenleaf Whittier and Henry Wadsworth Longfellow, poet-essayists like Ralph

[3] Alice F. Tyler, *Freedom's Ferment: Phases of American Social History to 1860* (Minneapolis, 1944), 175-224, 346-47, 419-512; Arthur Y. Lloyd, *The Slavery Controversy, 1831-1860* (Chapel Hill, N.C., 1939), 52, 62-65.

[4] Forrest Wilson, *Crusader in Crinoline: The Life of Harriet Beecher Stowe* (Philadelphia, 1941), 259-68.

Waldo Emerson, and poet-journalists like William Cullen
Bryant were counted in the antislavery camp. As editor
of the New York *Evening Post*, Bryant expressed ideas
similar to ex-President Martin Van Buren's. Emerson, a
celebrated lecturer, also opposed slavery's extension. Whittier and James Russell Lowell persistently attacked the
institution.[5] Not every writer, however, saw eye to eye
with such zealots as Whittier. Nathaniel Hawthorne, who
was dismissed in 1849 from the customs surveyorship in
Salem, Massachusetts, shortly thereafter wrote *The Scarlet
Letter* which had nothing to do with chattel slavery. Edgar
Allan Poe, a Southerner, who died that October, never
evinced much interest in the topic. Walt Whitman detested
slavery but, like Bryant, was no Garrisonian.[6] An examination of the major writers of the period would show that
antislavery sentiments by no means dominated the literary
scene.

3

JUST AS THE extremes of antislavery feeling had not pre-
empted all literature, so the wave of reform in the northern
states left many a businessman virtually untouched. The
miller, the chandler, the druggist, the banker, and the dry
goods merchant thought primarily in terms of profit and
investment. Those rural Americans who planted corn on
the rocky slopes of Vermont or harvested wheat in the
fertile quarter-sections of Illinois had just as little time for
agitation. Although many opposed the extension of slavery
into new western areas acquired from Mexico, this was not

[5] Howard R. Floan, *The South in Northern Eyes, 1831 to 1861*
(Austin, Texas, 1958), 24-25, 41-43, 54-55, 71-73, 149-51; Richmond
C. Beatty, *James Russell Lowell* (Nashville, Tenn., 1942), 75-93.
[6] Floan, *The South in Northern Eyes*, 83-85, 133-44, 167-72;
Ralph H. Gabriel, *The Course of American Democratic Thought*
(New York, 1956), 74-75, 128-29.

thought of as interfering with slavery in the southern states. There is no evidence that the average farmer or city dweller was an abolitionist or any other kind of radical in 1849.

In manufacturing and in commerce, there was a direct connection between northern profits and southern crops. The textile industry of Massachusetts depended on cotton produced by slave labor. New York merchants sold luxury items and plantation necessities to wealthy Southerners, who might be owners of fifty or five hundred blacks. The reliance of northern summer resorts on the patronage of southern families was only one facet of the sections' socio-economic interdependence. Northerners not only did business with Southerners but often looked on approvingly as their children chose mates from across the Mason-Dixon Line. The fact that the country was still young and the Northwest and Southwest had much in common was a bond of union. Although President Zachary Taylor owned over a hundred slaves, he had lived nearly as long in the Northwest as in the Southwest and was nationalistic to the core.[7]

It may be that industrial developments were a more fundamental cause of sectional friction than the annexation of Texas, the Mexican War, or the ardor of reformers and seers. Slowly the agricultural society, which Thomas Jefferson had valued so highly and on which he depended for democracy's development, was giving way in the North to mechanization and the urban growth that machinery bred. The tariffs sought by Massachusetts, Pennsylvania, and New Jersey were based on industries' demands and came into conflict with southern agriculture. The average white Southerner, however, seemed relatively satisfied with things as they were. If upcountry yeomen and their way of life appeared to be separated by a social curtain from the planter and his plantation, these two most important free southern elements were not without their community of

[7] Holman Hamilton, *Zachary Taylor: Soldier in the White House* (Indianapolis, 1951), 31, 386, 399-400, 408-10, 419.

interest.[8] Both planter and farmer were rural. Each had
fierce local and regional pride, and each responded favor-
ably to low-tariff doctrines of southern theorists and politicians. Other southern whites—the banker, the factor, the
lawyer, the physician, the merchant—usually shared the
attitude of farmers or planters who were their neighbors.
Frequently, too, the doctor himself was a planter and a
master of slaves. The factor might have an investment in
cotton, the attorney in sugar, the banker in hemp. Some
lived in columned mansions on their own plantations.
Others were absentee owners who delegated control of soil
and slaves to overseers. Whether they resided in town or
in the country—owning no Negroes or two, ten, or a hundred, most of the white people of the South accepted
slavery.

There were moves toward industrialism in the South.
The first United States railroad had been initiated in
South Carolina. William Gregg was producing cotton
clothing at Graniteville in that state, where he paid his
operatives an average weekly wage of three dollars and
five cents.[9] Edward McGehee of Mississippi, planter, phi-
lanthropist, and manufacturer-to-be, was a builder of the
West Feliciana Railroad on which a slave was the engi-
neer.[10] But the average planter was not industry-minded.
The average farmer let well enough alone. With incidental
exceptions, the South's society remained almost as rural
as when Jefferson was still expounding his ideas at Monti-
cello and Poplar Forest.

Qualities that appealed to Yankees—the aggressiveness,
the commercialism of the North—might not be present in

[8] Frank L. Owsley, *Plain Folk of the Old South* (Baton Rouge, La.,
1949), 5, 7, 133-34.

[9] Charles S. Sydnor, *The Development of Southern Sectionalism,
1819-1848* (Baton Rouge, La., 1948), 267-69; Broadus Mitchell,
William Gregg: Factory Master of the Old South (Chapel Hill, N.C.,
1928), 34.

[10] Charles S. Sydnor, *Slavery in Mississippi* (New York, 1933), 7,
24-25, 208-209, 233.

most of the South, but southern men and women did not
miss them. In contrast to the crush on the crowded side-
walks of New York, the peace and ease of the southern
landholder seemed precious indeed and well worth defending.[11] Pain and privation, of course, were present.
Northern and international bankers, with their strident
agents and their discount rates, intruded as disturbingly on
southern happiness as did the spectre of servile insurrec-
tion. Still, residents of Georgia, Alabama, Mississippi, and
Louisiana loved their region. Some southern forty-niners
trekked to California, and some of their brothers or cousins
clamored and schemed for jobs from the Washington Whig
regime. Most, however, remained content in the fields
where the cotton and sugar cane grew, where rice was
cultivated, where hogs were raised by Negro farm workers,
and where timber was cut and piled on the banks for use
as river packets' fuel.

4

If SOUTHERNERS as a whole were pleased with their land
and institutions, most men of the North—while preferring
their own section—were not disposed to interfere with
slavery in states where it was constitutionally protected.
There had been considerable objection before and during
1845, however, to the annexation of Texas in that year. For
annexing Texas had meant the addition to the Union of a
huge southwestern state where slavery was legal, and
slavery's *spread* was something to which large numbers of
Northerners were emotionally and politically opposed. This
opposition increased and began to be more strident during

[11] Lady Emmeline Stuart Wortley, *Travels in the United States
. . . during 1849 and 1850* (New York, 1855), 146: "Nothing and
nobody seem to stand still for half a moment in New York; the
multitudinous omnibuses, which drive like insane vehicles from morning till night, appear not to pause to take up their passengers."

the War with Mexico, which many in the North regarded
as a war brought on largely by southern expansionists.
Hostilities officially ended in February of 1848 with the
Treaty of Guadalupe Hidalgo, as a result of which approxi-
mately one-fifth of the United States of 1849 was ac-
quired by the victors. Then known as California, New
Mexico, and Deseret, the acquisitions eventually became
the modern states of California, Nevada, Utah, most of
Arizona and New Mexico, and parts of Colorado and
Wyoming.

Eighteen months before the signing of the treaty, the
Wilmot Proviso was first introduced, a move which came
to symbolize the hardening insistence of many Northerners
that slavery should not be permitted to expand. In the
House of Representatives, the Pennsylvania Democrat
David Wilmot tacked a fateful amendment onto a special
appropriation bill. This provided that the then President
James K. Polk, head of a Democratic administration, could
not have essential governmental funds unless slavery were
prohibited on any soil to be obtained from the enemy.
Although the specification never passed the Senate, the
House approved it a number of times—and the idea dominated many a debate. Wilmot himself left the Democratic
ranks to join such northern leaders as former Democratic
President Martin Van Buren in the new Free Soil party,
which in 1848 attracted several hundred thousand ex-Whigs
and ex-Democrats. The Pennsylvanian's action in Congress
also evoked pro-Proviso resolutions from fourteen of the
fifteen free-state legislatures. And the very names of
"Wilmot" and "Proviso" became red flags to irate Southerners, naturally resentful of any attempt to impede slavery's
extension into the new West.[12]

[12] Justin H. Smith, *The War with Mexico* (2 vols., New York,
1919), I, 58-261, 370-400, II, 17-188, 233-52; Robert S. Henry, *The
Story of the Mexican War* (Indianapolis, 1950), 15-63, 138-89, 238-
91; Herman V. Ames (ed.), *State Documents on Federal Relations*
(Philadelphia, 1900-1906), 241-78.

Although decisions made by the two major parties in the 1848 presidential contest were related to the problem of reconciling northern feeling against the growth of slave territory with southern fears for sectional equality, they did not solve it. Fundamental weaknesses in the Whig high command went back as far as ten or fifteen years, and the necessity of turning to a military hero was indicative of those intrinsic flaws. The White House claims of oft-defeated Henry Clay, of Senator Daniel Webster, and of other Whig civilians were set aside when the Whig National Convention nominated Zachary Taylor, the military man who had become popular at Palo Alto, Resaca de la Palma, Monterey, and Buena Vista. Running against Taylor was Lewis Cass, a Democratic politician from Michigan and (like Taylor) a veteran of the War of 1812. Both parties were even more corroded by factionalism than is customarily the case, and observers saw that strictly partisan allegiances were unquestionably conditioned by the broad stripe of sectionalism that appeared in many states.

The real issue in 1848 may best be summarized as follows: Would the lands in the West, recently Mexican, be open to slaveholders and their slaves—or would the vast areas become free territories and, subsequently, free states? But the issue was beclouded by the major-party candidates, who understood that their main aim was to win the election and hence felt they had to appeal in the same breath to both northern and southern voters. Cass fell back on his doctrine of popular sovereignty, which was designed to take pro- or antislavery judgments out of the control of Congress and leave them up to residents of the affected western regions. Taylor, too, failed to speak out boldly. Promising not to employ the veto power except on con-stitutional grounds, he depended on that assurance to woo Proviso-minded Northerners with their majority in the House of Representatives—while relying on his southern residence and his southern economic interests to persuade fellow Southerners that he was with them in mind and spirit. Van Buren, the Free Soilers' presidential nominee, was utterly unlike Cass and Taylor in that he explicitly opposed slavery's extension. The Free Soil effort was consequential because of its effect on the Whig and Democratic totals. Van Buren, however, had no chance of winning the race because the Free Soil party was too new and too loosely organized to disrupt all established voting habits of the masses.

In the November election, Whigs and Democrats each carried fifteen states. Taylor triumphed in the extremely close contest because he managed to secure a popular plurality in the North, a popular majority in the South, and with them a majority in the electoral college. Had Taylor lost either New York or Pennsylvania, Cass would have won in the nation, and this almost certainly would have been the outcome if Van Buren's Free Soil party had not split the New York Democratic vote.[13] The fact that Taylor's victory depended so significantly upon a combination of causes, together with the slenderness of his margin and the absence of clarity in his campaign, foreshadowed serious difficulties for the old Indian fighter in Washington.

5

NOT ONLY DID Taylor have no clear mandate from the people, but his presidential term could not avoid being affected by a growing conviction on the part of some Southerners that the North was bent on reducing them to a minority status. This sentiment dominated the thoughts of South Carolina's John C. Calhoun. In his "Southern Address" of January 1849, the Carolinian underscored the

[13] Hamilton, *Zachary Taylor*, 54-62, 70-133; Frank B. Woodford, *Lewis Cass: The Last Jeffersonian* (New Brunswick, N.J., 1950), 251-71.

North's "systematic agitation" against slavery itself. Here
he was hammering at the abolitionists. But Calhoun included other sectional grievances involving larger ·numbers
of Northerners: denial of the principle of equal rights in
the West, opposition to slavery in the District of Columbia,
and northern states' failures to help Southerners recover
Negroes who ran away from southern farms and plantations. Calhoun's Address likewise stated that a militant
North was attempting to destroy the very institution of
slavery through ultimate emancipation or war.[14]

While most southern Whigs and Democrats were less
aroused than Calhoun, almost all had grown up aware of
dangers—actual and potential—in northern attitudes toward
chattel slavery. It was true that slaveholding George Washington, more than threescore years before 1849, had hoped
to "see a plan adopted for the abolition" of slavery. "There
is only one proper and effectual mode by which it can be
accomplished, and that is by Legislative authority," the First
President had written, "and this, as far as my suffrage will
go, shall never be wanting." But when "happy" slaves are
"seduced" to leave their masters, and when tampering with
master-slave relationships "begets discontent on one side
and resentment on the other," even a humanitarian purpose
"introduces more evils than it can cure."[15]

In 1820, slaveholding Thomas Jefferson had described the
Missouri issue of that year as "a fire bell in the night"
which "awakened and filled me with terror." When men
talked of admitting Missouri into the Union as a slave state
and Maine as a free state and of excluding slavery from the
Louisiana Purchase north of 36°30' with the exception of
Missouri, Jefferson had considered the knell of the Union
hushed. "But this is a reprieve only, not a final sentence,"

[14] Charles M. Wiltse, *John C. Calhoun: Sectionalist, 1840-1850*
(Indianapolis, 1951), 378-88; *Niles' National Register* (Philadelphia),
February 14, 1849.
[15] John C. Fitzpatrick (ed.), *The Writings of George Washington*
(39 vols., Washington, 1931-1944), XXVIII, 407-408.

wrote Jefferson. "A geographical line, coinciding with a
marked principle, moral and political, once conceived and
held up to the angry passions of men, will never be oblit-
erated; and every new irritation will mark it deeper and
deeper." Jefferson had feared another Peloponnesian War
or a servile war. Together with James Madison and James
Monroe, the author of the Declaration of Independence
had reacted to the Missouri Controversy not as a liberal,
not as an apostle of the Enlightenment, but as a Southerner.
Thus he revealed to some extent the depth of southern
feeling.[16]

Although the years from 1820 to 1849 had come and gone
without the war foreseen by Jefferson, irritations remained
and (true to the Jeffersonian prophecy) marked the geographical line deeper and deeper. In 1832, nullification had
dramatized the discontent with which South Carolina
viewed the "Tariff of Abominations." The new tariff law
adopted in 1833 had contained provisions of moderation
reminiscent of the Missouri Compromise. But the abolition
movement, the fact and fancy of Negro insurrections, and
debates over the right of petition kept politics in a whirl.
Now a new and explosive element was added with the
question of containing slavery within fifteen states or allow-
ing it to expand in the West. Calhoun, deeply distrustful
of what President Taylor and Congress might do or fail to
do, used his influence to develop opinion in favor of holding
a southern convention. With dark forebodings, throughout
the spring and summer of 1849, he and others were to
correspond in detail on the subject. Kindred spirits were
found in Mississippi, and from that state in October of 1849
a call went forth for a sectional gathering in Nashville, Tennessee, the following June. All states where slavery was
legal, from Delaware to Texas, would be urged to send
delegates to the Nashville Convention—men reflecting the

[16] Paul L. Ford (ed.), *The Works of Thomas Jefferson* (12 vols.,
New York, 1904-1905), XII, 158; Glover Moore, *The Missouri Controversy, 1819-1821* (Lexington, Ky., 1953), 251-56.

convictions of southern voters and empowered to announce them to the country at large.[17]

6

WHILE THIS PLAN was being formulated and while tenseness increased in many quarters, there was no end of speculation regarding the probable policies of the new President. In background and in personality, Zachary Taylor was far from being a typical chief executive. In his day, he was unique in that he entered the White House without political experience of any kind in either elective or appointive civil office. Taylor had been a soldier during most of his adult life. Born in Virginia in 1784, he was taken to Kentucky as an infant and there he grow to manhood. A first lieutenant in 1808, his final promotion—to the grade of major general—occurred shortly after his second battle with the Mexicans. Spending nearly forty years in camp and field, the veteran of the frontier force never had been a state legislator, a congressman, a diplomat, a governor, or a Cabinet member.

Following his defeat of Cass and Van Buren, Taylor was confronted by a variety of vexing problems. The usual presidential challenge of Cabinet construction proved especially difficult for him, since he was personally acquainted with only a few of his party's leaders and ill feeling separated him from the two most influential Whigs—Clay and Webster. He also faced the disagreeable likelihood that, when Congress would convene in December of 1849, he could depend on a Whig majority neither in the Senate nor in the House of Representatives. Taylor's most serious handicap, however, lay in politicians' and voters' fresh recollection that during the campaign he and Cass had often been accused of talking out of both sides of their mouths

[17] Cleo Hearon, "Mississippi and the Compromise of 1850," Mississippi Historical Society *Publications*, XIV, 46-47, 50-63, 67-68.

with respect to slavery's extension in order to appeal to both Northerners and Southerners, who interpreted their statements in different ways. If this had seemed "smart politics" for a candidate in 1848, it made for trouble in the Presidency of 1849. As a further complication, Taylor was a slaveholder. His residence at the time of his election was at Baton Rouge, Louisiana, and he owned a cotton plantation and over a hundred Negroes in Jefferson County, Mississippi. Yet more than half of his electoral vote had come from northern states, and more northern than southern Whigs were to be members of the Thirty-first Congress.

Small wonder, then, that the March 5 Inaugural Address of this untried twelfth President of the United States was described as "negative and general." While taking cognizance of critical conditions in the country, Taylor stressed what he hoped would be the forthcoming contributions of the Senate and House, instead of enunciating a specific executive program. "I shall look with confidence" to Congress, he said, "to adopt such measures of conciliation as may harmonize conflicting interests and tend to perpetuate that Union which should be the paramount object of our hopes and affections. In any action calculated to promote an object so near the heart of everyone who truly loves his country[,] I will zealously unite with the co-ordinate branches of the government." There was nothing more definite than that in Taylor's speech—nothing to suggest that the President had or thought he had *the* solution, or even *a* solution, for the vexing slavery-extension problem.

President Taylor did stress the word "Union." Superficial analyses of twentieth-century Americans, however, may oversimplify the term in the context of 1849. If perpetuation of the Union was Taylor's paramount object, let it be recalled that definitions of "the Union" were then at variance with one another. Was the Union a national, consolidated state as interpreted by Daniel Webster? Or was it a joint enterprise of sovereign states, from which member states could withdraw at will under conditions specified by themselves? Not all Americans of the 1840s and 1850s were in agreement on the topic. And it was the unconsolidated, state-sovereignty Union—the Union as "our fathers" knew it —that loomed as the real Union of tradition, love, and glory to such Southerners as Calhoun.[18]

7

IN THE SPRING and summer of 1849, responsibility for governing California and New Mexico was entrusted to the Army. While this had been the natural result of acquiring from the Mexican War areas where neither states nor territories had been formed, a military government was makeshift at best. It proved particularly inadequate in California. There a handful of military officers, "supported" by small numbers of enlisted men who were strongly inclined to run off to the mines, could not control chaotic conditions stemming from the discovery of gold.

In San Francisco and at the placers themselves, gold-seekers were arriving—weekly by the hundreds and monthly by the thousands—from all parts of the globe. It was the Gold Rush—which would not have developed in a freshly-acquired region once in ten thousand times—that gave a special urgency to the problem of what to do with regard to the western lands. That some kind of civil government must be provided, and provided soon, was as obvious at the California capital of Monterey as in Washington itself. The creation of a Territory of California, however, could be accomplished only by Congress and would inevitably be preceded by a long debate on slavery's exclusion or extension there. It was also possible for California to petition for statehood with or without slavery, skipping the ter-

18 William H. Seward to Thurlow Weed, March 1, 1849, Thurlow Weed Papers, University of Rochester; Hamilton, *Zachary Taylor*, 156-58, 173-74.

ritorial stage. But such a move likewise would be controversial. Whether it was more or less explosive than the
territorial alternative was a question which even the most
objective American found hard to answer in 1849.

While Zachary Taylor made no speeches from March
through July on the western lands, he acted in a highly
significant way with respect to California. Early in the
spring, he selected Representative T. Butler King of Georgia
to go to the West Coast as his special agent. Sailing from
Savannah in April, King reached San Francisco on June 4
and straightway informed the Californians of the "sincere
desire of the Executive" to protect them in the "formation
of any government . . . hereafter to be submitted to Congress, which shall be the result of their . . . deliberate
choice."

The day before King disembarked, Military Governor
Bennet Riley at Monterey had called for a state constitutional convention which assembled on September 3. Although the Taylor-King language was guarded, it meant
in the context of California developments that the White
House favored immediate statehood. The President and his
advisers believed that, if the region aimed at becoming
a state rather than a territory, part of the prospective
long-drawn-out Congressional debate on slavery might be
avoided. Similarly, they surmised that the people of California—most of whom were from the North—would favor
the exclusion of slavery when their delegates drew up their
constitution. That Taylor, owner of slaves and cotton fields,
would approve of this prospect may seem remarkable.
However, he was showing that in his concept of the Union
what he thought was the national welfare bulked far larger
than interests of his section and class. The delegates at
Monterey eventually did what the President expected,
voting for a free-state constitution which in December went
into effect with a civil governor and other civil officials.
Then in 1850, California's petitioners would personally

knock on the doors of Congress, requesting that the thirty-first star—free California's—be added to the American flag.[19]

8

T. BUTLER KING's mission, featuring as it did the sending of a Georgia slaveholder by a Louisiana slaveholder to help bring a free state into the Union, aroused much adverse criticism in the South when publicized in the latter half of 1849. Taylor was stigmatized as a southern man with northern principles, just as Presidents Franklin Pierce of New Hampshire and James Buchanan of Pennsylvania were to be branded in the North of the 1850s as northern men with southern principles. Taylor's 1849 activity, moreover, was not limited to California. Through Indian Agent James S. Calhoun and Army Lieutenant Colonel George A. Mc-Call, the President sought to gain statehood for New Mexico with the territorial stage comparably avoided and the slavery institution specifically excluded.

The political oligarchy at Santa Fe, however, did not make much of an effort to emulate California's example until the spring of the following year. It was a matter of common knowledge that practical conditions in New Mexico differed from those farther west. Aside from Indians and Mexicans, few people lived there. No Gold Rush brought in a tide of immigration, and the fact that New Mexico's boundaries were undetermined greatly complicated the governmental outlook. Approximately the eastern half of twentieth-century New Mexico was claimed by the adjacent, pro-slavery state of Texas. Denying Texas' right to the disputed zone, most Northerners were inclined to view

[19] Cardinal Goodwin, *The Establishment of State Government in California, 1846-1850* (New York, 1914), 59, 80-88, 260; T. Butler King to John M. Clayton, June 20, 1849, John M. Clayton Papers, Library of Congress; *Congressional Globe*, 31 Cong., 1 Sess., 222 *et seq.*

nearly all of modern New Mexico and Arizona as belonging within the region governed by the Army at Santa Fe. Most Southerners, of course, saw justice in Texas' claim. Long before 1850 reached its halfway mark, this boundary dispute was to become at least as fraught with controversy as the California one, though it developed much more slowly.[20]

A third portion of the American West, theoretically part of New Mexico but actually not under Santa Fe's control, was the region having as its focal point the Great Salt Lake of modern Utah. Here the zealous denominationalists known as Latter-day Saints, or Mormons, had come from trial and terror in the East while the Mexican War was being fought. Here they began building Salt Lake City, where under the leadership of Brigham Young they and their sons would make barren land fruitful and create a thriving society in the desert. And here in March of 1849, on their own initiative, they drafted a constitution for a provisional "State of Deseret."

The dynamic Young was one of the nineteenth century's most audacious and masterful leaders. His boldness was never more vividly exemplified than in the document which he virtually dictated, for his "Deseret" encompassed all the country between the Sierra Nevada Mountains and the Rockies and between Mexico and Oregon Territory, as well as a large slice of California with the seacoast from San Diego to Los Angeles. Deseret differed from northern California in that its population was small, and from New Mexico in the absence of a threatened dispute with the state of Texas over boundaries. It had as a political asset the fact that slavery's flourishing there was inconceivable to most Southerners as well as Northerners. Still, it was scarcely logical that Congress would grant the Mormons' petition for Deseret's admission into the Union; even if the Mormon faith and polygamous practices had not proved

[20] William C. Binkley, "The Question of Texan Jurisdiction in New Mexico under the United States, 1848-1850," *Southwestern Historical Quarterly*, XXIV (July 1920), 1-6, 10-16.

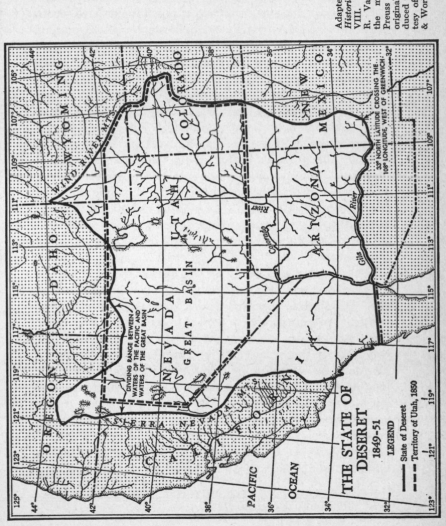

THE STATE OF
DESERET
1849-51

LEGEND

———— State of Deseret
- - - - Territory of Utah, 1850

Adapted from the *Utah Historical Quarterly*, Vol. VIII. Compiled by E. R. Varner 1940 from the map by Charles Preuss 1848 and other original sources. Reproduced through the courtesy of Harcourt, Brace & World, Inc.

suspect in many eyes, Deseret's expanse was simply too vast. Hindsight suggests that an idea with which the Taylor Administration toyed in 1849 was even more fantastic. So intent was the President on the desirability of avoiding interminable territorial debates that he sent John Wilson westward as an agent to broach a possible combination of California and Deseret in a single state. While nothing was to come of this scheme, and the Deseret petition met with stern disfavor, even the projection of such possibilities underscored the gravity of the land-and-slavery dilemma.[21]

Related to the boundary controversy between Texas and New Mexico was the Texas debt, nominally amounting to more than $11 million but prorated at $5.6 million by the auditor and comptroller of Texas. Anxious to discharge the debt on the pro rata basis, Texas considered the United States partly responsible for her failure to redeem bonds and notes issued in the era of the Texas Republic, for with annexation, Texas had lost substantial income in customs from its ports of entry. Thus the case was made that compensation from Washington was only fair under the circumstances.

Texas was proud. Her pride was shared by her congressmen, at least one of whom would long reject the proposal that Texas give disputed lands (also claimed for New Mexico) in return for federal assumption of her debt. Nevertheless, when a softened offer along the same line was made in the Senate and the House of Representatives, it would be accepted by the Texas delegation. Worth bearing in mind is the fact that some of the most widely-known lawyers, bankers, brokers, and public men in America acquired Texas securities. Nearly 200 individuals, partnerships, pools, and business institutions would eventually receive drafts on the United States ranging from $5,000 to hundreds of thousands. There was brisk trading in Texas

[21] Dale L. Morgan, "The State of Deseret," *Utah Historical Quarterly,* VIII (April-July-October 1940), 72-95.

Bonds in 1849 and 1850. Marked appreciation occurred. Welcome profits would be made by the lucky or the canny. Because of the particular interest of the owners of the securities in a favorable decision in the bond-and-land questions, their possible influence cannot be ignored in the outcome of events in Washington.[22]

9

LESS DIRECTLY connected with land in the West were the problems concerning fugitive slaves. The Constitution provided that, when escapes were made, American citizens of the North were bound to help remand the Negroes to their southern masters. Loopholes in the original provisions had led to a Fugitive Slave Law, signed in 1793 by President Washington. The law nominally was still in effect fifty-six years after its enactment. Its execution, however, depended upon the cooperation of enforcement agencies in northern states and localities. And Southerners launched charge after charge that northern officials were remiss in their duties and downright hostile to their southern brethren, when they failed to supply the necessary aid.

Northern antislavery extremists, sympathetic toward blacks in bondage, became active in a program for assisting runaways. Some formed what was called the "Underground Railroad." Not only were slaves encouraged to leave the plantations and farms of their owners, but transportation, clothes, and concealment were given them. Advancing stealthily from town to town, often under the cover of night, they stopped for a day or a week at "stations" located on the "underground" routes. While many Negroes

[22] Edmund T. Miller, *A Financial History of Texas* (Austin, Texas, 1916), 117-18; Texas Debt Claims and Warrants, Record Group 217, Records of the General Accounting Office; "Register of Texas Debt Warrants, 1856-1861," Record Group 39, Records of the Bureau of Accounts (Treasury), National Archives, Washington.

sought asylum in Canada, others settled in northern United States communities and acted as if they were just as free as their new neighbors.

The situation presented many white Northerners with moral and legal complications. There was a law to be enforced, and also a principle (as they saw it) in direct conflict with the law. Which should be heeded? Which obeyed? There was likewise a recurring threat to Negroes in the North who were legally free, and for whom the 1793 act offered no safeguards against seizure and kidnapping. Although trial by jury had been demanded in some states as early as the 1820s, emphasis on "personal liberty" became stronger after 1842 when the U.S. Supreme Court handed down a historic ruling. In *Prigg v. Pennsylvania*, it was asserted that state officials need not execute a constitutional requirement applying to federal authorities alone. Expanded "personal liberty laws" grew fashionable north of the Mason-Dixon Line. Proof of ownership, rigorously demanded, in many cases was hard to show. Then, too, northern public opinion (or the more vocal part of it) sided with the alleged fugitives and usually gave the benefit of the doubt to the Negroes rather than to their pursuers.

As in most quarrels, both parties to the contest over fugitive slaves had some justice in their cause. Slavery being legal in the South and an integral factor in southern economy, owners of that species of property could not be expected to cheer while money invested in labor vanished. Southerners resented the North's airy attitude toward something so near southern pocketbooks and hearts. Northerners, they felt, failed to keep faith with the spirit of compromise in the Constitution. To the familiar jabs of abolitionists, with their papers and pamphlets and provocative speeches, most Southerners had grown fairly accustomed. But having northern *officials* thwart them was particularly resented. Especially loud in their complaints were owners living in the borderland of Maryland, Virginia, Kentucky, and Missouri, whence most of the fugitives fled.

An added sectional irritation directly concerned the District of Columbia. Slavery existed in the cities of Washington and Georgetown, and the slave trade in the District— while exaggerated by northern orators—was known to have shocked sensitive onlookers. If not a few Americans in the South were eager to have a stronger Fugitive Slave Law, supplanting the one of 1793, their northern counterparts demanded the abolition of Washington's publicized "slave pen" and slave sales. Indeed, some critics in the North, not satisfied with aiming their weapons at the vulnerable target of the District slave trade, desired the elimination of slavery itself at the seat of the federal government.[23]

10

THESE THEN WERE the issues—California, Deseret, New Mexico, the Texas boundary, the Texas debt, conflicting attitudes toward fugitive slaves, and slavery and the slave trade in the District of Columbia. All were to have a part in the provocative debates throughout the crisis of 1850. It should never be forgotten by historian or reader that hundreds of thousands of average people were too busy earning a livelihood, making love, rearing families, building homes, and going about other activities of normally peaceful people to care a great deal about political matters. Yet the point Thomas Jefferson had made—that a geographical line which coincided with moral principles and was held up to angry passions would mark a deepening cleavage— held true as more and more Americans were pulled into the vortex of angry disputes which would reach a climax in the Civil War. That war, or one like it, *might* have

[23] Larry Gara, *The Liberty Line: The Legend of the Underground Railroad* (Lexington, Ky., 1961), 42-92; Wilbur H. Siebert, *The Underground Railroad from Slavery to Freedom* (New York, 1898), 20-22, 34-46, 259-67, 359-61, 370; Walter C. Clephane, "The Local Aspect of Slavery in the District of Columbia," Columbia Historical Society *Records* (Washington, 1900), III, *passim*.

broken out in 1850 instead of 1861. Contrasts in regional societies, in rival economic interests, and in moral outlooks had rapidly sharpened since the annexation of Texas in 1845. And some citizens may have remembered the respected Emerson's prediction: "The United States will conquer Mexico, but it will be as the man swallows the arsenic, which brings him down in turn. Mexico will poison us."[24]

Moods of statesmen, the temper of the times, legislative instructions to members of Congress, and partisan and factional contention would affect bills, speeches, and laws from December of 1849 through September of 1850. When the debates opened, a Whig President occupied the White House. A Whig vice president sat on the Senate's dais. A Democratic majority "controlled" the Senate, and Democrats organized the House—but only after sixty-three ballots and the choice of a Speaker by plurality vote. With the Presidency held by a man with no political experience and placed in office by a small electoral majority, with a Congress almost evenly divided along party lines, with divisive problems requiring some solution, men wondered what might be accomplished or what might befall on a national level in a sectional age.

[24] Edward W. Emerson and Waldo E. Forbes (eds.), *Journals of Ralph Waldo Emerson* (10 vols., Boston, 1909-1914), VII, 206.

CHAPTER II

The Rising and
the Setting Suns

.——⟨(O)⟩——.

NO CONGRESS of Jefferson's day—of Jackson's, Wilson's, or Franklin D. Roosevelt's—has matched the color of the one assembling in December, 1849. That was a month when Congressional generations joined in what has been described as a meeting of "rising, risen, and setting suns."[1] From the Bay of Fundy to Brownsville, Texas, and out to the gold mines and the Golden Gate, the newspaper reader, the idler, and the gossip watched from afar as young men and old displayed charm and ability on the Capitol stage. The tenseness of the sectional crisis alone was enough to capture attention. But the identity of the congressional actors, the prompters in the box, and the critics everywhere magnified the drama and the interest of a compelling performance.

The spotlight would often fall on the Senate during the winter, spring, and summer of 1849-1850. Small wonder, since three masters of eloquence and skill were once more on the scene of their earlier glory and dazzling colleague and spectator alike. From his Kentucky country place, Henry Clay had come back to the Senate which he entered as a neophyte in 1806. Now approaching his seventy-third birthday, Clay was physically less resilient than in former times. No longer could he play cards all night, then change to fresh linen and debate all day. Yet, once on the floor of the familiar chamber, the old verve returned and the music to his voice.[2]

Never as eloquent as Webster nor so close a reasoner as Calhoun, Clay throughout a long career was more consistent politically than his rivals. Clay, moreover, was a magnetic party leader—next to Andrew Jackson, his generation's greatest, and his skills would be tried to the utmost by the divisions within his party on the eve of 1850. It was in Congress (not on the hustings, and not in political conventions) that the Kentuckian appeared at his best. No other American surpassed his reputation for parliamentary finesse. Savoring the prospect of creating a peaceful resolution of a difficult problem, as he had conceived himself doing on two earlier occasions, it was inevitable that the resourceful Whig would shine in the events unfolding.

This was Clay's first appearance as a senator since his "retirement" seven years before. Webster, however, had returned in 1845 and hence seemed more of a congressional fixture. Like Clay, Webster had served both in House and Senate and as secretary of state, but was less the parliamentarian, less the party chieftain. There was a compelling quality about Webster's personality. His flashing eyes, his noble brow, his erect figure, his buff and blue waistcoat with its brass buttons caused him to stand out and led a British wit to exclaim, "That man is a fraud, for it is impossible for anyone to be as great as he looks."[3]

Webster was famous for his speeches, and his "Reply to Hayne" was already considered one of the greatest

[1] William E. Griffis, *Millard Fillmore: Constructive Statesman* (Ithaca, N.Y., 1915), 41.

[2] Henry Clay to Mrs. Clay, February 19, 1850, Thomas J. Clay Papers, Library of Congress; Glyndon G. Van Deusen, *The Life of Henry Clay* (Boston, 1937), *passim*.

[3] Theodore L. Cuyler, *Recollections of a Long Life* (New York, 1902), 126.

orations accomplished by an American. His critics (and there were many) found him deficient in high moral standards. Had Webster not accepted money from the Bank of the United States when he was engaged politically in promoting that establishment? Was his legislative record not damagingly inconsistent, the onetime low-tariff sectionalist becoming a high-tariff nationalist, his policy veering like a weathervane when public opinion in Massachusetts shifted? Careless in money matters, deeply in debt,[4] Webster still had numerous admirers. He worked long hours in 1850, appearing before the Supreme Court in the morning on behalf of his clients, then devoting afternoons and evenings to his senatorial labors. Although suffering from insomnia and often sick, he spoke as magnificently as ever, and packed galleries would hang on his rounded periods.[5]

Calhoun, the third member of that historic trio, had a rank not far from Clay's and Webster's. The South Carolinian's career as a national leader had once been extremely promising, but circumstances or convictions or both swerved him from the path of his early attainments. A graduate of Yale and of Tapping Reeve's law school, gifted as a congressman in the War Hawk days, Calhoun became secretary of war for eight years in Monroe's Cabinet and was twice elected to the vice presidency. Favoring the tariff of 1816 when Webster the sectionalist opposed it, the cotton planter of Fort Hill had advanced the cause of internal improvements in the House and in the Cabinet.[6]

Then Calhoun the nationalist became a sectionalist. His state's economic interests changing, he reversed Webster's switch—each henceforth occupying the other's old ground.

[4] Claude M. Fuess, *Daniel Webster* (2 vols., Boston, 1930), II, 383-96; Edgar D. Jones, *Lords of Speech: Portraits of Fifteen American Orators* (Chicago, 1937), 43-44; Daniel Webster to William W. Corcoran, March 7, 9, 1850, William W. Corcoran Papers, Library of Congress.

[5] Fuess, *Daniel Webster*, II, 207, 213.

[6] Charles M. Wiltse, *John C. Calhoun: Nationalist, 1782-1828* (Indianapolis, 1944), 29-154.

A nullifier on the issue of the tariff of 1832, foremost
champion of the right of secession, Calhoun wrote learnedly
in political theory and became an outstanding logician.
Like Clay and Webster he had his hour in the State Department, reentering Congress in 1845 after helping to arrange
the annexation of Texas. Though hailed as one of the most
notable thinkers among American statesmen of all time,[7]
much of his theory of concurrent majorities seems to have
been adopted from Timothy Ford, his law preceptor in
Charleston.[8] Tall, gaunt, stern, forbidding in mien, Calhoun became a victim of tuberculosis, and, as 1850 opened,
was near death. Yet he came to the Capitol on occasion.
There friends and followers clustered about him, for even
in his dying days he was the revered spokesman of many
Southerners.[9]

2

BORN IN 1782, the same year as Calhoun and Webster,
Senator Lewis Cass of Michigan, the recent Democratic
candidate for President, was often seen by visitors to the
Capitol passing quickly through the rotunda clad in a suit
of glossy black. Although a native of New Hampshire and
a schoolmate of Webster's at Exeter, he was as thoroughly
identified with the Old Northwest as Clay with Kentucky
or Calhoun with the cotton kingdom. Michigan's territorial
governor for eighteen years, then secretary of war and
minister to France, Cass first went to the Senate in 1845

[7] Vernon L. Parrington, *Main Currents of American Thought* (3
vols., New York, 1927-1930), I, 320.

[8] The author is indebted to Professor Fletcher M. Green of the
University of North Carolina for calling his attention to the writings
of Ford.

[9] Charles M. Wiltse, *John C. Calhoun: Sectionalist, 1840-1850*
(Indianapolis, 1951), 456-57, 460-61. For contrasting views of Cal-
houn's switch, *cf.* this and other writings of Wiltse, *passim;* Gerald M.
Capers, *John C. Calhoun, Opportunist: A Reappraisal* (Gainesville,
Fla., 1960), 103-65; Parrington, *Main Currents,* II, 67.

and had recently won a second election. This wealthy owner of Detroit real estate was the chief exponent of popular sovereignty, which he equated with his White House hopes and prospects for 1852.[10]

A competent contemporary of Cass, Webster, and Calhoun was Thomas Hart Benton, the senior senator in point of service. Foe of the Bank of the United States, of internal improvements, of the cheapened dollar, and of Calhoun, the Missourian had a distinguished background as a Jackson-Van Buren stalwart. A nationalist now as in the past and a Jacksonian to the core, Benton was to become an exponent of Zachary Taylor's policies. Although a partisan Democrat, Benton was convinced that he must support the Whig President in order to prevent slavery's extension. If his remarks were likely to prove interminable and his arrogance offended, auditors were loath to underrate his bludgeoning tactics in debate.[11]

Quite as famous as Benton was Sam Houston of Texas, whose name had become a household word. Sporting a buckskin suit and a leopardskin vest, the two-time president of the Texas Republic usually sat silent in the Senate, content to whittle little wooden hearts from blocks of pine while his peers orated. But people listened when "The Raven" spoke, for the glory of San Jacinto and the wounds of two campaigns lent luster to Houston's reputation and made him a legend in his lifetime.[12] Other Democrats of the older generation exhibited nearly every variant of that diverse party, from Henry Dodge of Wisconsin (who followed free soil instructions) to Andrew P. Butler of South Carolina (a slaveholder of the state-rights school).

[10] Philadelphia *Pennsylvanian,* May 2, 1850; Frank B. Woodford, *Lewis Cass: The Last Jeffersonian* (New Brunswick, N.J., 1950), 3, 11-16, 90-271.
[11] William N. Chambers, *Old Bullion Benton: Senator from the New West* (Boston, 1956), 146, 158-368; Philadelphia *Pennsylvanian,* May 2, 1850.
[12] Llerena Friend, *Sam Houston: The Great Designer* (Austin, Texas, 1954), *passim;* Christian F. Eckloff, *Memoirs of a Senate Page* (New York, 1909), 42-43.

Among the older Whigs, most Southerners inclined measurably toward such adjustments as Clay and Webster would soon be sponsoring, with variations represented by John Bell of Tennessee, John M. Berrien of Georgia, and Joseph R. Underwood of Kentucky. Men like Bell and Underwood were more conservative in their outlook than Whig senators from the North, who, excepting Webster and Pennsylvania's James Cooper, would stand to a man with Zachary Taylor.

In noteworthy contrast to Webster and Clay was a Washington newcomer, William H. Seward, junior senator from New York. The 48-year-old Whig was no novice in the art of practical politics, but he was notable for his enthusiastic following among dedicated antislavery men. Able as a lawyer and twice governor of the most populous state, Seward was a northern extremist, yet close to Taylor of Louisiana and influential as a White House adviser. Another figure of the days to come was the Mississippi Democrat, Jefferson Davis. Davis' life had been a strange one. Kentuckian by birth, West Point cadet, army lieutenant on the frontier, he suffered an almost crushing bereavement in the death of his first wife who was Taylor's second daughter. Retiring to his plantation for eight years— pathetically alone with books, brother, slaves, and grief— Davis emerged to remarry and become a hero under Taylor in the Mexican War. Now 41, slender and handsome, Davis shared many of Calhoun's ideas as well as his regional devotion. Week in and week out, Senator and Mrs. Davis would be received with parental affection by the Taylors at the Executive Mansion, notwithstanding the President's disagreement with Davis on the major issue before the country.[13]

[13] Frederick W. Seward, *Seward at Washington as Senator and Secretary of State . . . 1846-1861* (New York, 1891), 105 and *passim;* New York *Tribune,* March 16, 1850; Holman Hamilton, *Zachary Taylor: Soldier of the Republic* (Indianapolis, 1941), 100-109, 201, 209, 237-38, and *Zachary Taylor: Soldier in the White House* (Indianapolis, 1951), 172, 236-38.

No senator in 1850 proved more pugnacious than the other Mississippian. Forty-nine years old, diminutive and fragile, Henry S. Foote had a whiplash tongue and was relentless in attack. Foote had corresponded sympathetically with Calhoun during the previous summer. On a superficial basis, one might assume that anything smacking of nationalism or compromise would repel this fiery controversialist. But his personal antipathy toward his rival Davis, his intimacy with Lewis Cass, and his ability to find common ground with Clay exerted influences on Foote regarding the sectional situation. Thus in Foote there was a combination of methods usually attributed to radicals, coupled with conservative aims.[14]

Without the energy and common sense of Stephen A. Douglas, compromise efforts might have ended in collapse. Douglas was a Vermonter by birth but long had lived in Illinois and, at 36, was one of the three youngest members of the Senate. Only five feet four, nicknamed "the Little Giant" and "a steam engine in britches," Chicago's first citizen had an extraordinary capacity for directing political operations.[15] If the Northwest and his Democratic party were to be decisive factors, it was clear that Douglas might be given at least some of the credit or blame.

Consistently opposed to Douglas and Foote were the Senate's two Free Soilers. The eloquent and witty John P. Hale of New Hampshire had advocated the principle of the Wilmot Proviso even before the Mexican War. Southerners might detest Hale's opinions and moderate Northerners inveigh against them, yet he was rather well liked by his colleagues and his humor softened the impact of his sallies. No such saving grace characterized his Ohio associate. The pompous Salmon P. Chase possessed much of the moral courage which up to now marked Hale's career, but

[14] James D. Lynch, *The Bench and Bar of Mississippi* (New York, 1881), 286-88; Henry S. Foote, *War of the Rebellion; or, Scylla and Charybdis* (New York, 1866), 69-70, 172-75, 389-95.

[15] George F. Milton, *The Eve of Conflict: Stephen A. Douglas and the Needless War* (Boston, 1934), 2-3, 15-47.

geniality rarely relieved his puritanical intensity. These
political insurgents owed their senatorial elections to state
legislative coalitions—Hale to Whigs and independent Democrats, Chase to Democrats and Free Soilers. Although
their backgrounds were partly Democratic, neither was
counted in Democratic ranks or admitted to the Democratic
caucus.[16]

3

FROM THE STANDPOINTS of vitality and staying power, it
may be significant that over half the Democratic senators
were below the age of 50. James M. Mason, a Calhoun
lieutenant from Virginia, was one year older. But among
the relatively young Democrats of more than average
ability were David R. Atchison of Missouri, Jesse D. Bright
of Indiana, Daniel S. Dickinson of New York, Hannibal
Hamlin of Maine, Robert M. T. Hunter of Virginia, and
Thomas J. Rusk of Texas. Adding variety were Florida's
David L. Yulee, the West Indies-born Jew; Illinois' James
Shields, an Irish Catholic from County Tyrone; and Louisiana's Pierre Soulé, the swarthy Paris revolutionary turned
New Orleans criminal lawyer. Of the five Whigs under 50,
New Jersey's William L. Dayton and Jacob W. Miller were
enrolled in the Taylor camp. Not so Cooper of Pennsylvania
or the adjustment-minded Marylanders, James A. Pearce
and Thomas G. Pratt, who joined Clay's compromise
contingent.

There never was any doubt of the Democrats' organiza-
tional control. Even if the two Free Soilers had voted
regularly with the twenty-five Whigs, the thirty-three mem-

[16] Allen Johnson et al. (eds.), *Dictionary of American Biography*
(22 vols. and index, New York, 1928-1958), VIII, 105-107, IV, 27-34;
Reinhard H. Luthin, "Salmon P. Chase's Political Career Before the
Civil War," *Mississippi Valley Historical Review*, XXIX (March
1943), 520-21.

bers of the Democratic party would have been in a
dominating position so far as organization was concerned.
Douglas won reelection to the chairmanship of the important Committee on Territories, and Butler succeeded
himself as head of the Judiciary Committee. Almost all the
committees were five-man affairs, with Democratic majorities and Democratic chairman.[17]

Senatorial analyses also reveal that eighteen of the thirty-
three Democrats and twelve of the twenty-five Whigs lived
in slave states. This situation is significant when studied in
conjunction with the caucuses (especially the Democratic
caucus), and it may be related to the exclusion of the most
radical antislavery senators—Chase, Hale, and Seward—
from committee assignments. Worth noting was the residence of half the southern Whigs in Delaware, Kentucky,
and Maryland, which were strongly inclined toward adjustment of differences. Two-thirds of the northern Democrats, moreover, represented northwestern states. Tradi-
tionally, the Northwest had close economic and political
ties with the South, so it was no surprise to find most of
the Democratic Northwesterners willing to go along with
Whig border-staters in a compromise direction.

In fact but not in name, the Senate comprised not two
but four principal parties: (1) Whigs from the North who,
except for Webster and Cooper, wanted slavery specifically
excluded from the whole West; (2) most of the Democrats
from the South, who insisted on slavery's extension into at
least part of the West; (3) nearly all northern Democrats
and some southern Democrats, who favored compromise on
a popular sovereignty basis; (4) almost all southern Whigs
and two northern Whigs, who, likewise stressing peace,
were coming to accept the Democrats' popular sovereignty
prescription. Leaders of the first group (to which Chase
and Hale often attached themselves) were the southern
Whig President Taylor, the northern Whig Senator Seward,

[17] *Congressional Globe*, 31 Cong., 1 Sess., 39-41, 44-45.

and the southern Democratic Senator Benton. Principal
spokesmen for the second group were Calhoun and Jefferson Davis; for the third, Cass, Douglas, and Foote; and for
the fourth, Clay and Webster.

Although not every detail of each zone of demarcation
was clear at the start of the session, the general attitude of
many a senator could be approximated. Before long it
seemed certain that backers of the Administration policy
were at least sixteen in number. Southerners to whom
Calhoun's strictures had the greatest appeal constituted a
total of fourteen. The moderate Democrats similarly numbered about fourteen, and Clay and Webster soon assumed
that they themselves could count on nine votes including
their own. The positions of the remaining senators did not
become clear at once. From the recapitulation it is evident
that something more than a mere listing of names under
party labels is essential to an understanding of 1850 strategy.
Neither partisanship alone nor sectional preoccupation
alone accounts for speeches, actions, and votes of all men
or groups. In an era when the Whig party was disintegrat-
ing and Democratic regularity was jeopardized, when some
Southerners as well as Northerners owed their seats to
legislative coalitions, motives were exceedingly complex
and elusive. Ambition, gratitude, jealousy, hope, selfishness,
esprit de corps, and the power of personalities played their
parts, as well as instructions from state assemblies.

4

WHAT KINDS OF men were those who sat in the House of
Representatives? Never before, in six decades under the
federal Constitution, had the House been more chaotic.
People who otherwise would have busied themselves with
constructive programs busied themselves with words. For
three hectic weeks the House could not organize because

no Speaker could be elected. Rules called for a majority
decision, but not enough representatives to form a majority
could agree. And so, during most of that critical December,
orators ranted and members voted ineffectually while the
mere clerk of the previous session presided and sought a
semblance of order. At night, when adjournment came,
caucuses met in the same hall, and southern, northern, western, and eastern partisans raged as tempestuously as before.
The House of December, 1849, was truly a cave of political
winds.

Yet capable politicians were members of that House. One
of the most popular was a stout Georgia Democrat of
medium height and ruddy complexion. Very young when
he first came to Washington in 1843, Howell Cobb had
mastered procedural niceties and advanced to the responsi-
bilities of floor leader. Though he was now barely 34 years
old, he conducted himself with a veteran's assurance, while
not the least of his assets was a sense of humor. The fact
that he was one of four southern Democrats who had
refused to sign Calhoun's "Southern Address" affected his
chances for the speakership, with Northerners admiring
him on that account and most Southerners of his party
supporting him in spite of it.[18]

Linn Boyd of Kentucky, Cobb's senior by fifteen years,
had been a congressman fully twice as long. The two
Democrats had much in common from the standpoint of
problems and solutions, their careers being marked by
devotion to southern rights and also by insistence that
issues be settled on the basis of national—not sectional—
principles. Like Cobb, Boyd had withheld his signature
from the "Southern Address." Their economic roots, however, were dissimilar. Lacking Cobb's cultural and financial advantages, the tall, handsome, seven-term idol of
western Kentucky was the son of poor parents and a farmer

[18] Zachary T. Johnson, *The Political Policies of Howell Cobb*
(Nashville, 1929), 81-84.

who really farmed. Eventually, Boyd would be Speaker in
the Thirty-second and Thirty-third Congresses.[19] In 1849,
he proved less popular than Cobb, perhaps because the
younger man did more to ingratiate himself with Northerners.

A Democrat from a western state on intimate terms with
Boyd and Cobb was John A. McClernand of Illinois. A
native of Kentucky, left fatherless at four, McClernand as a
youth helped to support his widowed mother and went on
to enlist in the Black Hawk War, edit a newspaper, practice
law, and win four elections to Congress. Now one of the
Northwest's two senior Democratic representatives, this
energetic Jacksonian was Douglas' top lieutenant in the
House. It is worth noting that his district lay in "Egypt,"
the southernmost part of Illinois; many of his constituents
were southern-born, and their and his politics reflected a
sympathetic understanding of southern problems. Throughout the session McClernand's long, thin face would be seen
in the midst of procompromise conferences, while his
occasional boldness on the floor commanded attention in
the galleries.

Thomas H. Bayly of Virginia was another of the prominent younger Democrats. Bayly had climbed the political
ladder from his state's general assembly to a circuit judge-
ship and finally to the House in Washington. Tempera-
mentally, he was by no means as stable as Cobb, Boyd, or
even McClernand. In the debates of 1850, he would lose
his temper, hurling terms like "snarling puppy" and "spite-
ful little meddler" at a fellow Democrat who crossed him,
and exclaiming, "If you keep objecting to this bill, I will
wring your neck for you, God d—n you." The slaveholder
from the Eastern Shore was well connected, due in part
to his association with the editor of the Washington
Union. Bayly's devotion to Cobb during the tense Speaker-

[19] *Congressional Globe,* 30 Cong., 1 Sess., 21; Holman Hamilton,
"Kentucky's Linn Boyd and the Dramatic Days of 1850," Kentucky
Historical Society *Register,* LV (July 1957), 185-95.

ship struggle endeared him to the successful contender, who would hasten to repay him with the chairmanship of the Ways and Means Committee.[20]

5

THE ATTITUDE of the leading Whig in the House, Robert C. Winthrop of Massachusetts, provided a partial contrast to that of the principal Democrats. A graduate of the Harvard that bred an Edmund Quincy and a Theodore Parker, Winthrop might have been as intransigent as his alma mater's most dogmatic sons. Or he might have joined the Free Soilers, aspiring to the political mantle which Charles Sumner was soon to wear. Instead, remaining faithful to the Whig organization which had made him Speaker of the last two sessions, the aristocratic Winthrop sought reelection to the chair as a Taylor adherent. Tall, slender, and bespectacled, Winthrop was liked by many congressmen. But neither his fine mind nor his sociability dissuaded some southern Whigs from opposing his ideas as too extreme, or Free Soilers from considering them too moderate. Such reactions, on the part of persons holding the balance of power, contributed to the deadlock in the December contest.[21]

Was there somebody who might have appealed more than Winthrop to the Whig representatives as a whole? Each of the men suggested as substitutes was fatally handicapped. One had a weak voice, a factor of importance in a

[20] Johnson *et al.* (eds.), *Dictionary of American Biography*, XI, 587-88, II, 78-79; Thomas J. McCormack (ed.), *Memoirs of Gustave Koerner, 1809-1896* (2 vols., Cedar Rapids, Iowa, 1909), I, 480; New York *Herald*, September 3, 1850.

[21] Robert C. Winthrop, Jr., *A Memoir of Robert C. Winthrop* (Boston, 1897), *passim; Congressional Globe*, 30 Cong., 1 Sess., 2; Philadelphia *Pennsylvanian*, April 30, 1850; Robert C. Winthrop to John P. Kennedy, December 4, 1849, John P. Kennedy Papers, Peabody Institute, Baltimore.

chamber where acoustics were wretched. Another had a
reputation for involvement in vituperative disputes. A third,
the epitome of border-state moderation, received a kiss of
death in the form of too obvious sponsorship by the
Toombs-Stephens faction. And Winthrop was preferred by
those Whig newcomers to Congress who were not well
acquainted with his rivals and whom the Bostonian's
prestige impressed. A peculiar feature of the situation was
the small number of Southerners (fewer than thirty) on the
Whig side of the aisle. This meant that southern Whig
Speakership aspirants could not depend on much help from
residents of their own section.

Disconcerting to Whig nationalists was the stand taken
by Alexander H. Stephens and Robert Toombs. "Little
Ellick" Stephens, slight and sickly with a shrill treble voice
and the face of a lad grown prematurely old, looked under-
developed alongside the leonine Toombs. These Georgia
Whigs in their late thirties had won places among Taylor's
trusted advisers between his election and inauguration.
They were even chiefly responsible for two appointments
to the Cabinet. But they had been disillusioned by Taylor's
California-New Mexico policy and now broke with the
President and with Northerners like Winthrop, bolting the
Whig caucus on December 1 because it refused to grant
guarantees respecting the South's rights in the West. Nor
were the two dissidents unsupported. Four other Southerners joined them in withdrawing. Henceforth, unbound by
caucus nominations, five and often six Whigs from Georgia,
Florida, Virginia, and Alabama would make up an irritating
splinter group and would irk Whig regulars by voting as a
unit.[22]

Nine and sometimes ten Free Soilers likewise darkened

[22] Robert Toombs to John J. Crittenden, April 23, 1850, John J.
Crittenden Papers, Library of Congress; Alexander H. Stephens, *A
Constitutional View of the Late War Between the States* (2 vols.,
Philadelphia, 1868-1870), II, 199-200; Philadelphia *Pennsylvanian*,
April 30, 1850; New York *Herald*, December 4, 1849.

majority prospects. Their usual leader was Joshua R. Giddings, an ex-Whig from Ohio who had left his old moorings to back Van Buren for President against Taylor and Cass. A seven-term legislator, this "perfect bull-dog in debate" was influential. His associates included Preston King, an upstate New Yorker with a rolling gait and "fat heavy figure," and Ohio's Joseph M. Root whose voice was harsh but whose arguments incorporated anecdote and repartee. Others were Charles Allen of Massachusetts, a grandson of old Samuel Adams, and the forceful and famous but slovenly ex-Democrat, David Wilmot of Pennsylvania.[23] Like the Toombs-Stephens clique, the veteran Giddings and his friends customarily cast ballots as an independent bloc.

To do justice to all the House personalities would require a lien on the rest of this study. Three of the most colorful were Thaddeus Stevens of Pennsylvania, free soiler in principle though elected as a Whig, his cold face rarely lighted up unless by a sardonic grin; Isaac E. Holmes, six-term Democrat from South Carolina, whose expression seemed pensive as he examined the papers on his desk through a glass suspended from a guard chain; and the hulking William A. Richardson, Democrat from Illinois and a tobacco-chewing intimate of Senator Douglas. Others were Horace Mann, an antislavery Massachusetts Whig and noted public school pioneer; William J. Brown, Indiana Democrat, who would achieve notoriety as a candidate for Speaker, and Thomas L. Clingman of North Carolina, nominally a Whig but veering toward the Democrats and cordially cooperative with Stephens and Toombs. Clingman's fellow Carolinian, David Outlaw, was a rather typical southern Whig whose letters to his wife are among our best sources of developments in Washington. The lone spokesman for the Native American party was Lewis C. Levin, a Philadelphian of Jewish antecedents.

Spectators were frequently informed of marriages, blood

[23] Philadelphia *Pennsylvanian*, April 30, May 2, 18, 1850.

ties, and old friendships connecting various congressmen. For example, James McDowell, a Virginian so eloquent that he could hold the House spellbound for two hours, was a brother-in-law of Senator Benton who was Mrs. Henry Clay's first cousin. Representative Daniel Breck of Kentucky had boarded at the residence of Senator Chase's father when little Salmon was four years old. Two senators and one representative had attended Bowdoin College together. Four senators had been contemporaries at Transylvania University. Senator Pratt of Maryland was an early schoolmate of Senator Foote. There were two sets of brothers in the House, and Senators Thomas Corwin of Ohio and Jackson Morton of Florida also had brothers there. Senator Augustus C. Dodge of Iowa was the son of Senator Henry Dodge of Wisconsin.

Like senators, many House members had seen one another regularly during previous sessions. Ten could point to four or more terms, prior to the present one. Nineteen were beginning their fourth terms, twenty-three their third, fifty-seven their second. However, the most arresting statistic is that 117 representatives (more than half) were congressional freshmen. It is almost as illuminating to discover that 44 percent of the 117 either would not seek reelection or would meet defeat when they ran. The House was green, a notable example being the New York delegation which contained twenty-two first-term men and nine second-termers in its aggregate of thirty-four. Equally noticeable was the youth of the House, the average age being 43 with only two members over 62. As in the Senate, there were many more old Whigs than old Democrats and more young Democrats than young Whigs. The House also had more old Northerners than old Southerners. Followership was involved, as well as leadership. The legion of freshmen made it probable that office-holders with authority or background—the President, senior senators, the Speaker and his associates—could exert great influence on the average legislator.

6

AT THE OUTSET, such forces failed to do much more than cancel each other. Even if initially combined, it is doubtful whether they could have compensated for the absence of a Whig or Democratic majority. Had a dozen or a score of House leaders possessed the competence of Winthrop and Cobb, and had rank-and-file representatives been more experienced than was the case, there still would have been difficulty in achieving the election of a Speaker. Although some congressmen reached Washington late, nearly all of the House seats were occupied from the beginning. Of the members answering the roll call on the first ballot and the last, 108 were Democrats, 103 Whigs, one a Native American, and 9 Free Soilers. The principal candidates for the Speakership were Cobb and Winthrop. In the course of sixty-two ballots over a three-week span, the total vote ranged from a high of 226 to a low of 217, of which the Georgian's maximum was 103 and the Bostonian's 102.[24]

From time to time, on their own volition or as a result of pressure, Cobb and Winthrop withdrew their names to give others an opportunity for preferment. But, with the single exception of William J. Brown, no rival surpassed the Cobb-Winthrop crests. During the session's first fortnight, there was ample evidence for Winthrop's October assertion that "the Whigs are in a sad state," and for Cobb's report to his wife that both Democrats and Whigs were in "a stew." "Bluster and nullification have their way," Winthrop wrote his Baltimore friend, John P. Kennedy. Over in Philadelphia, another Whig was pessimistic. "No one can say how soon we may be involved in the dangers & calamities of disunion," brooded Sidney G. Fisher. "The house is not yet organized & parties are becoming inflamed," with slavery and related topics cloaking "the ambitious

[24] *Congressional Globe*, 31 Cong., 1 Sess., 2-39, 41-44, 46-48, 51, 61-67; Hamilton, *Zachary Taylor: Soldier in the White House*, 247-52.

designs of demagogues & to delude & excite the people—
who . . . are victims & tools."[25]

A few months later, a South Carolina representative
would characterize the House as "not a Hall" but "a
cavern—a mammoth cave, in which men might speak in
all parts, and be understood in none."[26] Certainly the
acoustical drawbacks of the chamber, the echo and confusion and buzz of conversation, were not conducive to an
orderly transaction of business. The size of the member-
ship, too, tended to make the body unwieldy. And yet the
first three weeks would have been far more productive
(regardless of communication defects) if the nine Free
Soilers and five Toombs-Stephens Whigs had been willing
to back either Winthrop or Cobb.

On the sixty-third ballot, the impasse ended. The winds
in the cave subsided. Hostile elements bowed to reason,
finding a way out of their blind alley by resorting to a
plurality decision. Howell Cobb won the Speakership on
December 22, with 102 votes to Winthrop's 99. The van-
quished Whig cordially congratulated his successor. Boyd
administered the oath of office. Then, the last day of the
year, Speaker Cobb named southern and northern Democrats (Bayly of Virginia, James Thompson of Pennsylvania,
McClernand of Illinois, and Boyd of Kentucky) as chair-
men of major House committees.[27] With Cobb now occupying the chair and selecting the committees' personnel, the
Democratic party found itself in control of both House and
Senate organizations. The protracted struggle in the lower
chamber over the Speakership, however, suggested that
troubles would develop when the House tried to legislate.

---

[25] Winthrop to Kennedy, October 18, 1849, Kennedy Papers;
Ulrich B. Phillips (ed.), *The Correspondence of Robert Toombs,
Alexander H. Stephens, and Howell Cobb,* American Historical As-
sociation *Annual Report . . . for the Year 1911* (Washington, 1913),
II, 177; Winthrop to Kennedy, December 16, 1849, Kennedy Papers;
Sidney G. Fisher, manuscript diary, December 16, 1849, Historical
Society of Pennsylvania, Philadelphia.
[26] *Congressional Globe,* 31 Cong., 1 Sess., 1425.
[27] *Ibid.,* 66-67, 88-89.

CHAPTER III

The Appeal
of a Venerable
Kentuckian

IT WAS IN THE House that the first rumblings of the thunder of 1850 were heard. Before Cobb's election as Speaker, a spirited verbal exchange had occurred between Edward Stanly of North Carolina and several other congressmen. Stanly referred disparagingly to "Free Soilism, Wilmot Provisoism, and all such tomfoolery," insisting that the Union was not in danger while Clay and Benton remained in the Senate and Taylor at the west end of Pennsylvania Avenue. Bayly of Virginia answered the southern Whig by blaming party distraction on Taylor's "doubtful" position in the last campaign. Joseph M. Root then felt prompted to assert that, when brought before their constituents, nine out of ten northern Whigs would not brand the Proviso "a humbug" or "tomfoolery." Robert Toombs also spoke. Stung by charges that he and Stephens were recusants, he declared that northern violators of the Constitution imperiled southern interests. "I do not . . . hesitate to avow before this House and the country, and in

the presence of the living God," Toombs boomed, "that if
by your legislation you seek to drive us from the territories
of California and New Mexico . . . and to abolish slavery
in this District . . . , *I am for disunion.*"[1]

"Sir, we do not believe the Union *can ever be dissolved,*"
avowed an Illinois Whig, who served notice that "we shall
not be intimidated by threats of violence." "The South is
prepared to teach the North that she is in earnest," a
Calhounite from South Carolina replied. ". . . If any bill
should be passed at this Congress abolishing slavery in
the District of Columbia, or incorporating the Wilmot proviso in any form, I will introduce a resolution in this House
declaring . . . *that this Union ought to be dissolved.*" The
first day after the Christmas recess, Joshua R. Giddings,
a Free Soiler, fired away at northern Whig leadership.
"For two years," he asserted, ". . . the people of the North
have been defrauded, deceived, and imposed upon . . . ,
and the voice of northern philanthropy has been stifled by
the votes of northern Whigs." That was too much for a
fellow Ohioan, Robert C. Schenck, who praised orthodox
Whiggery and pictured Giddings as resembling Toombs in
obnoxiously delaying House organization.[2]

Early in January, 1850, Senator Calhoun privately reported the "common opinion" that the South should not
remain in the Union without full recognition of its equality
and ample security for the future. The hour of decision
had come, he warned. "If the South is to be saved[,] now
is the time." "The Union trembles at its base," wrote the
New York Whig diarist, Philip Hone. A Georgia correspondent informed Speaker Cobb that "the Union feeling in
this State has given way . . . & I very much fear that any
offensive action of Congress would be the signal for a
rupture." James Buchanan agreed. "The blessed Union
of these States," the Pennsylvania Democrat said, "is now

---

[1] *Congressional Globe,* 31 Cong., 1 Sess., 18-28.
[2] *Ibid.,* 28-30; *ibid., Appendix,* 35-43.

in greater danger than it has ever been since the adoption of the federal Constitution." Northerners "are just now beginning to believe the South to be in earnest," he told a Tennessee friend on New Year's Day.[3]

Ill-will in the House was not the only source of pessimism, which, as it deepened, could also be traced to Senate speeches and maneuvers. On January 8, William Upham of Vermont provoked a fiery debate with the submission of a set of resolutions adopted at Montpelier. Defining slavery as "a crime against humanity, and a sore evil in the body-politic," the document instructed Upham and his colleague Samuel S. Phelps unswervingly to oppose extension. Yulee of Florida objected to printing language so "offensive, opprobrious, and reprehensible." As the discussion grew more tense and participants' remarks more torrid, Hale attacked the South and Calhoun the North—each for encroaching on the other's rights. Solon Borland of Arkansas, Chase of Ohio, Jeremiah Clemens of Alabama, Butler of South Carolina, and Hunter of Virginia joined in the fray. No philippic was more bitter than that of Clemens, who found Northerners circulating "incendiary publications among our slaves" and transforming Christian pulpits into "sanctuaries of slander." None was more graphic than that of Borland, who compared Yankee radicals to hardened criminals, declaring: "I cannot argue with the robber, who meets me upon the highway and demands my purse; I cannot consent to argue with the assassin, who seeks to stab me in the dark; I cannot argue with the midnight incendiary, who stands ready to apply the torch to my dwelling, and to consume my wife and children."

[3] John C. Calhoun to James H. Hammond, January 4, 1850, James H. Hammond Papers, Library of Congress; Philip Hone, manuscript diary, January 7, 1850, New-York Historical Society, New York City; William H. Hull to Howell Cobb, January 9, 1850, Howell Cobb Papers, University of Georgia, Athens; James Buchanan to Nimrod Strickland, December 24, 1849, New-York Historical Society; Buchanan to Cave Johnson, January 1, 1850, copy, James Buchanan Papers, Historical Society of Pennsylvania, Philadelphia.

At one stage of this forensic battle, Jefferson Davis
chastised northern voters who sent Free Soilers to Washington. Such abusers of the suffrage were responsible for
demagogues' attaining lofty posts, in which they did untold
harm through the medium of emotional harangues. "I
came to this session of Congress," Davis continued, "with
melancholy forebodings . . . that it might be the last of our
Government. I still trusted, however, in the intelligence
and patriotism of the masses, for I . . . put no faith in
politicians." But, "if the representatives of that people think
proper to sow the seeds of disunion, and to inflame the
passions and prejudices of one section, whilst they drive the
other by every possible provocation to the point of civil
war, then all I have to say is, that the representatives of
the South . . . are prepared to meet the issue here and
now."[4]

2

To a Congress already embroiled with sectional attacks
and recriminations President Taylor submitted, on January
21, his special message on California and New Mexico.
The President pointed out that, on entering office, he found
a military commander acting as governor of California.
Taylor had not disturbed this situation. To the people of
the West Coast, however, he had expressed his desire that
they draw up a constitution and petition Congress for
admission as a state. The Californians had been clearly
told, the Chief Executive emphasized, that they were to
originate their own domestic policy without interference
from Washington. Their constitution later was drawn up.
As soon as it reached the national capital, Taylor recommended that it be given the sanction of the Senate and the
House.

[4] *Congressional Globe*, 31 Cong., 1 Sess., 119-23, 133-37; *ibid.*,
Appendix, 52-54.

Respecting New Mexico, which was also under military rule and where (as in the case of California) Mexican legislation had made slavery illegal, the President doubted the expediency of setting up a territorial government. After New Mexico became a state, the boundary dispute affecting Texas could be resolved judicially. No court, however, could pass on a suit between a state and the United States. It was his belief, Taylor added, that New Mexico at no distant period would ask for entrance into the Union. What could be more natural, he implied, than for the voters of the region to take the initiative through a constitutional convention—or for Congress to endorse their wishes? Previous times of controversy had been safely passed. The President believed that the 1850 crisis would also subside if his countrymen heeded his December admonition to avoid "exciting topics of a sectional character." In other words, Taylor proposed that Congress do nothing until California and New Mexico petitioned for statehood, though he suggested that Congress should approve these petitions. The President, at this time, left untouched the question of the Texas boundary and debt retirement.

Superficially, the special message was reasonable in tone. Few could find fault with Taylor's appeal to patriotism or devotion to duty. Few could deny that argument and dissension might "endanger or impair" the Union's strength, the vital element in which was "the regard and affection of the people for each other."[5] But when the President told Congress to do nothing about organizing the West until the government heard from the West, he placed himself in opposition to extending the 36°30' line and also to the principle of popular sovereignty with its provision for a territorial stage. The virtual certainty that New Mexico as well as California would have a free-state constitution (and

[5] James D. Richardson (ed.), A Compilation of the Messages and Papers of the Presidents, 1789-1897 (10 vols., Washington, 1901), V, 27-30.

the "state of Deseret," which had already petitioned for
admission to the Union, was assumed to be unsuited for
slavery) meant that Taylor's plan would in effect limit the
expansion of the South. Such a proposal could not fail to
stir southern passions, already aroused by the verbal exchanges in Congress.

The very next day, Clingman of North Carolina, speaking
in the House, demanded a share in the West for the South.
Sentiment sampled the previous summer, in the course of
a northern journey, had convinced him that his section
must defend its rights. Clingman did not openly condemn
the President, but the very idea of southern exclusion
shocked the Whig from the Asheville district. With California and New Mexico leading the way, a procession of
free states would file into the Union to the end that large
congressional majorities finally could enable the North to
abolish slavery whenever it saw fit. As this would be
grossly unfair, it was essential that portions of the West
must at once be opened to slavery. "Do us justice,"
Clingman said, "and we continue to stand with you;
attempt to trample on us, and we part company."[6]

Volney E. Howard, a Texas Democrat, was the next
member of the House to speak. A native of Maine but for
some years prominent as a lawyer and editor in Mississippi,
Howard had moved to San Antonio shortly before Texas'
annexation. Taylor's New Mexico policy alarmed him. Re-
asserting Texan claims to eastern New Mexico, Howard
related the Santa Fe question to California developments.
The Monterey convention had been coerced by the Administration, he said, and it was now recommended that
"the intervention of the *non-intervention* of the President"
should apply to New Mexico as well. What was this if not
the Wilmot Proviso, camouflaged but real and ever odious?
A southern occupant of the Executive Mansion was attempt-

ing to prostrate his own section and, in the case of the
boundary, to violate established treaties and laws! "The
South is aroused and will act as one man," the caustic
Texan exploded.[7]

James A. Seddon was equally vehement. Although the
Virginian's voice did not carry well, his speech was readable
and significant. Seddon's tactics were subtler than Clingman's or Howard's. Asserting his confidence in Taylor,
Seddon went on to attack the members of the Cabinet; it
was they who were responsible for sending King to California, assuming "high legislative powers" and thereby cir-
cumventing Congress. The story that a Louisiana slaveholder intended to bar the South from the West seemed
to the Richmond Democrat "like the crude fantasy of a
crazed brain, rather than . . . reflection and wisdom."
Thus Seddon sought to drive a wedge between the Presi
dent and his advisers.[8]

As indicative of tension as any address were the petty
and protracted corollaries of the Speakership problem.
Representatives voted twenty times before managing to
elect a clerk. Three ballots were taken to choose a chaplain,
and eight were necessary for selection of a sergeant-at-arms.
None of the fourteen candidates for the exalted post of
doorkeeper could win that office after fourteen trials. Calhoun continued to believe that there was small chance for
preserving the Union. On January 12, he informed his son
that southern congressmen were bolder "than I ever saw
them"; many "avow themselves to be disunionists." Berrien, the second oldest senator, urged the general assembly
of his state to prepare a memorial indicative of Georgia's
resistance to northern aggression. George W. Julian, an
Indiana Free Soiler, was ill and therefore refrained from

[7] *Congressional Globe*, 31 Cong., 1 Sess., 205-209; James D. Lynch,
The Bench and Bar of Mississippi (New York, 1881), 250-51.
[8] *Congressional Globe*, 31 Cong., 1 Sess., *Appendix*, 74-78; David
Outlaw to Mrs. Outlaw, January 24, 1850, David Outlaw Papers,
Southern Historical Collection, University of North Carolina, Chapel
Hill.

debate. But "I can hardly sit still," the Hoosier admitted, "after hearing a rabid Southern speech."[9]

3

WHILE REPRESENTATIVES declaimed and grumbled, members of the Senate attempted to devise constructive legislation. In December, Douglas had presented a memorial of the Deseret provisional government, seeking admission as a state with a territorial alternative. The first week in 1850, Mason came forward with a new and stronger fugitive slave bill, which he modified at the month's end in hope that the revision would win northern acceptance. Benton introduced a measure on January 16 giving Texas $15,000,000 for retirement of her debt in return for a cession of 200,000 square miles to the United States. Foote proposed setting up territorial governments for California, New Mexico, and Deseret without explicit reference to slavery; agreeing with Benton that Texas was "too large for a single State," the Mississippian wished to divide it into two slave commonwealths called Texas and "Jacinto." The Deseret memorial and the Foote proposal were referred to Douglas' Committee on Territories, while the Mason and Benton plans went to Senator Andrew P. Butler's Judiciary Committee.

It would be misleading to leave the impression that all these developments occurred smoothly. Yulee temporarily blocked the reference of the Mormon memorial. Foote had earmarked his Texas bill for Butler's committee, not that of Douglas, and the division defeating him showed 22

[9] *Congressional Globe*, 31 Cong., 1 Sess., 95, 106-107, 117, 124-26 138, 140, 156-57, 161-62, 174-75, 186-94, 223-24, 274-75, 277-78; J. Franklin Jameson (ed.), *Correspondence of John C. Calhoun,* American Historical Association *Annual Report . . . for the Year 1899* (Washington, 1900), II, 780; John M. Berrien to Charles J. Jenkins, January 7, 1850, John M. Berrien Papers, Southern Historical Collection, University of North Carolina, Chapel Hill; George W. Julian to Isaac Julian, January 25, 1850, Giddings-Julian Papers, Library of Congress.

Northerners and the Delaware Whigs for Douglas while 22 Southerners voted for Foote. Sectionalism was also evident when Seward gave notice that he intended to amend Mason's first bill in such a way as to guarantee alleged fugitives a jury trial in the judicial district where they were captured. Everybody knew that this would make the rendition of runaways next to impossible. Foote, in defense of the South, immediately branded Seward a crafty, malevolent, fanatical demagogue. Seward's strategy was termed an attempt "to spoliate upon the known and undeniable rights and interests of all the southern States of the Confederacy with pointed disapprobation, with hot contempt, with unmitigated loathing, and abhorrence unutterable."

Contrasted with such abrasive rancor and protesting against the "evil spirit of sectionalism" was the soothing speech of Daniel S. Dickinson. Touching lightly on fugitives, slavery in the West, and special problems in the District of Columbia, the senior senator from New York asked whether the Union was not of priceless value and exhorted northern and southern statesmen to "treat each other with kindness, and courtesy, and conciliation"; if they would do this, the "Republic will be able to outride the dark lowering storms which threaten its existence."[10] In similar fashion Lewis Cass took a position against extremism. The Michigan Legislature had instructed him to support the Wilmot Proviso, and interest was widespread as to how so clearly committed an anti-Provisoist would react to the Lansing edict. Analyzing the question in a 45,000-word oration, Cass said that the Proviso was unconstitutional and inexpedient and made it clear that, confronted with the obligation of his instructions, he would resign before he would vote for the Proviso. He thus dealt a blow to extremists by his willingness to sacrifice his Senate seat rather than submit to pressure. Substantial restraint likewise characterized Phelps when he defended

[10] *Congressional Globe,* 31 Cong., 1 Sess., 86-87, 103, 165-71, 183-84, 211-13, 233-37.

Vermont's resolutions. Butler was mild in commenting on
fugitive slaves. On the surface, even Chase seemed some-
what conservative, denying that his views were sectional.
And the words of Mason, speaking for his fugitive slave
proposal, were temperate compared to Seward's amendment
or Foote's rejoinder.[11] By January 29, therefore, the Senate
atmosphere was less electric than it had been a fortnight
before. Would this work to Clay's advantage as the 72-
year-old Whig introduced a program of "adjustment" on
"one of the most bright and beautiful days" a contemporary
"ever saw"?

4

HENRY CLAY was a logical spokesman for a congressional adjustment or compromise. Twice before in his long
career, he was credited with taking a prominent part in
a compromise when the Union had been threatened by
sectional forces. In the debates of 1819-1821, when Clay
was the Speaker of the House, the Missouri Compromise
had added Maine's star to the flag as a free state, Missouri's
as a slave state, and the agreement that slavery would not
be permitted in the Louisiana Purchase north of 36°30′
except in Missouri. Again in 1833, when Clay was a
senator, he was one of a group of statesmen devising the
Compromise Tariff of that year. Providing for a gradual,
annual reduction of customs schedules, this tariff was a
principal cause of ending the nullification controversy which
had flared in South Carolina in 1832. "The Great Pacifi-
cator" was a title Clay enjoyed, and many Americans looked
to him to promote—or help promote—a third major program
of pacification in the critical year of 1850.

But, actually, compromise had deeper roots in American

[11] Floyd B. Streeter, *Political Parties in Michigan, 1837-1860*
(Lansing, Mich., 1918), 107, 115-16; *Congressional Globe,* 31 Cong.,
1 Sess., *Appendix,* 58-74, 79-83, 91-97.

political soil than the ones suggested by Clay's own experience or by Congress' course in the three decades immediately preceding 1850. National independence, revolution, and audacious constitutional innovations were not the only significant ingredients in the slightly more distant political past of the United States. The give and take of compromise were evident in the fundamental law. The very structure of government involved adjustments affecting (1) interests of thinly *and* thickly populated states, (2) claims of states with or without slaves, and (3) states' rights as well as federal authority. Students of the Constitutional Convention and of the Constitution itself were well aware in 1850, as they are in the twentieth century, that without the element of compromise there could have been no Constitution and no United States government as they historically developed.

All this is not to say or infer that compromise is always practical, always applicable. But coming down to them from 1833 and 1820, from the Constitutional Convention of 1787, from the Articles of Confederation before that, and from centuries of Anglo-Saxon precedent in England and the colonies, compromise of some sort seemed logical to many leaders—including Senator Clay—in the Washington of 1850. Whether this was a year for compromise, and whether a basic adjustment or merely "patchwork" expedients could be achieved, only time and testing could decide. But that compromise should be attempted in the midst of crisis seemed as natural to moderate people as their day-to-day reliance on representative government and free elections as guarantors of both majority and minority rights.

5

THAT LAST TUESDAY in January, the Senate galleries were crowded and the Capitol lobbies full, but "not a sound above a breath could be heard" when Clay's "clear and distinct voice" opened his historic presentation.[12] His first resolution called for admitting California as a state. The second specified territorial governments for New Mexico and Deseret without any slavery restriction or condition. The third and fourth were designed to reduce Texas' area and to pay her debt, but the amount of the payment was purposely left unspecified. The fifth and sixth resolutions denied the expediency of abolishing slavery in the District while providing for termination of the slave trade there. In the seventh, the Kentuckian advocated a more effective fugitive law. The last and eighth resolution was a simple assertion that Congress had no power to obstruct the slave trade of the southern states.

In defending his program, Clay set a pattern for much that followed in succeeding weeks. His main appeal was aimed at the North, which he thought would have more to concede than the South. While philanthropy might dominate northern feeling about the institution of slavery, "habit, safety, property, life, everything is at hazard" below the Mason-Dixon Line. The northern majority should be magnanimous and try to see things from the southern standpoint. Clay mentioned that he recently had been given a fragment from the coffin of George Washington. Holding up the "precious relic," Clay said that "the venerated Father of his Country" was warning Congress from Mount Vernon to "pause" and "reflect" before destroying the Union he did so much to create. "I now ask every Senator," Clay entreated, ". . . in fairness and candor . . . to examine the plan of accommodation which this series of resolutions proposes, and not to pronounce against them until convinced after a thorough examination."[13]

Eight senators, all Southerners and seven of them Democrats, immediately replied to several points. Rusk of Texas

[12] Henry Clay to Thomas B. Stevenson, January 26, 1850, copy, Historical and Philosophical Society of Ohio, Cincinnati; Outlaw to Mrs. Outlaw, January 29, 1850, Outlaw Papers; New York *Express*, January 31, 1850.
[13] *Congressional Globe*, 31 Cong., 1 Sess., 244-47.

resented the idea of making Texas soil "a peace-offering" to northern "encroachment." Foote objected to the assumption of state debts and wanted specified western zones opened to slavery. Mason and Davis joined Rusk and Foote in the ranks of the opposition. Solomon W. Downs of Louisiana considered the "compromise" no compromise at all, and Berrien the Whig called for modifications. While Butler did not "blame" Clay for "this effort to preserve the Union," he counseled that it could not be saved "by the mere name of compromise." The only real encouragement which Clay then received came from Alabama's William R. King, and even King was not wholly in accord.[14]

All this was but prelude to Clay's major speech of the next Tuesday and Wednesday, February 5 and 6. The old master's return to the center of the stage had been anticipated. By 9 o'clock Tuesday morning, the galleries were jammed. By 10, approaches to the floor were choked. People impatiently awaited the chance of being admitted into the aisles and the constricted area just outside the bar. Visitors congested the rotunda, overflowed into the congressional library, and even into the House where Clay could be neither seen nor heard. In the small, cramped Senate itself with its columns and crimson carpets and draperies, seats were arranged for privileged womenfolk. Ex-Senator Buchanan was in Hamlin's curule chair, chatting amiably with Benton and bowing to the richly attired wives and daughters of his friends. "No pageant was expected," wrote an observer. There was none of the glitter and show, the pomp and display which in other countries "draw crowds to witness . . . a royal speech or an imperial coronation." Fashionable Washington was drawn "to hear an old man speak!" It was a "spontaneous offering" to an "illustrious orator."[15]

[14] Ibid., 247-52.
[15] New York Herald, February 7, 1850; New York Tribune, February 7, 1850; Peter Harvey, Reminiscences and Anecdotes of Daniel Webster (Boston, 1877), 218; Philadelphia Inquirer, February 7, 1850.

And what of Clay himself? Suffering from a cold, he gamely made his way up Capitol Hill, pausing now and again to cough, while a fellow Kentuckian proffered a supporting arm. He entered the chamber "erect, calm and serene, the dignity of his manner happily conforming to the power of his reasoning." Beginning the address at 1 o'clock, Clay talked for two and a half hours and did not resort to Lundyfoot snuff till the afternoon's effort was almost over.[16] Stressing the concern he felt for the country, Clay said he had found Congress anxious and appalled. Parties and party spirit he accused of being at the root of the trouble. He deemed a comprehensive adjustment essential, and only "passion, passion—party, party—and intemperance" could prevent its realization. Do away with these, he pleaded, and tranquillity would be restored.

In the course of a detailed exposition, Clay did not dwell long on California. Delegates to a constitutional convention, backed by voters in a referendum, could determine whether their fledgling state would accept or reject slavery. "If . . . a decision of California has taken place adverse to the wishes of the southern States, it is a decision respecting which they cannot complain to the General Government." Californians made it, he reminded his auditors, and Californians "incontestibly" had a right to make it. Respecting territorial stipulations, Clay first referred to the Wilmot Proviso. It was true that northern states "put their hearts upon the adoption of this measure," but "I call upon them to waive persisting in it" and "to see, as they must see, if their eyes are open, the dangers which lie under it." Slavery could not exist under Mexican law, and in Clay's view the same prohibition applied to land formerly Mexican but now American. Furthermore, "according to all the probabilities of the case, slavery will never be introduced into any portion" of it.

[16] Clay to Mrs. Clay, January 11, 21, February 7, 19, 1850, Thomas J. Clay Papers, Library of Congress; Calvin Colton (ed.), *The Works of Henry Clay* (10 vols., New York, 1904), III, 129-31; New York *Tribune*, February 7, 1850.

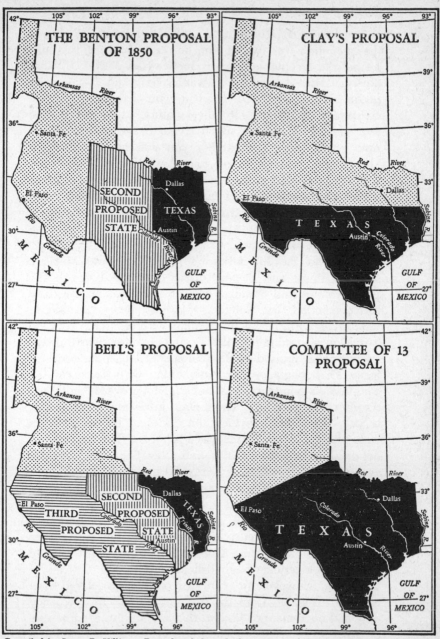

FOUR PROPOSALS FOR DIVIDING TEXAS SOIL

Developing this theme at length, Clay explained that if the institution was barred from fertile California, it would scarcely be acceptable in unproductive New Mexico. "What do you want?—what do you want?" he asked, "—you who reside in the free States. Do you want that there shall be no slavery introduced into the territories acquired by the war with Mexico? have you not your desire in California? And in all human probability you will have it in New Mexico also. What more do you want? You have got what is worth more than a thousand Wilmot provisos. You have nature on your side—facts upon your side—and this truth staring you in the face," that there is no slavery in that area.

Solution of the New Mexico problem hinged in part on the Texas boundary, which, as described by Clay, would extend from the Rio Grande's mouth to New Mexico's southern limits and thence to the 1819 line between the United States and Spain. The week before, Senator Rusk had contended that Congress was no more warranted in interfering with Texas' limits than with Kentucky's. Clay denied this, arguing that the Texas boundary "was unfixed, and remains unfixed at this moment." The residents of Santa Fe strongly opposed any union with Texas, and a compromise boundary was essential to prevent "agitation, disorder and anarchy." The federal government ought also to pay "the debt for which the duties of foreign imports were pledged" when Texas was a republic. The sum should not be less than $3,000,000, and Clay would be "greatly surprised" if the people of Texas did not approve it.

Clay agreed to an adjournment at this point in his argument, but the following day he resumed his remarks with courtly recognition of the "vast assemblage of beauty, grace, elegance, and intelligence"—the ladies and gentlemen who had come to hear him. Congress had the constitutional power, he asserted, to abolish slavery in the District of Columbia. However, an expression on this subject had been carefully excluded from the fifth resolution. Inexpediency only had been mentioned, and that was due to the interests of adjacent Maryland. The District slave trade, on the other hand, was "repugnant" to both Southerners and Northerners. Abolish it, and adopt the other measures, and "I venture to predict that, instead of the distractions and anxieties which now prevail, we shall have peace and quiet for thirty years hereafter."

As to fugitive slaves, it was the Northerners' duty to aid Southerners in securing them. Instead, Negroes were being urged to run away (often to their own disadvantage), and a southern citizen no longer could travel safely with his servant in the North. Actions of individuals and actions of states were irritating and inflammatory. Northern state laws, with obstructive devices, were unneighborly and unconstitutional. Without pledging adherence to Mason's bills, Clay pounded home the need of increasing the effectiveness of federal regulations. "I will go with the furthest Senator from the South . . . to impose the heaviest sanctions upon the recovery of fugitive slaves, and the restoration of them to their owners." On the self-explanatory eighth resolution, the sponsor spoke briefly. Then he scrutinized and rejected the pet project of many Southerners—extension of the 36°30' provision of the Missouri Compromise to the Pacific.

Near the close of his remarks, as at the outset, Clay exhorted fellow senators to concede and forbear. He emphatically opposed secession, equating the end of the Union with war. "Sir, we may search the pages of history, and none so furious, so bloody, so implacable, so exterminating, from the wars of Greece down . . . none, none of them raged with such violence . . . as will that war which shall follow that disastrous event—if that event ever happens—of dissolution." And after civil war? A tyrant would arise, extinquishing the light of liberty. "I conjure gentlemen . . . solemnly to pause . . . at the edge of the precipice, before the fearful and disastrous leap is taken into the yawning abyss below." Looking skyward, Clay begged the best blessing of Heaven that, if dissolution should indeed occur, he would not survive to behold it.[17]

[17] *Congressional Globe,* 31 Cong., 1 Sess., *Appendix,* 115-27.

6

EXTREMISTS on both sides reacted in character to Clay's
proposals. "Sentiment for the north," sniffed Senator Chase,
and "substance for the south—just like the Missouri Compromise." Beverley Tucker disagreed. The South would
concede everything and the North very little, in the judgment of the angry Virginia professor, who called Clay a
"humbug" and a "charlatan." Orlando Brown, close friend
of Taylor's, held that the influence of the resolutions would
be greater in the North than in the South. Outlaw, the
misnamed mild North Carolinian, found that Clay's ideas
"do not seem to meet with much favour." And Philip Hone
thought pessimistically that faction had got beyond the
control of reason.[18] Clay, however, was cheered by re-
sponses from Daniel Ullman and others in New York City.

Such Whig newspapers as the New York *Express* and the
Lexington *Observer & Reporter* enthusiastically lauded
Clay. The Washington *Union,* Democratic and national
in its outlook, gave qualified approval to the two-day
speech; it was happy that Clay said "grace over the whole
barrel" in contrast to the President's "dilatory, temporizing,
timorous policy." Nevertheless, Speaker Cobb feared that
"no good is to result" from words that would have a "bad
effect" on Northerners—leading them to think that Clay
"expresses southern sentiment, which is very far from being
the fact." On February 7, Clay himself wrote: "I have been
yesterday and the day before making a Speech of near four
hours and three quarters, in the Senate, on my proposition

[18] *Diary and Correspondence of Salmon P. Chase,* American Historical Association *Annual Report . . . for the Year 1902* (Washington, 1903), II, 200-201; Beverley Tucker to Hammond, February 2,
1850, Hammond Papers; Orlando Brown to John J. Crittenden,
February 1, 1850, John J. Crittenden Papers, Library of Congress;
Outlaw to Mrs. Outlaw, January 30, 1850, Outlaw Papers; Colton
(ed.), *The Works of Henry Clay,* V, 600; Philip Hone, manuscript
diary, February 18, 1850, New-York Historical Society.

to compromise the Slavery questions. It has exhausted me very much, but I hope to recover my strength in a day or two. Whether my specific propositions will be adopted or not is uncertain, but all agree that my movement and Speeches have done good."[19] The Hone diary and the Cobb, Outlaw, and Tucker manuscripts show that Clay was sanguine when he used the word "all."

Two developments, one prompt and the other cumulative, gave heart to Clay and his admirers. The bipartisan nature of compromise sentiment was exemplified by Sam Houston, who delivered a well-timed Union eulogy in the Senate. Although preferring the extension of 36°30′ and disagreeing with Clay on the boundary matter, the Texan was amicable and his contribution welcome. Like Clay, Houston closed with a stirring peroration: "I wish, if this Union must be dissolved, that its ruins may be the monument of my grave, and the graves of my family. I wish no epitaph to be written to tell that I survived the ruin of this glorious Union."[20] Comparably important was the progress of arrangements for procompromise public meetings, which Clay held to be vital. As early as December 22, Clay had urged his fellow-townsman Leslie Combs to drum up conciliatory spirit in Kentucky. On February 2, he counseled Ullman to do the same thing in New York. "Large public meetings (one at New York especially), indorsing my plan substantially, would do much good," Clay wrote. "I am glad to hear of the contemplated popular movement in the city of New York," he later told the same correspondent. Its beneficial effects would "depend much upon its being conducted as a local and spontaneous assemblage, without any

[19] New York *Express*, February 5, 6, 1850; Lexington (Ky.) *Observer & Reporter*, February 6, 1850; Washington *Union*, February 2, 1850; Ulrich B. Phillips (ed.), *The Correspondence of Robert Toombs, Alexander H. Stephens, and Howell Cobb*, American Historical Association *Annual Report . . . for the Year 1911* (Washington, 1913), II, 183-84; Clay to Mrs. Clay, February 7, 1850, Thomas J. Clay Papers.

[20] *Congressional Globe*, 31 Cong., 1 Sess., *Appendix*, 97-102.

ground for the imputation of its being prompted from any
exterior source." Both Democrats and Whigs should attend,
the partisan of old insisted.[21]

In a sense it was ironic that Foote, not Clay, first presented a plan for handling in the Senate the measures which
Clay had advanced and which have become associated with
his name. After Clay had proposed his solutions, Foote
called for a select committee to pass upon the sectional
problems and unite most or all of them in a single bill.
Foote said he made this move on the assumption that Clay
favored just such strategy in his speech of February 5 and
6, expanding on the January 29 resolutions. Clay, however,
denied this. "My desire," he said, "was that the Senate
should express its sense upon each of the resolutions,
beginning with the first and ending with the eighth. . . . I
never did contemplate embracing in the entire scheme of
accommodation and harmony . . . all these distracting questions, and bringing them all into one measure."

No other remarks at the time throw brighter light on the
evolutionary nature of developments during 1850 than those
of the Mississippi Democrat and the Kentucky Whig. Foote
accused Clay of "throwing into the hands of his adversaries
all the *trump cards* in the pack." Clay disparaged Foote's
"omnibus speech, in which he introduced all sorts of things
and every sort of passenger, and myself among the number."[22] It was thus, on Clay's initiative, that the word
"omnibus" was incorporated in standard 1850 congressional
language. Superficially, it seemed that the two men's
strategies were as far apart as their figures of speech. In a
matter of weeks, however, these senators and their plans
would be in close conjunction.

[21] Louisville *Journal*, July 21, 1860; Colton (ed.), *The Works of
Henry Clay*, V, 593, 600-601.
[22] *Congressional Globe*, 31 Cong., 1 Sess., 356, 365-69.

CHAPTER IV

Equilibrium or Union—Calhoun or Webster?

.———◀(O)▶———.

D URING THE fortnight when Senate attention re-
volved around Clay's resolutions, all five of the
formal House orations were delivered by followers
of Calhoun. On January 30, Albert G. Brown of Mississippi
stressed his section's economic strength and threatened
secession if Northerners failed to substitute fairness for
oppression. Among those who took the same line were
Alabama's Samuel W. Inge and Tennessee's Frederick P.
Stanton. Of the twenty-two set speeches in the House in
February, nine were delivered by southern Democrats, four
by southern Whigs, three by northern Democrats, five by
northern Whigs, and one by a northern Free Soiler. At
least one person argued for every shade of partisan and
sectional opinion. If the declamatory efforts of the Browns
and the Inges were saturated with grievances and studded
with threats, they were countered by the equal intransigence
of Thaddeus Stevens and Horace Mann.[1] It was noteworthy
that six of the nine northern spokesmen supported either

the Wilmot Proviso or the Taylor program set forth in the
President's special message to Congress. The greatest support for compromise in the House came from northwestern
Democrats and southern Whigs, but even they premised the
adjustments they deemed acceptable on stipulations which
extremists thought intolerable.

The tide of feeling that ran so strong in the House had in
the Senate not been abated by the submission of Clay's
resolutions. Berrien of Georgia saw his Southland endan-
gered by repeated assaults on her way of life. Perils had
been generated by the "madness of fanaticism," by the
"calculating . . . spirit of political demagogues," and by the
"excited feelings of a wronged and insulted people." Explicitly denying the authority of Congress to shut slavery
out of the West, the old Whig affirmed the right of any
Southerner to take slave property there. "If you seriously
believe that slavery is a stain upon the land where it exists
—that it will pollute the soil—that you cannot dwell among
slaveholders—if this be your real belief," Berrien challenged,
then "make a partition of the country." For himself, he
valued the Union highly. "I owe, nevertheless, a duty to
my State, which I will endeavor to fulfill."

Jefferson Davis, the next Senate speaker, charged Clay
with performing a disservice to the South by surrendering
her claim to equal rights and by minimizing abolitionism.
How to allay the excitement and dispel the tempest?
Surely not by submission to "a self-sustaining power"
steadily advancing toward "unlimited supremacy." Davis
denied Clay's assumption that, in the concessions he was
sponsoring, the North yielded more than she received.
Slavery was a blessing, Davis continued. It wa a godsend
to Africans brought from a benighted region to a Christian
land. Unlike degraded free Negroes in the North, slaves
were comfortable and happy. Factious, revolutionary firebrands who warred against this beneficial institution were

<hr>

[1] *Congressional Globe,* 31 Cong., 1 Sess., 257-61, 336-40, 348-50,
358-61, 388-89; *ibid., Appendix,* 102-15, 138-43, 157-65, 177-93,
195-201, 211-28.

backed by scheming northern politicians. Davis did not say precisely what would be acceptable, so far as slavery was concerned, in the West. But he implied that the extension of the Missouri line to the Pacific constituted the "substantial security" which might satisfy the South.[2]

Equally critical of Clay, Louisiana's Senator Downs talked in terms of—but did not definitely advocate—the founding of a Southern Confederacy. Painting plantation life as idyllic, Downs berated Taylor for interference in California. He prayed that Northerners "will listen to us" so that "strife between us will cease forever." To some extent Downs was seconded by Rusk of Texas, who defended the southern position, urging men of the North to pause and reflect before proceeding to extremities. An expert on areas, treaties, and titles, the Texan discussed the southwestern boundary; finding fault with Clay's statistics, he claimed the maximum for Texas. The speech of Jacob W. Miller of New Jersey, who pledged his state to uphold the Union until the silencing of the last gun, noticeably irritated Rusk. The northern Whig senator, a strong Taylor adherent, lauded the President as a patriotic pilot capable of weathering stormy seas—a tribute that did not please the southern Democrats. Neither Downs nor Rusk was so conclusive as Miller when it came to specific recommendations. The latter recommended the Administration policy as suiting the nation's needs, while the Southerners were content to blast both Taylor's and Clay's proposals without offering alternatives of their own.[3]

2

THOUGH MUCH of the oratory in both chambers portended no foreseeable compromise, significant maneuvering occurred in the House or outside the Capitol. Northern extremists were jolted on February 4, for when the House

[2] *Ibid., Appendix,* 149-57, 202-11.
[3] *Ibid., Appendix,* 233-39, 310-18.

took up Root's resolution to apply the Wilmot Proviso to all
new western land except California, the Free Soiler's project
was tabled by a safe majority, 105 to 75, with eighteen
northern Democrats and fourteen northern Whigs sustaining the South in this crisis. The Douglas lieutenants,
McClernand and Richardson, joined Boyd and Bayly in the
tabling vote. Thus it appeared that the Northwesterners
and the Southerners had achieved a *modus vivendi*. On
February 10, a different sort of victory was scored for the
compromise cause. At the National Hotel, Henry Clay and
Congressman Bayly met privately with Clay's old foe
Thomas Ritchie. An acknowledged leader of the Democratic party and the editor of the *Union*, white-haired
"Father" Ritchie had made overtures to Clay in the
columns of his newspaper. The coalition of these erstwhile
foes symbolized the growing strength of the compromise
forces.[4]

The next day in the National Hotel there was a larger,
perhaps equally important, meeting—an assemblage of investors and speculators whose holdings included Texas
bonds, securities which might soon be redeemed if Washington paid the Texas debt. Chief sponsor of the gathering
was General James Hamilton, former governor of South
Carolina and attorney for owners of over half the bonds.
Minutes of the meeting have never been found, but circumstantial evidence strongly suggests that agreements
were reached concerning the establishment of an effective
bondholders' lobby. As the year went on, the work of the
lobbyists was apparent at the Capitol. And Hamilton was
to boast that "no man in or out of Congress . . . contributed
more to the adjustment of [the] Texas question at Washington than myself."[5]

[4] *Ibid.*, 276; Richmond *Enquirer*, September 10, 1852; Henry S.
Foote, *A Casket of Reminiscences* (Washington, 1872), 24-26. James
W. Simenton of the New York *Courier & Enquirer* helped with the
preliminaries.

[5] Austin *Texas State Gazette*, January 12, 1850; James Hamilton to
Thomas J. Rusk, September 27, 1850, and Rusk to Hamilton, September 29, 1850, Thomas J. Rusk Papers, University of Texas, Austin.

Later in February, at Cobb's residence on Third Street, seven members of the House subscribed to a course of action which Douglas and his aides initiated. It was understood that McClernand would introduce bills for Territories of New Mexico and Utah on a popular-sovereignty basis; California was to be admitted free, and slavery retained in the District of Columbia, with all these measures interdependent. McClernand also promised that Douglas would follow the same procedure in the Senate. While no immediate legislative achievements developed from the conference, it was significant that two of the seven representatives were southern Whigs. The fact that Robert Toombs and Alexander H. Stephens were willing to work for a Democratic program encouraged Cobb, McClernand, and Douglas.[6]

Meanwhile, as in the defeat of Root, moderate men removed a worrisome barrier from the floor of the House. James D. Doty, a Wisconsin free-soil Democrat, had proposed that a California statehood bill unlinked with other legislation be reported by the Committee on Territories, a move that angered Southerners, who saw a bargaining point slipping from their grasp. Thirty roll calls in close succession took place on the proposal, with Speaker Cobb and his associates dextrously using delaying tactics, for it was clear that if Doty succeeded, the compromisers would be hamstrung. With Bayly demanding "resistance at all hazards," the Democratic chieftains and a few Whigs stalled and dodged with agility, their every motion sustained by the Georgian in the chair. For the better part of a day, from early afternoon till midnight, the pro-California majority was deprived of a showdown vote. Finally, the House adjourned without acting. Other business supplanted Doty's the next day, and the authority of the Speaker for the first time was fully felt.[7]

[6] Alexander H. Stephens, A Constitutional View of the Late War Between the States (2 vols., Philadelphia, 1868-1870), II, 202-204.
[7] Congressional Globe, 31 Cong., 1 Sess., 375-85; Alice E. Smith, James Duane Doty: Frontier Promoter (Madison, Wis., 1954), 319-20.

3

DURING THE MONTH of February reactions to Clay's proposals and to the crisis, both in Washington and in the
country at large, were as mixed as those on the floor of
Congress. The newspapers of the capital, except for the
abolitionist *National Era,* tended to marshal moderate
opinion favorable to the spirit of compromise. Readers
of the Whig *National Intelligencer* and the Democratic
Union were encouraged to support an adjustment while
even the *Republic,* which was the Administration "organ,"
praised Clay as well as Taylor. In other quarters, however,
the opinions on Clay's measures were by no means encour-
aging. "I do not think much of Clay's compromise as a
whole," wrote Edward Everett, and he added, "Unless some
southern man of influence has courage enough to take
ground against the extension of slavery, and in favor of its
abolition in the jurisdictions of the United States, we shall
infallibly separate; not perhaps immediately but before
long." A friend of Thurlow Weed was more pessimistic:
"Clay's compromise is as dead as herrings that are red. He
has offended the South without appeasing the North—He
should retire from that kind of business."[8] And Seward
defined Clay's "scheme" as a "magnificent humbug." On
the other hand, so irate were New York merchants at the
Seward-Weed Whig faction's opposition to a Clay adjustment that they helped launch an Albany paper as a rival to
Weed's *Journal.* A few of the merchants pledged nearly
$10,000 in a single evening, and the wealthy William B.
Astor added $1,000. Businessmen issued a call for a mass
meeting in New York to encourage Congress in settling

[8] Washington *National Intelligencer,* Washington *Union,* Washington *Republic,* February-March, 1850, *passim;* Edward Everett to
Robert C. Winthrop, February 1, 1850, Everett letterbook, Massachusetts Historical Society, Boston; D. H. Abell to Thurlow Weed,
February 1, 1850, Thurlow Weed Papers, University of Rochester.

"great questions now agitating the nation." In three days promoters secured the signatures of 2,500 merchants, so alarmed was the business community by the possible loss of southern trade.[9]

Other events and opinions emphasized the anxieties and divisions which were pervading the nation. Between February 6 and 13, several southern states approved the Nashville Convention and arranged to send delegates. The Georgia Legislature appropriated $30,000 for a state convention to review the course of Congress and to request a redress of grievances. Stephens of Georgia saw "no prospect of a continuance of this Union long." "Everything here is uncertain," he wrote from Washington; "we are like a set of fellows at sea, trying to make a port in a storm." Hone, the New Yorker, thought the outlook bleak. So did Henry H. Sibley, the delegate to Congress from the Territory of Minnesota.[10] Indicative of the uncertainties of the time were the vacillations of Edward Everett and Horace Greeley. The ex-president of Harvard was swayed by each scrap of news blowing in from Washington. To Winthrop he said one thing, to Webster another, to Nathan Appleton a third; he seemed to have no purpose other than ingratiation.[11]

[9] William H. Seward to Weed, February 2, 14, 1850, Simeon Draper to Weed, July 22, 1850, Weed Papers; Jerome Fuller to Millard Fillmore, February 18, 1850, John L. Bush to Fillmore, February 23, 1850, Hugh Maxwell to Fillmore, February 25, 1850, Millard Fillmore Papers, Buffalo Historical Society.

[10] Philip M. Hamer, *The Secession Movement in South Carolina, 1847-1852* (Allentown, Pa., 1918), 43-45; Richard H. Shryock, *Georgia and the Union in 1850* (Durham, N.C., 1926), 217-32; Henry T. Shanks, *The Secession Movement in Virginia, 1847-1861* (Richmond, 1934), 30-31; Lewy Dorman, *Party Politics in Alabama from 1850 through 1860* (Wetumpka, Ala., 1935), 37-38, 43; Richard M. Johnston and William H. Browne, *Life of Alexander H. Stephens* (Philadelphia, 1884), 247-48; Philip Hone, manuscript diary, February 9, 1850, New-York Historical Society, New York City; Henry H. Sibley to Alexander Ramsey, February 9, 1850, Alexander Ramsey Papers, Minnesota Historical Society, St. Paul.

[11] Everett to Winthrop, February 18, 28, March 1, 21, 1850, Everett to Nathan Appleton, February 4, 1850, Everett to J. C. Warren, February 14, 1850, Everett to Daniel Webster, March 12, 22, 1850, letterbook, Everett Papers.

Although Greeley stood with Clay most of the time, in the spring he defected to Taylor, then changed back to Clay again. Optimistic the first seven weeks of 1850, the New York editor was suddenly petrified at the thought of disunion. Sixty members of Congress "this day desire . . . a Dissolution of the Union . . . and are plotting to effect it," he wrote on February 23.[12] The indecisiveness of such leaders as Everett and Greeley did little to further a settlement of the crisis.

In the midst of this flux Taylor continued to stand firm, although on February 21 the Boston *Advertiser* quoted the New York *Herald* to the effect that Taylor's Cabinet was upset by developments. After Horace Mann dined at the White House, he reported to his wife that Taylor seemed childlike when he talked about plans for levying an embargo and blockading southern harbors. "I can save the Union," the President told Mann, "without shedding a drop of blood."[13] Southern congressmen found Taylor just as determined when, in an interview at the Mansion, they threatened secession in certain contingencies. According to some accounts, he looked on them as traitors and said he would personally take the field if troops were ordered out to smash a rebellion. He also expressed satisfaction that the South itself would react adversely and patriotically if a drive was made to destroy the Union. Regardless of details, all versions of this interview depict the President as inflexible.[14]

Tempers were sizzling when Taylor left on a trip to Richmond, where he dedicated the cornerstone for a monument to George Washington. Taylor's remarks at Virginia's

[12] New York *Tribune*, February 20, 23-25, March 9, April 19, May 10, July 9, 1850.
[13] New York *Herald*, quoted in Boston *Advertiser*, February 21, 1850; Mary Mann, *Life of Horace Mann* (Boston, 1891), 292-93.
[14] Thurlow W. Barnes, *Memoir of Thurlow Weed* (Boston, 1884), 176-78; James F. Rhodes, *History of the United States from the Compromise of 1850* (7 vols., New York, 1893-1906), I, 134; New York *Tribune*, February 25, 1850.

capital were innocuous enough, but, reaching Fredericks-
burg on the way home, the Chief Executive minced no
words. "As to the Constitution and the Union," he said,
"I have taken an oath to support the one, and I cannot do
so without preserving the other, unless I commit perjury,
which I certainly don't intend to do. We must cherish the
Constitution to the last. There may be and will be local
questions to disturb our peace; but, after all, we must fall
back upon the farewell address of the father of his country.
Near this spot he spent a large portion of his . . . life, and
near here his parents lie buried. Let us remember his
farewell advice, and let us, in all time, preserve the Union
at all hazards." Thus, publicly as well as privately and in
a slave state as well as at the White House, the President
refused to alter his position.[15]

4

THOUGH CALHOUN commented in his letters that the only
alternative for the South was secession,[16] on other occasions
he was more reserved. Even on March 4, when he exerted
himself to the utmost, tottering into the Senate on the arm
of James Hamilton, the words he brought to the Capitol
were punctuated with caution. Wrapped in flannels, he
was so feeble that he could not speak for himself. And so,
sinking into his chair, he listened as Mason of Virginia read
what he had written. A throng of visitors had come to
hear what many thought would be the sick man's last
speech. The womenfolk were again on hand in their bon-

[15] Washington *Republic*, February 23, 25, 1850; Richmond *Enquirer*, February 26, 1850; Richmond *Whig*, February 26, 1850; Boston *Post*, March 2, 1850; New Orleans *Weekly Picayune*, March 11,
1850.
[16] J. Franklin Jameson (ed.), *Correspondence of John C. Calhoun*,
American Historical Association *Annual Report . . . for the Year
1899* (Washington, 1900), II, 781.

nets and rustling skirts, for they anticipated drama. Webster
and Clay were in their places, and a hush encompassed the
chamber as the principal sponsor of the Fugitive Slave Bill
delivered Calhoun's crisp sentences.[17]

In Calhoun's interpretation, the primary reason for the
Southerners' discontent was the disappearance of an equilibrium once existing between the South and the North. It
no longer existed, he asserted, because of piecemeal destruction through the years, beginning in 1787 with the
Northwest Ordinance. The Missouri Compromise had followed, and then the creation of Oregon Territory, those
three enactments excluding slaveholders from a million
and a quarter square miles. Small wonder that, in the
House, the South's representatives were less numerous than
the North's. If the trend continued, and especially if California were admitted free, the Senate balance would dis-
appear. Hence southern men were unhappy and fearful,
and the Union was "in danger."

The equilibrium having vanished, according to Calhoun,
free states had dominated Congress and passed tariff laws
for their own benefit. The North got more than its rightful
share from customs duties, and in the development of
industries which were financed by the agricultural South.
As a result, the North's capital had pyramided, attracting
immigrants to the Northeast and Northwest. The immigrants swelled northern majorities in the House and the
electoral college, and the North could do more and more
as it pleased. With the North ever more imperious, could
the South safeguard the Constitution's guarantees? If no
state-rights recourse remained, then the character of the
government had changed from a federal republic into a
consolidated national democracy.

17 Charles M. Wiltse, *John C. Calhoun: Sectionalist, 1840-1850*
(Indianapolis, 1951), 460, 552; New York *Herald,* March 5, 6, May
3, 1850; New York *Tribune,* March 5, 1850; Charleston *Courier,*
March 9, 1850; Charlotte Everett to Edward Everett, [March 6,]
1850, Everett Papers.

The North's "absolute control" might be endured, said Calhoun, if no vital question divided the sections. There was such an issue, however, and in scattering incendiary pamphlets through the South, in pressing the battle for abolition petitions and interfering with delivery of fugitive slaves, the North worked toward the goal of eliminating slavery everywhere. As proof of deteriorating relations, Calhoun cited what was happening to churches. Methodist and Baptist denominations had divided sectionally over slavery. The Presbyterians were following suit, and the governmental cord binding the Union fared no better than the spiritual. The cry of "Union!" could no more prevent disunion than the cry of "Health!" could save a patient lying desperately ill. Nor could the Administration plan prevent it. The "Executive proviso" was plotted to do covertly what the Wilmot Proviso would do openly: deprive the South of her rights in the West. Legally there was no state of California, which was only an offspring of presidential interference. Did senators think that shutting Southerners out of land acquired from Mexico "is an object of so paramount a character . . . that right, justice, constitution, and consistency must all yield when they stand in the way of our exclusion?"

"But . . . what is to be done?" The stronger North should concede to the weaker South an equal right in the new West. It should fulfil stipulations on fugitive slaves and agree to a constitutional amendment, restoring to the South the power she possessed before the equilibrium was destroyed. If this was to be refused, northern spokesmen should say so and let states separate in peace. "We shall know what to do, when you reduce the question to submission or resistance." If the North stood silent, the inference would be plain. Then California would become the test, and her admission would point to the intention of destroying the equilibrium irretrievably. "We would be blind not to perceive, in that case, that your real objects

are power and aggrandizement, and infatuated not to act
accordingly."[18]

As Senator Mason spun Calhoun's syllogisms, occupants
of the gallery who could see the principals strained to study
the author's face. None could know what passed through
the mind of the veteran of the War Hawk days, the man
who had served as secretary of war, vice president, secretary of state, and had reached thrice toward a higher
office. If he cherished regret or if pride surged swiftly,
Calhoun gave no sign of it. Eyes narrowed, shoulders
sagging, gray hair framing his sunken cheeks, he resembled
a graven image. When Mason finished reading, there was
silence for a moment. Then, one by one, defender and
detractor gripped the hand of the "cast-iron man." And
old friends came to take his arm, helping him return to
boardinghouse and bed.[19]

5

SOME REACTIONS to the speech were favorable, Calhoun's
ideas were "the only safe and sound ones," said James H.
Hammond. The former governor of South Carolina believed
that, if Northerners did not consent to permanent equality
in the Senate, "we should . . . kick them out of the Capitol
& set it on fire." Calhoun's argument was powerful and
"very patriotic," Richard Rush of Pennsylvania wrote to
Mason. Ex-President John Tyler, however, thought the
sentiments "too ultra." And Senator King of Alabama
reported to Buchanan that in general the speech was "able"
but "in some particulars met with no approval from a large
majority of Southern men." A distinguished Maryland Whig
declared that "a more peevish and feeble manifesto was
never put forth in a wretched cause." Especially significant
was the attitude of Mississippi's Foote, who had been a

18 *Congressional Globe*, 31 Cong., 1 Sess., 451-55.
19 New York *Tribune*, March 5, 1850.

Calhoun correspondent the preceding summer but now prepared to chip away at the speech in the Senate.[20]

The next afternoon a 40-year-old Democrat from Maine, Hannibal Hamlin, became the first New England senator to deliver a set speech in the "Great Debate." For the most part, his views coincided with Taylor's and Benton's. A combination of measures did not interest him, for "each question" should "depend upon itself" without resort to "entangling alliances." Scoffing at the "state of alarm" produced with the aid of "stage machinery," Hamlin defended the California record of the Administration and said that Berrien and Calhoun once advocated what they now deplored—the very action Californians had taken. Hamlin's place has been minimized in most accounts of Senate developments. This is surprising, for he was important as a Taylor adherent in 1850 and eventually became a Republican leader, serving as Abraham Lincoln's vice president.

A senator whose part in the 1850 proceedings is of interest as illustrative of the influence of legislative instructions and who has received slight attention from historians was Isaac P. Walker, a Democrat from Wisconsin. Walker had been subjected to a barrage of criticism from the Wisconsin Legislature on the grounds that he had favored the South during the Thirtieth Congress. Now, with instructions to support the Wilmot Proviso, he tried to make amends by justifying federal exclusion of slavery from the western domain. In a series of exchanges with Cass, and with Butler and Davis, he seemed to be beyond his intellectual depth, however, in dilating on constitutional nu-

[20] James H. Hammond to John C. Calhoun, [March 6,] 1850, James H. Hammond Papers, Library of Congress; Charles H. Ambler (ed.), *Correspondence of Robert M. T. Hunter, 1826-1876,* American Historical Association *Annual Report . . . for the Year 1916* (Washington, 1918), II, 106; Lyon G. Tyler (ed.), *The Letters and Times of the Tylers* (3 vols., Richmond, 1884-1896), II, 481; William R. King to James Buchanan, March 11, 1850, James Buchanan Papers, Historical Society of Pennsylvania, Philadelphia; John P. Kennedy to Joseph Gales, March 9, 1850, author's collection; *Congressional Globe,* 31 Cong., 1 Sess., 461-64.

ances. As a result of pressure from home and warnings
from his colleague Dodge, Walker on test after test would
later vote alongside Dodge, Hamlin, and Benton.[21]

                                    6

BETWEEN THE START and finish of Walker's performance
came one of the most widely discussed orations in American
annals. This was what soon came to be known as the
"Seventh of March Speech" of Daniel Webster. As when
Clay had spoken, the Senate was crowded long before it
convened. Edward Everett's daughter, who surrendered
her chair to the wife of Ex-Speaker Winthrop, leaned
against a column and kept track of the time which she
noted was exactly three hours. Other ladies were also
conspicuous, and latecomers were disappointed to find that
not even standing space was available. Soon those who
jammed the galleries were hearing something schoolboys
have since memorized: "Mr. President, I wish to speak
to-day, not as a Massachusetts man, nor as a northern man,
but as an American, and a member of the Senate of the
United States. . . . I speak to-day for the preservation of
the Union. 'Hear me for my cause.'"

Reviewing the history of the Mexican War, the discovery
of gold, and the adoption of the California constitution,
Webster also discussed slavery's place in ancient and modern times. He stressed changing attitudes in the two main
sections of the country. Did not the Northwest Ordinance
bear the hand and seal of every southern member of the
Congress of the Confederation? Had not earlier Americans
looked upon slavery as a political rather than a moral evil?
Current southern economic interests and the religious sentiment of the North altered policies respecting the present
and the future, and also interpretations of the past. Rifts in

[21] *Congressional Globe,* 31 Cong., 1 Sess., *Appendix,* 242-48, 277-
90; Merle Curti, "Isaac P. Walker: Reformer in Mid-Century Politics,"
Wisconsin Magazine of History, XXXIV (Autumn 1950), 3-6, 58-62.

the churches, to which Calhoun had alluded, were indicative of sectional cleavages. Emotionalists now were holding that right could always be distinguished from wrong "with the precision of an algebraic equation."

Remarks like these were not likely to endear Webster to antislavery zealots. He compounded the felony in their eyes by attacking the abolitionists and by criticizing the Wilmot Proviso as unnecessarily offensive to the South. Emotional views, like selfish economic ones, could not restore harmony. The law of nature, Webster insisted, excluded slavery from the West; this was the heart of his argument. California's action had already been taken. As for New Mexico, if required to vote on a territorial government there, he would not inject a prohibition into it. Speaking slowly, as was his wont, Webster came to another quotable sentence, which he pronounced with effective deliberation: "I would not take pains to reaffirm an ordinance of nature, nor to reënact the will of God."

Throughout his speech, Webster kept in mind fellow senators' love of recognition. Friendly references sprinkled his remarks. And, once aware that Calhoun had belatedly entered the chamber, the old adversary twice referred with the utmost kindness to the invalid. Four times Webster evoked laughter. Apt were his reference to Texas (an "immense territory, ever which a bird cannot fly in a week") and his assertion that "the vernacular tongue of the country has become greatly vitiated, depraved, and corrupted, by the style of our congressional debates." Except for such instances, however, he was as serious as the nation's mood. Gravely he summarized grievances. This brought him to the problem of fugitive slaves, and here he took the southern position, promising to support Mason's bill in an amended form.

Critics have pounced on Webster's statement at a dinner party that he had not read Mason's measure when he gave it his assent. Less has been said of his reference to amendments. Unquestionably, what he contributed in this regard was as acceptable to Southerners as his anti-Proviso position.

It is just as true that nothing else in the address did more to arouse resentment in the North. For the rest of his life and long after his death, Northerners held Webster blameworthy for the Fugitive Slave Bill he qualifiedly endorsed. On March 7, however, most of the auditors seemed chiefly interested in the drama of the occasion. The master who twenty years before had electrified the Senate in the "Reply to Hayne" could still be both prophetic and eloquent. "I hear with pain, and anguish, and distress, the word secession," he declared. ". . . Secession! Peaceable secession! Your eyes and mine are never destined to see that miracle." Webster would not say "what might produce the disruption of the States; but, sir, I see it as plainly as I see the sun in heaven—I see that disruption must produce such a war as I will not describe."

Adverting to the Nashville Convention, urging conciliatory counsels there, and advising payment of the Texas debt, Webster concluded: "Never did there devolve, on any generation of men, higher trusts than now devolve upon us for the preservation of this Constitution, and the harmony and peace of all who are destined to live under it. Let us make our generation one of the strongest, and the brightest link, in that golden chain which is destined, I fully believe, to grapple the people of all the States to this Constitution, for ages to come. . . . Large before, the country has now, by recent events, become vastly larger. This Republic now extends, with a vast breadth, across the whole continent. The two great seas of the world wash the one and the other shore. We realize on a mighty scale the beautiful description of the ornamental edging of the buckler of Achilles—

> Now the broad shield complete the artist crowned,
> With his last hand, and poured the ocean round;
> In living silver seemed the waves to roll,
> And beat the buckler's verge, and bound the whole."[22]

[22] Charlotte Everett to Edward Everett, [March 8,] 1850, Everett Papers; *Congressional Globe*, 31 Cong., 1 Sess., *Appendix*, 269-76.

7

JOURNALISTIC PRAISE for the Seventh of March Speech emanated from nearly every quarter.[23] It was the "theme of almost universal eulogy," exclaimed the Boston *Post's* Washington reporter. At the capital, the *National Intelligencer, Union,* and *Republic* lauded it. Even the Charleston *Mercury* said that, "with such a spirit as Mr. Webster has shown, it no longer seems impossible to bring this sectional contest to a close." Letters and diaries contain comparable estimates. "Salutary" was Representative Outlaw's adjective. Even Calhoun was impressed. To him, the Massachusetts senator "shows a yielding on the part of the North, and will do much to discredit Mr Clay" and others offering "less favorable terms." Philip Hone noted that the exordium "is in every man's mouth." "I need not tell you with what satisfaction I read . . . your speech," Webster was assured by Everett, who added, however, that he feared the northern extremists would not like it. Rufus Choate, Benjamin R. Curtis, and William H. Prescott were among nearly a thousand Bostonians signing a congratulatory letter to Webster which was printed in a local paper and copied far and wide.[24]

But not every politician complimented Webster, and

[23] Philadelphia *Inquirer,* March 9, New York *Herald,* March 9, Boston *Courier,* March 12, 13, Baltimore *Sun,* March 8, Augusta (Ga.) *Chronicle,* March 12, New Orleans *Delta,* March 16, Louisville *Journal,* March 15, Knoxville *Whig,* March 30, 1850.

[24] Boston *Post,* March 13, Washington *National Intelligencer,* March 8, Washington *Union,* March 8, 9, Washington *Republic,* March 8, Charleston *Mercury,* March 11, 1850; David Outlaw to Mrs. Outlaw, March 9, 1850, David Outlaw Papers, Southern Historical Collection, University of North Carolina, Chapel Hill; Jameson (ed.), *Correspondence of John C. Calhoun,* II, 784; Philip Hone, manuscript diary, March 14, 1850, New-York Historical Society; Everett to Webster, March 12, 1850, letterbook, Everett Papers; Claude M. Fuess, *Daniel Webster* (2 vols., Boston, 1930), II, 226; Boston *Advertiser,* April 3, 1850.

eastern editors were cold. Garrison observed that never
had a speech been delivered in Congress which "so power-
fully shocked the moral sense, or so grievously insulted the
intelligence of the people of the North." The Hartford
Courant expressed "astonishment and regret." "Unequal
to the occasion and unworthy of its author" was Horace
Greeley's characterization in the New York *Tribune*. In
Boston, the *Atlas* led the attack. In that city, the *Journal*
complained because Webster failed to adopt "President
Taylor's compromise." The *Atlas* said that only six Whig
papers in New England outside Boston sided with Webster,
while over seventy found fault.[25] Emerson, Longfellow,
and Whittier looked down on Webster as on a fallen angel
and were as scornful as Theodore Parker, who likened the
statesman to Benedict Arnold.[26] What Webster uttered on
March 7 was tailored to southern, not northern, taste. With
rare exceptions like George Ashmun of the Sixth Massachusetts District, no "Northern Whig member of Congress"
concurred "with Mr. Webster in the propriety of establishing territorial governments for New-Mexico, &c., *without*
the Wilmot."[27]

Certain details respecting Webster's preparation, his publication of the manuscript, and the reception of the speech
help to make the picture three-dimensional. Besides con-
sulting Calhoun and other Southerners before delivery, the
orator discussed his composition with his son and his
friends Edward Curtis and Peter Harvey. Winthrop said
that Webster's speech "was *tremendously* Southern" as
"made in the Senate," but he "added some points" in the

[25] Boston *Liberator*, May 3, Hartford *Courant*, March 12, New
York *Tribune*, March 9, 1850; Boston *Atlas* cited in Boston *Advertiser*,
March 12, 1850; Godfrey T. Anderson, "The Slavery Issue as a Factor
in Massachusetts Politics from the Compromise of 1850 to the Out-
break of the Civil War" (Unpublished doctoral dissertation, University
of Chicago, 1944), 6.
[26] Holman Hamilton, *Zachary Taylor: Soldier in the White House*
(Indianapolis, 1951), 311-12, 447-48.
[27] Boston *Courier*, March 11, 1850.

printed version to reduce its one-sidedness.[28] In appreciation of his "golden chain" allusion, one admirer made him a gift of a "massive chain of pure California gold." Other friends bought him a superb gold watch. William W. Corcoran, the Washington banker and heavy investor in Texas bonds, sent Webster a letter of congratulation and a check for $1,000 and cancelled the senator's notes amounting to more than $5,000.[29]

8

As to the full effect of the last major Senate speeches of Webster and Calhoun, the commentator must be careful neither to exaggerate nor to underrate. There is no proof that Webster's words changed a single Senate vote. James Cooper, the sole northern Whig senator aligned with Webster during Taylor's lifetime, was pro-Webster long before March. Six Whig senators from slave states looked more to Clay than to Webster for leadership, and in June the five remaining southern Whigs did not follow either of them.[30] As late as July 9, Webster and Cooper excepted, all northern Whig senators supported the President. Several southern Whig representatives appear to have been influenced,[31] but it is doubtful that they would have sided with

28 New York *Herald*, April 13, 1852, January 14, 1859; Fuess, *Daniel Webster*, II, 210; Boston *Advertiser*, February 26, 1850; Winthrop to John H. Clifford, March 10, 1850, Robert C. Winthrop Papers, Massachusetts Historical Society, Boston.

29 Frankfort *Commonwealth*, April 9, 1850; Webster to William W. Corcoran, March 7, 9, 1850, William W. Corcoran Papers, Library of Congress; W. W. Corcoran, *A Grandfather's Legacy* (Washington, 1879), 84-85.

30 John H. Clarke to William M. Meredith, June 1, 1850, William M. Meredith Papers, Historical Society of Pennsylvania; Lewis Cass to Henry Ledyard, June 13, 1850, Lewis Cass Papers, William L. Clements Library, Ann Arbor, Michigan.

31 Outlaw to Mrs. Outlaw, March 9, April 18, 21, 1850, Outlaw Papers.

Webster if he had not identified himself with Clay. A few
northern representatives went along with him, and one can
give Webster the benefit of the doubt by granting that they
followed him. Though Webster and Clay on dramatic
occasions stood for adjustment, Democrats were more po-
tent strategically and numerically in Congressional maneuvering.

This is not to imply that Webster had no influence at all.
There were enough southern Democratic extremists in both
houses to make Democratic recruitment of some Whig
adherents vital in constructing a compromise majority.
If Webster and Clay had turned thumbs down on the
middle road, the anticompromise forces would have re-
joiced. The grandeur of Webster's personality and his
boldness in challenging his New England were a valuable
and undeniable encouragement to compromisers. Webster,
too, spoke at a time when Union rallies were being arranged
in northern cities. Organized principally by Clay men and
by Democrats, they capitalized on the force of Webster's
memorable rhetoric. Foote, in his account of the crisis,
emphasized these big public meetings in "every part of the
republic." Webster, like Clay, was more influential in the
country at large than on Capitol Hill.[32]

If Webster's impact was limited, Calhoun proved even
less successful in advancing the cause he had at heart. He
made few converts, and it seems probable that he even lost
lieutenants. While not many Southerners denounced his
speech, immediate endorsement of his position proved a
rarity in Senate and House. Calhoun was sick, and that
consideration should give pause to any critic. What should
he have done? If he had concentrated on 36°30', he might

[32] Louisville *Journal,* July 21, 1860; Nicholas Dean to James B.
Clay, February 28, 1850, Henry Clay Papers, Library of Congress;
Boston *Courier,* February 25, 1850; John P. Kennedy, manuscript
diary, March 1, 4, 1850, Kennedy Papers, Peabody Institute, Balti-
more; Frankfort *Commonwealth,* March 12, 1850; St. Louis *Missouri
Republican,* March 5, 7, 19, 20, 1850; Henry S. Foote, *War of the
Rebellion; or, Scylla and Charybdis* (New York, 1866), 147.

at least have held together men on the periphery of his camp as well as those die-hard followers who were ready to go anywhere he led. The latter he could not lose. The former he could not afford to lose.

Equilibrium or Union? Two titans had spoken. Now the setting was prepared for the younger men of tomorrow.

CHAPTER V

A Pattern Defined

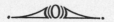

WHEN WILLIAM Henry Seward rose in the Senate on March 11, 1850, a spectator might have assumed that the New Yorker belonged to a lesser breed. One newsman, not unsympathetic, wrote that "never were two heads more unlike each other". than Webster's and Seward's. Webster's "ample brow, broad forehead, and lofty bearing" made you think you saw "a literary giant with corporeal dimensions to suit." Not so Seward, who "looks thin and studious" and "has a compact, well-made head, with nothing extraordinary about it to the casual observer." The voice and manner of the younger Whig were so commonplace that few were surprised to find many empty chairs in the chamber. Seward spoke in a monotone. In an age of declamation, he read his speech. Webster and Clay, however, were present. And Benton, Douglas, Foote, and even the pathetic Calhoun had come to hear the famous freshman senator.[1]

Seward was a Northerner, yet many Northerners could not subscribe to his more extreme assertions. He was a Whig, yet many Whigs called his ideas radical. He was Taylor's intimate, but the President would be upset by his speech, and the newspaper edited by the President's friends would condemn him. And why? There was nothing astonishing in his defense of the White House record on

California, in his taking Calhoun to task for the notion of sectional equilibrium, in his opposition to the capture of fugitive slaves, or in his argument that the Texas boundary issue should be separated from other questions. It was anticipated that he would deny slaveholders their right to carry their chattels into the West, that he would object to a division at 36°30′, and that he would define the Constitution as a compact among the people instead of the states. What ruffled the temper of Seward's critics was his bland introduction into the debate of "a higher law than the Constitution."

Equating his "higher law" with God's opposition to slavery extension, Seward shocked constitutional experts by departing from orthodox legal standards. For all his appeal to the law of nature, and to Baconian and related precedents, his moralistic generalities struck expedient men as irresponsible. In after years, the public forgot that the rest of his speech bore close resemblance to those of Miller, Hamlin, and other Northerners. When Seward insisted that Congress had the power to legislate on slavery in the territories, he cited the Constitution itself. Like Hamlin, he said that the Union was unshaken, the national crisis notwithstanding. Slavery, he predicted, would soon be eliminated by constitutional and peaceful means. Let timorous souls, who distrusted the Union, make compromises to save it. Their wisdom should not be impeached, nor their patriotism doubted. "But indulging no such apprehensions myself, I shall vote for the admission of California directly, without conditions, without qualifications, and without compromise."[2]

The storm that beat about Seward was of hurricane force. In the Deep South, he was termed an "unscrupulous demagogue." A Kentucky editor consigned him to "eternal execration." "Hateful" was the word selected by William G.

[1] New York *Tribune*, March 16, 1850; Boston *Courier*, March 21, 1850.

[2] *Congressional Globe*, 31 Cong., 1 Sess., *Appendix*, 260-69.

Brownlow's Knoxville *Whig*.[3] Philip Hone of Seward's state
found the speech "great" but "wild," right in some things,
wrong in more. "If Mr. Seward's doctrines were to be
endorsed by the people at large," said a Democratic paper
in New Hampshire, "there would be an end not only of
the Union but of every rational form of government." The
New York *Herald* was of the same mind.[4] The Washington
Republic attacked Seward. An associate of Weed's wrote
the Albany boss that "Gov S should have said nothing about
God's laws." Weed sadly agreed, confessing to the senator:
"Your speech which I read carefully last night, sent me to
bed with a heavy heart." Approval, however, came from
such sources as the Boston *Atlas* and New York *Tribune*.[5]
And Seward benefited from the mediocrity of the next
Southerner to address the Senate. Hopkins L. Turney was
a second-rate debater. Indeed, the paragraphs of the Tennessee Democrat sound as if penned long in advance and
then hastily revised to bring the New Yorker into range.[6]

2

SEWARD'S CRITICS were still sputtering when Stephen A.
Douglas gratified the moderates with a speech. Implicit in
nearly everything he said was the national Democrats'
established strategy of full cooperation with Clay. At times
the Little Giant was deferential, handing verbal bouquets

[3] New Orleans *Weekly Picayune*, March 25, 1850; Lexington (Ky.)
Observer & Reporter, March 27, 1850; Knoxville *Whig*, April 13,
1850.

[4] Philip Hone, manuscript diary, March 12, 1850, New-York Historical Society, New York City; Concord *New Hampshire Patriot*,
March 21, 1850; New York *Herald*, March 13, 1850.

[5] Washington *Republic*, March 15, 1850; John C. Clark to Thurlow
Weed, March 17, 1850, Thurlow Weed Papers, Weed to William H.
Seward, March 14, 1850, William H. Seward Papers, University of
Rochester; Boston *Atlas*, March 15, 1850; New York *Tribune*, March
13, 1850.

[6] *Congressional Globe*, 31 Cong., 1 Sess., *Appendix*, 292-97.

to the Kentucky Whig. Assailing Taylor as well as Seward, Douglas saw the crisis ended if the issues were entrusted to the public (and, inferentially, to Clay and himself) instead of to office-holding sectionalists. "The tide has already been checked and turned back," the stocky Illinoisan proclaimed. "The excitement is subsiding, and reason resuming its supremacy." The people simply would not allow reorganization of parties on geographical lines. They "will not sanction any such movement. They know its tendencies and its danger. The Union will not be put in peril; California will be admitted; governments for the territories must be established; and thus the controversy will end, and I trust forever."[7]

Clay was extolled more fulsomely by George E. Badger of North Carolina, who was the first of six other senators making set speeches in March. Deflating Calhoun's equilibrium theme, Hale of New Hampshire reminded his listeners that the single dissenting vote against the Northwest Ordinance in 1787 had been cast by a Northerner. Both Dayton of New Jersey and Hale opposed new fugitive-slave legislation. Dayton put in a good word for Taylor, serving notice that he might sustain the Wilmot Proviso under certain conditions. Counterbalancing these men was Hunter of Virginia, who resented "constant assaults" on the safety and peace of southern society. Philanthropists ought to turn their attention to white boys hitched by dog chains to carts in English colleries, or to young white children working sixteen hours daily as attendants of spinning machines. Morally and physically, was not the slave more fortunate than these? Let agitation cease, Hunter warned, and let warfare on the South abate.[8]

After Hunter came Salmon P. Chase, who offered a historical recapitulation to show that national policy on slavery was originally one of restriction and discouragement. A "remarkable change of feeling and action" was due to

[7] *Ibid., Appendix*, 364-75.
[8] *Ibid., Appendix*, 382-92, 1054-65, 435-43, 375-82.

"*first,* the political power derived by slaveholders from the representation of three-fifths of their slaves; and, *secondly,* the augmented value of slaves arising from the sudden increase of cotton culture." Objecting to formation of an "omnibus committee," the Ohioan declared that Congress "might as well" leave the Texas debt and boundary topics "to be disposed of when they arise." The last March orator, Roger S. Baldwin of Connecticut, agreed with Chase and Dayton that the California issue ought not to be connected with any other. His observations on the fugitive question, with their emphasis on the rights of free Negroes, grated harshly on southern ears. "I fear no danger to the Union," said Baldwin. But, "if there be any who . . . are ready to cry out disunion, and encourage the formation of sectional combinations to promote it, they have only to turn their eyes in any direction to see the hand-writing on the wall."[9]

That same month, twenty-two speeches were delivered in the House, about equally divided between northern and southern representatives, with only about a third of them favoring compromise. The Southerners generally were fearful for the Union and critical of President Taylor and his policy, while Northerners took the opposite stance, affirming the strength of the Union and upholding the President.[10]

Possibly the strongest House speech in March was that of the Oregon delegate. Samuel R. Thurston held the unique credential of having been in California when the Monterey convention was under way. As the Oregonian remembered events, T. Butler King's mission "was not the cause of the convention, had no effect on its deliberations . . . and should have no influence in the decision of this question of admission." Thurston's report thus ran counter to charges leveled against the President.[11] Aside from

[9] *Ibid., Appendix,* 468-80, 414-23.
[10] *Congressional Globe,* 31 Cong., 1 Sess., 444-48, 497-500, 543-45; *ibid., Appendix,* 228-33, 239-42, 248-60, 290-92, 297-310, 318-29, 336-45, 354-64, 392-401, 410-14.
[11] *Ibid., Appendix,* 345-54.

Thurston's, these House performances were unimpressive. They furnished no support for Douglas' statement that the waves of controversy were receding. In fact, the contrary seemed to be true. Union mass meetings might be held in New York and Raleigh, Baltimore and St. Louis, but in Washington Senate and House alike continued the unproductive pattern of the preceding weeks.

3

OTHER DEVELOPMENTS in Washington attracted more attention than the words of politicians. In the Senate John Bell offered a set of resolutions as an alternative to those of Clay. Foote wanted them referred to a committee of thirteen, which was not yet in existence but had often been recommended. On March 25, as chairman of the regular Committee on Territories, Douglas reported bills for California statehood and Utah (Deseret) and New Mexico territorial governments.[12] Congressmen also were hearing rumors of a scandal concerning an old and controversial claim which involved three heads of departments, including the secretary of the treasury. The Cabinet had grown very unpopular, and it was said that several members would resign. While Administration forces continued to be divided by the *Republic's* hostility to Senator Seward, moderates were discouraged by the prospective establishment of a new Washington paper favorable to southern extremists.[13] Fisticuffs enlivened the capital routine. In a hotel lobby, the second assistant postmaster general bloodied the face of Representative Levin. And Senator Foote got the same

[12] Joseph H. Parks, *John Bell of Tennessee* (Baton Rouge, La., 1950), 244-47; *Congressional Globe,* 31 Cong., 1 Sess., 436-39, 461, 508-10, 587, 592.

[13] Robert C. Winthrop to John P. Kennedy, [March 29,] 1850, John P. Kennedy Papers, Peabody Institute, Baltimore; Francis P. Blair to Martin Van Buren, March 24, 1850, Martin Van Buren Papers, Library of Congress.

treatment when he gave offense to Senator Borland as they encountered each other on a Washington street.[14]

Gossips were still talking about a threatened duel between Jefferson Davis and an Illinois congressman, which President Taylor was supposed to have prevented, and the antagonism between Benton and Foote was common knowledge.[15] The "Papers are full of horrors, political & personal," Representative Winthrop wrote. Senator Corwin of Ohio longed to wander by "some tributary brook of Hippocrene, with the barefooted Muses" until "this eternal 'Babel' of Speech Makers should be 'in the Lord's own good time' dispersed."[16]

While Corwin yearned for such a classical retreat, his brother congressmen sought relaxation at the legendary "Hole in the Wall," where liquor could be bought in the Capitol. There was much joviality in public bars and at private gatherings of congenial friends. Speaker Cobb relished the story of a new Georgia representative, a Savannah "Colonel" at one such gathering. *"The Col was horrified*—At my dinner he supposed that such revered seniors as Berrien & Butler would be grave and dignified in their deportment.—but he opened his eyes *wide* when he found that they too were but children of a larger growth."[17]

Milder amusements appealed to the ladies. The wife of a senator from Massachusetts commented on seeing at a White House reception "men with calico shirts—& women with satins & laces—men without cravats, and women with naked shoulders, arms &c." "I think we shall soon be saved the trouble of dressing at all," she went on to say. "If a

[14] St. Louis *Missouri Republican*, February 19, 1850; New York *Tribune*, March 16, 1850.

[15] Donald F. Tingley, "The Jefferson Davis-William H. Bissell Duel," *Mid-America*, XXXVIII (July 1956), 146-55.

[16] Winthrop to Kennedy, [March 29,] 1850, Kennedy Papers; Thomas Corwin to James A. Pearce, March 22, 1850, James A. Pearce Papers, Maryland Historical Society, Baltimore.

[17] Howell Cobb to Mrs. Cobb, March 25, 1850, Howell Cobb Papers, University of Georgia, Athens.

Lady appears with more than a shoulder strap, be sure she has nothing worth exhibiting. Grandmother or not—it is all the same."[18]

This climate of general cynicism, naïveté, small talk, and fustian was disturbed the last day in March with the death of John C. Calhoun. Neither intimate friends nor Americans as a whole were unprepared when tuberculosis claimed him. Almost to the end, however, the mind and will of the southern leader remained as acute and powerful as ever. "He had no idea of dying" when, at 11 o'clock the previous night, his amanuensis was reading to him and discussing politics. "Well—read the rest to me tomorrow," Calhoun had said. But, as fellow senators were sitting down to breakfast on the morning of March 31, word reached them that he was dead.

In a sense, the passing of Calhoun marked the beginning of an era's end. Nearly four decades had elapsed since he first served in Washington. Henry Clay was elected Speaker in that year of 1811, and two years later, young Daniel Webster came on from the New Hampshire hills. Now foes, now friends, they had long and deservedly shared public attention. Had America adopted a parliamentary system on the British model, any one of the three might have been a prime minister. Perhaps because of turns of sudden chance or personal limitations, not one had gained the highest prize of office, which each had sought. Now one was gone. Gloom pervaded the capital. No regular business was transacted in Congress until after the eulogies and the funeral, but practical men were asking how Calhoun's death would affect the crisis.[19]

[18] Mrs. John Davis to Mrs. Paine, February 10, 1850, John Davis Papers, American Antiquarian Society, Worcester, Massachusetts.
[19] James Hamilton to James H. Hammond, March 31, 1850, Joseph A. Scoville to Hammond, April 18, 1850, James H. Hammond Papers, Library of Congress; New York *Herald*, May 3, 1850; New York *Times*, December 11, 1857; Salmon P. Chase to Mrs. Chase, March 31, 1850, Chase Papers, Library of Congress; Kennedy to Winthrop, April 1, 1850, letterbook, Kennedy Papers.

4

LEGISLATIVE ODDS and ends occupied much of the Senate's
time between the services for Calhoun on April 2 and the
April 22 departure of six senators appointed to accompany
his body to Charleston. Throughout the three-week period,
even when minor matters supervened, Foote never flagged
in his promotion of the select committee project. Clay, who
had come around to side with Foote on tactics, did everything in his power to assist him. Against this plan were
forces led by Benton.

Benton delivered a set speech on April 8 and repeatedly
insisted that faster action could be obtained through "open
and independent voting" than by "hugger-mugger" behind
closed doors.[20] Most of the northern senators were with
him, and even Webster and Douglas made it clear that the
committee method was not to their taste. Webster, however,
said he would support Clay and Foote notwithstanding his
personal preference. Cass gave the procommittee group
encouragement when he announced that the Michigan Legislature had rescinded its Wilmot Proviso instructions,
thereby making him a free agent. By a division of 28 to 26,
Douglas' motion to table the long-pending Foote referral
was defeated. Hale's motion to entrust the whole subject
to the Committee on Territories was lost. The third test
came when, after protracted delays, a Benton-sponsored
tabling resolution was rejected. In general, Southerners
were winners and Northerners losers in the successive
votes. But consistently moderate throughout was the attitude of three northwestern Democrats (notably Bright of
Indiana) and Daniel Dickinson of New York. It was they
who held the balance of power.[21]

Following the three trials of strength, Douglas bowed out

[20] *Congressional Globe*, 31 Cong., 1 Sess., 640-43, 652, 655-65, 670,
704.
[21] *Ibid.*, 702-714, 747-48, 751-59.

of the struggle. "If I cannot have my own way," he declared, "I will not delay the Senate by preventing the majority from having theirs."[22] It was now a foregone conclusion that Benton's cause was lost. But when Hamlin offered an amendment to Foote's motion, Benton proposed amending the amendment with fourteen points of instruction to govern the committee from the hour of its authorization. Incidentally, he described Calhoun's 1849 Southern Address as "agitation." This gave Foote an excuse to attack Benton.

It was ironic to find Foote in the role of a Calhoun defender, as earlier he had denounced and broken with the Carolinian. But now, on April 17, the "lamented" Calhoun was "illustrious" and his address "holy work." And who was the "calumniator" (a fighting word in 1850)? "By whom is this extraordinary denunciation hurled against all those individuals who subscribed this address? By a gentleman long denominated the oldest member of the Senate—the father of the Senate. By a gentleman who, on a late occasion—"

Benton apparently had heard enough. Contrary to his action in January when Foote belabored him with insults, the proud Missouri Democrat was seen walking, not out of the chamber but toward his assailant. Foote then backed down the aisle in the direction of the dais, in his hand a revolver loaded and cocked. Colleagues, however, intervened. "Let the assassin fire!" Benton cried. "A pistol has been brought here to assassinate me."

"I brought it here to defend myself," replied Foote, who meanwhile had surrendered the weapon to Dickinson.

"Nothing of the kind, sir," Benton thundered. "It is a false imputation. I carry nothing of the kind, and no assassin has a right to draw a pistol on me."

The little Mississippian sought to explain: "Threatening language was used, menacing gestures indulged in, and an advance made towards me, with the view, as I supposed,

of putting violent designs into effect. I therefore retreated
a few steps, with a view to . . . act in my own defence, and
not to shoot him. So help me God, such alone was my
intention."[23]

Seven senators investigated the outrage, but, despite
demands for expelling Foote, there was no expulsion and
never a hint of contrition on his part. This offended many
Americans but was taken for granted by Washington in-
siders, as the compromisers were in control of operational
machinery—though not usually in command of votes on
precise measures—and Foote was one of their foremost
leaders.

In the next two days Benton's amendments were
eliminated, and at last the Senate created its special Committee of Thirteen. As had been expected, Clay became
chairman. Three of his associates—Willie P. Mangum of
North Carolina, Berrien, and Webster—were among his
oldest brother Whigs. Cass and King qualified as Democratic veterans, while Bell, Bright, Cooper, Dickinson,
Downs, Mason, and Phelps rounded out the group. Seldom,
if ever, did all the members (six Democrats and seven
Whigs) attend committee meetings simultaneously. The
work of composing a report was principally performed by
Clay over the line in Maryland at the estate of Charles B.
Calvert.[24] While the Kentuckian was thus engaged, numerous congressmen took advantage of the lull to go home and
mend their political fences. Those senators who were left
lectured empty galleries on such topics as the coinage of
gold and removals from office. House activities were nearly
as humdrum. Clay, in fact, prolonged the strange interlude

[23] *Ibid.*, 760-63; William N. Chambers, *Old Bullion Benton:Senator
from the New West* (Boston, 1956), 359-62.
[24] *Congressional Globe*, 31 Cong., 1 Sess., 763-64, 769-74, 779-82;
Henry Clay to Mrs. Clay, April 25, 1850, Thomas J. Clay Papers,
Library of Congress; David Outlaw to Mrs. Outlaw, May 6, 1850,
David Outlaw Papers, Southern Historical Collection, University of
North Carolina, Chapel Hill; Boston *Advertiser*, May 1, 1850; Kath-
erine Scarborough, *Homes of the Cavaliers* (New York, 1930), 77-78.

because of disagreements with Berrien and others and also
because of a delay in Webster's return from Boston and
Marshfield.

5

ON WEDNESDAY, May 8, a packed Senate finally heard Clay
read the report. The Committee of Thirteen's main recommendation consisted of the so-called "Omnibus Bill." This
not only provided for California statehood and for the two
territorial governments but also offered solutions for the
Texas boundary and debt questions. Kept separate were a
fugitive slave measure and another limiting the District
slave trade.[25] Comments came in a flood from seventeen
senators, including Phelps and Mason (who explained that
they did not concur in all respects) and Berrien (who
wanted California divided at the line of 35°30'). Cooper,
Mangum, and other members of the Committee sustained
the report, while Clemens and Yulee were among those
against it. Downs' observations were tantalizingly vague.
Bright closed the debate with an emphatic endorsement.[26]
It was on the thinking and votes of forgotten men like
Downs, as well as on the judgment of a Douglas or a Clay,
that success or failure would ultimately hinge.

Clay stepped forward again the following Monday with
an elaborate exposition. Once more the galleries were
crowded, and "ladies and their cavaliers" besieged the
doors. Clay was at his most convincing, though not always
completely frank, first in discussing California and secondly
in dealing with differences between the new and earlier
bills. A provocative six-word phrase, "nor in respect to

[25] Outlaw to Mrs. Outlaw, April 26, 1850, Outlaw Papers; Chase to
Mrs. Chase, April 10, 1850, Chase Papers; Austin *Texas State Gazette,*
June 8, 1850; *Congressional Globe,* 31 Cong., 1 Sess., *Appendix,* 401-
546 and *passim; ibid.,* 944-49.
[26] *Congressional Globe,* 31 Cong., 1 Sess., 948-56.

African slavery," was the chief alteration in proposals
previously sponsored by the Committee on Territories. The
insertion was designed to prevent the New Mexico and
Utah assemblies from legislating for or against slavery.
Clay appeared deceptively casual about the whole thing,
saying that he attached little importance to it even though
he had been outvoted when the Committee of Thirteen
sanctioned its addition. Similarly, he minimized the elimination of two statements in his own January resolutions—
that slavery "does not exist by law" and "is not likely to be
introduced" into the land acquired from Mexico. While he
said he believed in those "two truths," Clay attributed their
omission to the offense they gave southern Democrats.

The new fugitive slave bill contained a guarantee of
trial by jury in the state whence the Negro allegedly fled.
Slaveholders or their agents were to be made responsible
for carrying a written record containing the fact of slavery,
the fact of escape, and a description of the fugitive. In
advocating these new features, Clay said that the committee had considered "feelings and interests on both sides
of the question." He assailed the notion that "there is a
higher law . . . which entitles a man, under whose roof a
runaway has come, to give him assistance, and succor, and
hospitality." On the subject of the Texas debt, the Kentuckian avoided some details. He did not name the sum
"to be given to Texas" for relinquishing disputed soil, as
that "might lead to improper speculation in the stock
markets." Clay pitched his principal appeal on a patriotic
note: "Sir, I believe that the crisis of the crisis has arrived,"
and the fate of the committee's report "will, in my humble
judgment, determine the fate of the harmony or continued
distraction of this country."

Clay's treatment of the President was revealing. In one
breath, he proclaimed his anxiety to cooperate with the
White House. In the next, he advertised his purpose to
follow the dictates of his own ideas. The aims were com-
patible respecting California, but New Mexico was a

different matter. At first Clay said that Taylor had made no recommendation concerning New Mexico; on this assumption, "we take up the subject" where the Chief Executive dropped it. After developing this thesis, however, Clay bethought himself of the presidential message in which Taylor "tells us" he "had reason to believe" that the Santa Fe people might form a state government and apply for admission to the Union. Was this a recommendation? Not according to Clay, who chose to ignore accumulating evidence that statehood for New Mexico as well as California was in line with Administration hopes.[27]

Clay's position can be understood only when the observer comprehends the odd four-way involvement affecting Taylor, the Cabinet, the Kentucky senator, and the Washington *Republic*. The *Republic's* editor, Alexander C. Bullitt, lauded both the President and Clay *and* cordially disliked the Cabinet *and* praised the Committee of Thirteen. The *Republic* was supposed to be the Administration organ. So long as it remained friendly to Clay, there seemed a chance that Taylor might unbend. This in itself was reason enough for Clay's relative mildness on May 13. On May 14, however, the long-inconsistent Bullitt announced his resignation. The next week, his successor—Allen A. Hall— described Taylor's plan as "the best practicable" and denied that the President "now wavers, or has wavered, in his opinion on this subject."[28]

At once there came a change in the tone of Clay's public statements. Five bleeding wounds, he said, threatened the body politic. The Committee of Thirteen would heal all five; the Chief Executive, only one. Yet Taylor persisted in his own "peculiar" plan, whereas "I think" he "ought, without any dissatisfaction, to permit us to consider what is best for our common country." The alternative to the committee's arrangements, in the opinion of the senator, was no plan at all for dealing with New Mexico, Utah, the

[27] *Ibid., Appendix,* 567-73.
[28] Washington *Republic,* May 14, 20, 1850.

boundary, the fugitives, or the slave trade in the District.[29]

In a detailed rejoinder, Hall pointed out that Taylor's January message had been sent in response to a House resolution limited to California and New Mexico. Therefore, it naturally contained no reference to fugitive slaves or the District trade. Did Taylor oppose bills dealing with those subjects? On the contrary, he offered not the "slightest impediment" to the healing of these "wounds." Turning to New Mexico, the editor said that Taylor had "contemplated the *immediate* formation" of a constitution there. With New Mexico a sovereign state, not only would the Proviso be avoided but the Supreme Court could settle the boundary issue. The Deseret provisional government was "perhaps as well or better suited" to its people than any Congress might devise. Thus the President's policy met the trials of the times as comprehensively as the committee's. Hall concluded that Clay came to Washington "to lead, not to follow," with the "laudable ambition" of gaining "the glory of a third compromise." If so, in the light of events, the senator was at least partly to blame for the absence of "peace and concord" in White House-Capitol relations.[30]

6

DURING JUNE, sixteen senators made twenty-eight attempts to amend sections of the Omnibus Bill. Of the six successful ones, all four of importance pertained to the territories. The most significant was Berrien's, which substituted "establishing or prohibiting African slavery" for "in respect to African slavery." A departure from the popular sovereignty principle, this was not in line with the

[29] *Congressional Globe,* 31 Cong., 1 Sess., *Appendix,* 612-16. Clay combined New Mexico and Utah in one "wound," and the boundary and debt issues in another.

[30] Washington *Republic,* May 28, 1850.

views of the committee's majority. It empowered territorial legislatures to protect slave property in the event that a judicial decision should prove favorable to the institution. The next amendment was Yulee's. Specifying that the Constitution extended to a territory by its own force, it would have relieved slaveholders of "embarrassment" on a technical point. The third amendment, that of Hale, put the appellate power of the Supreme Court on the same footing in territories as in states. The fourth, introduced by Pierre Soulé, provided that a future state formed from a western territory would be granted admission into the Union regardless of its free or slave status.

Berrien, Soulé, and Yulee were Southerners who favored the extension of 36°30'. But, if that division could not be obtained, they wished to do what they could for slaveowning Southwesterners in the event of an Omnibus victory. In case the South should have its way on the Berrien and Yulee amendments, Hale wanted to be sure that jurisdiction would go beyond an inferior tribunal. There was no roll call on the Hale Amendment, the logic of which was indisputable if one granted the Berrien premise. Opposition to the other three came largely or exclusively from the North. Nevertheless, they were adopted by margins of 30-27, 30-24, and 38-12.[31]

While the South appeared to be making some little progress in the Senate, such was not true in the House proceedings. From May 8 to June 11, hour-long set speeches were delivered by fifty-eight representatives. Thirteen of these were in complete accord with Clay's committee. Six others inclined in that direction. Nineteen favored the President's Plan in essence or in substance. Five were for the Wilmot Proviso. Four adhered to 36°30', while nine seemed inclined to a 36°30' settlement but spent more time objecting to middle-road policies than advocating other ideas. One congressman stressed his disappointment that

[31] *Congressional Globe,* 31 Cong., 1 Sess., 1134, 1145-46; *ibid.,* *Appendix,* 902, 911.

the Senate and House had not created a joint committee of twenty-six persons. Finally, one of these fifty-eight was unreported in the *Globe*. It is doubtful that many representatives were as interested in flexible debate as in couching their opinions for home consumption. So as to give each orator his due, House sessions were repeatedly held at night, with attendance sparse. Some of the printed speeches were never delivered. Others were dressed-up versions, for the record, of informal unwritten addresses which had been met with their share of laughter or boredom.

Underlying the Senate amendments and causing the stalemate in the House was the basic fact that the compromisers were unable to make headway. Foote admitted in mid-May that the spirit of accommodation was lacking. Orlando Brown, who sympathized with Taylor, wrote Kentucky Governor John J. Crittenden: "Mr. Clay is sustaining all his former reputation and power in Congress, and true to his hates he has flung down the defiance to the friends of General Taylor. . . . I am glad myself that he has at last stept out with his armor on—an avowed enemy though formidable can be met."[32] A Missouri Whig stated the case more simply: "Hurrah for old Zack, and Dam his enemies." "We are not so secure from civil war at home as we imagine," wrote a correspondent of the Philadelphia *Bulletin;* "the elements grow darker and darker, and will burst presently with a terrible crash."[33] The first week in June, Senator Corwin found the "Compromise Bill an impracticable remedy" and the President's Plan "the only permanent cure." Clay declared on June 19: "A hundred times almost . . . have I been quite ready to yield." He had never seen a measure so much opposed. Well-nigh insuperable difficul-

[32] *Ibid.*, 1110, 1123, 1151, 1167, 1173-78, 1182-91, 1193-1201; Orlando Brown to John J. Crittenden, May 23, 1850, John J. Crittenden Papers, Library of Congress.

[33] David D. Mitchell to Brown, May 28, 1850, Orlando Brown Papers, Kentucky Historical Society, Frankfort; Philadelphia *Bulletin,* quoted in New York *Express,* June 4, 1850.

ties, on points "of no earthly practical consequence, start up from time to time, to discourage the stoutest heart."[34] The same day, Webster was of the opinion that "our prospects brighten," the "amount to be given to Texas" being "one difficulty to be got over." At the end of the month, however, he was blue—while Thurlow Weed advised a friend that "Old Zack's stock is looking up."[35]

From May through June of 1850, the crisis had provoked, in addition to House speeches and Senate amendments, Senate speeches and House amendments—amendments of amendments, motions to adjourn, and nudges toward indefinite postponement. Out of this welter of words and maneuverings a congressional pattern was clearly defined—a pattern whose emergence Clay had sought to prevent. At one extreme stood the southern Hotspurs—at the other, Free Soilers, northern Whigs, the few Benton Democrats, and (most powerful) the President of the United States. Contrary to the wishes of Douglas and Webster and to the earlier ideas of Clay, the strategy of the omnibus had been adopted. And now the vehicle seemed permanently stalled.

[34] Corwin to Crittenden, June 4 [7?], 1850, Crittenden Papers; *Congressional Globe*, 31 Cong., 1 Sess., *Appendix*, 929.

[35] *The Writings and Speeches of Daniel Webster* (18 vols., Boston, 1903), XVIII, 374; *Congressional Globe*, 31 Cong., 1 Sess., *Appendix*, 968; Weed to George Harrington, June 25, 1850, Henry E. Huntington Library, San Marino, California.

CHAPTER VI

The Wreck
of the Omnibus

F ROM OUTSIDE Washington came two encourage-
ments to the compromisers' hopes. The delegates to
the Nashville Convention took no irrevocable step in
the direction of secession. True, most of the convention
members approved resolutions opposing a compromise and
favoring the 36°30' scheme. But they hedged before
advocating anything like overt disunion, being content to
wait and see what action Congress would take.[1] Equally
heartening to Clay and the compromisers were the ever-
louder demands for peace, voiced in the North by businessmen in general and seaboard merchants in particular.
Petitions, sponsored by the business community, bore the
names of thousands of signers. Letters filled columns in
the commercial press. Blending organizations and labels,
Democrats and Whigs together promoted enthusiasm for
their national leaders—provided those leaders were pledged
to moderation. This was epitomized in June, when the
powers of Tammany Hall let the rafters ring with praise of
Clay. Again, in the second week of July, a burgeoning
eagerness for tranquillity was the watchword of a bipartisan rally at the Chinese Museum in Philadelphia.[2]

Meanwhile, the President found himself facing additional troubles. At a time when Congress and the domestic crisis challenged him every day, foreign affairs weighted the burden of Taylor and his secretary of state. One serious diplomatic problem grew out of a recent assault by filibusters on the Spanish island of Cuba. A second involved stiff demands against Portugal in connection with long-overdue claims. A third was temporarily eased when, on July 5 after months of negotiation, Taylor affixed his signature to the Clayton-Bulwer Treaty, abating American and British rivalry in Central America.[3] On the domestic front, the Galphin Claim, involving the reputations of three Cabinet members, received two conflicting reports from a House investigating committee. And all the time the President and Congress anxiously awaited the latest news from Santa Fe bearing on the danger of a civil war between the United States and Texas.

Events in New Mexico had been hurrying to a climax ever since March 21, when Lieutenant Colonel George A. McCall joined Military Governor John Munroe at Santa Fe. Acting on the basis of McCall's instructions from the War Department, the officers began a campaign to intensify sentiment for statehood. In mid-April, word was sent to Taylor's private secretary that New Mexico's old territorial party would unite with the rival statehood clique in creating a state government.[4] This resulted to some extent from the pressures of the military men. Civilian leaders, however, who were suspicious of anybody and anything Texan, were angered by a commissioner whom the Texas governor had assigned to work for Texas in the disputed

[1] Dallas T. Herndon, "The Nashville Convention of 1850," Alabama Historical Society Transactions, V (1906), 216-26.

[2] Philip Hone, manuscript diary, June 18, 1850, New-York Historical Society, New York City; Philadelphia Bulletin, July 9, 1850.

[3] Holman Hamilton, Zachary Taylor: Soldier in the White House (Indianapolis, 1951), 345-52, 357-71.

[4] George A. McCall to William W.S. Bliss, April 15, 1850, George A. McCall Papers, Library of Congress.

area.[5] After a number of New Mexico citizens had asked
for a constitutional convention, Munroe arranged for the
election of delegates. In May they met, emerging from
their deliberations with an antislavery state constitution.
The document was duly ratified in June, with nearly 8,000
ballots cast in its favor and only 39 opposing.[6]

Texas, however, was not idle. Her governor, P. Hans-
borough Bell, early in the year made no secret of his
intention to defend the "rights" of Texas in and near Santa
Fe, regardless of whatever action the United States commander might take, but to his great disappointment the
general assembly did not authorize his plan to dispatch
Texas troops into the region under federal control. In June,
using the Texas commissioner's rebuff as a means of
mobilizing opinion, he decided to push his scheme again
and summoned the assembly members to return for a
special session, which he scheduled for the month of
August. Bell hoped and planned that, with legislative backing, he could confront Colonel Munroe with substantial
armed opposition.[7]

                                    2

NEWS FROM AUSTIN and especially Santa Fe took a long
time in reaching Washington. Even at that, by the end of

[5] Loomis M. Ganaway, *New Mexico and the Sectional Controversy,
1846-1861* (Albuquerque, N.M., 1944), 47-49; Kenneth F. Neighbours, "The Taylor-Neighbors Struggle over the Upper Rio Grande
Region of Texas in 1850," *Southwestern Historical Quarterly*, LXI
(April 1958), 431-63.

[6] Ganaway, *New Mexico and the Sectional Controversy*, 49-52;
McCall to Bliss, May 21, July 16, 1850, McCall Papers; Neighbours,
"The Taylor-Neighbors Struggle," 450-52; William A. Keleher, *Tur-
moil in New Mexico, 1846-1868* (Santa Fe, N.M., 1952), 124.

[7] William C. Binkley, "The Question of Texas Jurisdiction in New
Mexico under the United States, 1848-1850," *Southwestern Historical
Quarterly*, XXIV (July 1920), 22-24, 26-31; Neighbours, "The Taylor-
Neighbors Struggle," 455-59.

June, many Easterners appreciated the situation's gravity. In the nation's capital, on the Fourth of July, the *National Intelligencer* printed an unrestrained letter by Alexander H. Stephens. The first federal gun illegally fired against the people of Texas, he predicted, would signal "freemen from the Delaware to the Rio Grande to rally to the rescue." And "when the 'Rubicon' is passed, the days of this Republic will be numbered." If the *Intelligencer* was "sorry to see" the Georgian "indulging in such bloody visions,"[8] less conservative papers were patently alarmed. The Hartford *Courant* feared that, if Texas tried to establish her authority over Santa Fe by force, the move would lead to "civil war and, perhaps, disunion." The Richmond *Republican* said a solution of the controversy could not be delayed without the "hazard of a collision," possibly involving "the whole Union." And the New York *Express* thought "there would be other parties to the fray than Texans and New Mexicans, before it ceases."[9]

Critical concern grew when Taylor proposed sending additional soldiers to Santa Fe as reinforcements for Munroe. On hearing this, Stephens went to the President's office and argued for a change in policy. With Toombs at his side, he also informed Secretary of the Navy William Ballard Preston that "if troops were ordered to Santa Fe, the President would be impeached."

"Who will impeach him?" Preston asked.

"I will if nobody else does," said Stephens.[10]

Toombs and two other southern Whigs broached the same problem on a White House visit. The three were either old friends of Taylor or original Taylor partisans in the campaign of 1848. They now heard the same statements that the President previously made to Stephens, and

8 Washington *National Intelligencer*, July 4, 1850.

9 Hartford *Courant*, July 2, 1850; Richmond *Republican*, July 9, 1850; New York *Express*, July 10, 1850.

10 Myrta L. Avary (ed.), *Recollections of Alexander H. Stephens* (New York, 1910), 26-27.

after the interview they left, concluding there was "no longer any hope."[11] There is still another illuminating story, involving Secretary of War George W. Crawford of Galphin Claim notoriety. Crawford advised the Commander-in-Chief that he would not sign a contemplated order to Colonel Munroe to resist any Texan attempt to exercise jurisdiction in New Mexico. Thereupon Taylor calmly replied to his appointee that he would sign it himself.[12]

Taylor, whose role was so vital at that juncture, appeared to be in robust health on Independence Day. A few weeks before, an associate had noted that he seemed "dejected & haggard," which was not strange in view of the challenges great and small. He had been very sick the preceding summer in Erie, Pennsylvania. But in June of 1850 and the onset of July, acquaintances described his "smiling countenance" and "fine spirits," while his opponent Clay looked "worn and thin" and felt "jaded and exhausted."[13] July 4 was hot. A torrid sun beat down on the Potomac flats where, at the unfinished Washington Monument, Senator Foote delivered an address lasting over an hour. When the Mississippian concluded and the applause subsided, the President beckoned to him and said: *"Why will you not always speak in this way?"* Taylor then left the protecting canopy and walked over, in the July sun, to listen to yet another speaker.[14]

The 65-year-old President experienced intense thirst and hunger when at length he departed from the monument

11 J. F. H. Claiborne, *Life and Correspondence of John A. Quitman* (2 vols., New York, 1860), II, 32-33.

12 *Ibid.*, 33. *Cf.* Thurlow W. Barnes, *Memoir of Thurlow Weed* (Boston, 1884), 180-81.

13 Albert T. Burnley to John J. Crittenden, May 8, 1850, John J. Crittenden Papers, Library of Congress; Frederick W. Seward, *Seward at Washington as Senator and Secretary of State . . . 1846-1861* (New York, 1891), 141; New York *Express*, July 10, 1850; John P. Kennedy, manuscript diary, June 21, 1850, John P. Kennedy Papers, Peabody Institute, Baltimore; Boston *Advertiser*, June 28, 1850.

14 Hamilton, *Zachary Taylor*, 388, 454; Henry S. Foote, *War of the Rebellion; or, Scylla and Charybdis* (New York, 1866), 149.

grounds. Returning home, he consumed quantities of raw fruits and vegetables, washing them down with liberal draughts of iced water or iced milk or both. The next day he was unwell but managed to sign both the Clayton-Bulwer Treaty and a letter thanking a Bostonian for two "delicious salmon" which "arrived most opportunely."[15] Belatedly the family sent for a physician, who found Taylor a victim of "cholera morbus" or acute gastroenteritis. On July 7 and 8, the patient was much worse, and consultants were called but could do nothing. On the night of July 9, the Chief Executive died. The political impact can hardly be exaggerated, for suddenly the plan of the Committee of Thirteen had lost an unflinching enemy.[16]

3

MILLARD FILLMORE of New York, who succeeded Taylor as head of the nation, had, during earlier phases of his career, caused Southerners to be suspicious of his attitude toward slavery and related topics. As recently as April 1850, he had confided in a private letter that he stood with Taylor in the sectional battle.[17] But Fillmore afterward wrote that in July he told Taylor that his vice-presidential vote "might" be cast for the Omnibus Bill in the event of a Senate tie.[18] Superficially, it may seem peculiar that a Northerner like Fillmore would favor compromise. However, the new President's enmity toward the Whig faction headed by Seward and Weed and his recent change of ideas brought renewed optimism to adjustment-minded men.

It became common knowledge almost at once that Fillmore relied heavily on the advice of Clay and Webster.

[15] Zachary Taylor to H. S. Favor, July 5, 1850, author's collection.
[16] Hamilton, *Zachary Taylor,* 388-93, 454-55.
[17] Historical and Philosophical Society of Ohio *Quarterly Publications,* XIII (April-June 1918), 43-44.
[18] Frank H. Severance (ed.), "Millard Fillmore Papers," Buffalo Historical Society *Publications,* XI, 321-34.

The Whig giants were closeted with him, and undenied rumors about their conferences spread word that a new Cabinet would be installed. Later in the month, Webster became secretary of state and Senator Corwin secretary of the treasury, while their vacated Senate seats were occupied by Robert Winthrop and Thomas Ewing. Most consequential was Clay's unofficial assignment as White House spokesman at the Capitol. Administration prestige and patronage were now thrown on the side of compromise.[19] There were reports that some northern representatives would readily respond to the Fillmore leadership. In the Senate, too, there might be a few shifts to the compromise.

The votes in the Senate during the third week in July showed quickened progress on the Omnibus Bill. The closest margin came on one applying to Utah the controversial phrase "establishing or prohibiting African slavery" which Berrien in June had inserted into the New Mexico legislation. (See p. 98.) Clay acquiesced in this concession to the South, and six Northerners made possible its adoption. After several days of oratory and balloting on the Texas question, the idea of Maine Senator James W. Bradbury to entrust the boundary dilemma to a joint United States-Texas commission seemed most favored by the Senate. Final action on this did not come immediately, but extremists lost four times when Rusk, Hale, Benton, and Mason could not alter the Bradbury project. In reply to criticism, Clay proudly said he saw no "incongruity" in the freight or passengers "on board our omnibus."[20]

On Monday, July 29, Bradbury's solution of the boundary problem failed to pass but then was revived in a slightly different form. On Tuesday, William C. Dawson of Georgia offered a modification stipulating that New Mexico Territory would not have jurisdiction east of the Rio Grande

[19] Robert J. Rayback, *Millard Fillmore: Biography of a President* (Buffalo, 1959), 224-47.

[20] *Congressional Globe*, 31 Cong., 1 Sess., 1378-83, 1398, 1410-11, 1448, 1456-57; *ibid.*, *Appendix*, 1397, 1404-1408, 1415-26, 1436-47.

until the commission defined the boundary, an arrangement
that would allow Texas to control the civil government of
most New Mexicans. After considerable debate, the senators endorsed by a vote of 30 to 28 the Bradbury commission plan as amended by Dawson. On Wednesday,
July 31, Moses Norris of New Hampshire eliminated Berrien's "establishing or prohibiting" phrase from the New
Mexico resolution. The Committee of Thirteen's original
preference, "nor in respect to African slavery," was thereupon restored to both the Utah and New Mexico provisions.
To observers unfamiliar with delicate legislative shadings,
everything seemed to be arranged for Clay's success on
that final day of July. Not only were compromisers glad
to see the troublesome Berrien phrase eliminated, but the
Bradbury-Dawson contribution was supposed to guarantee
the support of the whole measure by the two Texas
senators. With these obstacles removed, would the Omnibus
Bill now pass, bringing the crisis to an end?

4

To CLAY'S DISGRUNTLEMENT and eventual disgust, the surface appearances were deceptive. Kaleidoscopic voting
shifts in the critical last week of July showed that neither
Clay nor any other compromiser on the floor really controlled the situation. There had been many striking incon-
sistencies, especially on the part of senators who had supported Dawson on the jurisdiction question and then turned
around to oppose Bradbury's plan after Dawson amended
it to their presumed satisfaction. Clay's Kentucky colleague,
Joseph R. Underwood, was disenchanted and later charged
that some senators' backing of Dawson was merely a
"manoeuvre" and not a genuine movement to make Bradbury's plan acceptable to themselves.[21]

[21] *Congressional Globe*, 31 Cong., 1 Sess., 1481-82, 1490; *ibid.*,
Appendix, 1456, 1463, 1473; Louisville *Journal*, November 18, 1851.

The final events of Wednesday saw the sudden destruction of the Omnibus. First, James A. Pearce of Maryland took the lead in destroying the Dawson proposition. "Incongruous," "lop-eared," "crippled," and "deformed" were some of the terms with which Pearce branded Dawson's contribution. Clay begged Pearce to reconsider. Foote, Rusk, Shields, Dawson, Benton, and Houston joined in the debate. Then a 33-22 vote did away with the New Mexico territorial part of the Omnibus in its entirety, in order (as Pearce explained) to get rid of the obnoxious Dawson feature. This was a tremendously significant decision, as it doomed the plan of the Committee of Thirteen.

Soon, on the motion of Florida Senator David L. Yulee, a 29-28 vote struck from the bill everything related to Texas. Next, Pearce failed to restore the Bradbury version of the New Mexico sections with the Dawson provisions left out —Pearce's total being three short of a majority.[22] David R. Atchison of Missouri, who long had sided with the compromisers, now moved that California statehood be eliminated—and this was done by a vote of 34 to 25.[23] Clay, defeated on the Yulee and Atchison motions as well as the first one of Pearce, had been in the minority except on one vote which he sidestepped. Now he walked out of the chamber.

"The omnibus is overturned," Thomas Hart Benton gloated, "and all the passengers spilled out but one. We have but Utah left—all gone but Utah! It alone remains, and I am for saving it as a monument of the herculean labors of the immortal thirteen." So it was that thirty-two of the fifty senators left on the floor ordered the Utah bill alone to be engrossed for a third reading, with passage assured the following day. Darkness had fallen. Statesmen were weary. The Senate's approval of Utah Territory was

[22] *Congressional Globe,* 31 Cong., 1 Sess., *Appendix,* 1473-81; *Congressional Globe,* 31 Cong., 1 Sess., 1490.

[23] William E. Parrish, *David Rice Atchison of Missouri: Border Politician* (Columbia, Mo., 1961), 104-105.

small compensation to Clay and his friends. That night Horace Greeley wrote: "And so the Omnibus is smashed —wheels, axles and body—nothing left but a single plank termed Utah. I even saw the gallant driver abandoning the wreck between six and seven this evening, after having done all that man could do to retrieve, or rather to avert the disaster. . . . There was nothing left but to grin and bear it."[24]

5

AN ANALYSIS of the July 31 reckoning shows that only five Whigs joined Clay in opposing Pearce's critical anti-Dawson move, while sixteen Democrats "followed" Clay's "lead" in this regard. When the Yulee motion eliminated the Texas sections, Clay and ten other Whigs went down to defeat alongside seventeen Democrats. On the California question, only six Whigs voted with Clay, who drew three-fourths of his support from Democrats and Free Soilers. Eight of the nine men aligned with Clay all three times were Democrats. Thus, individually as well as collectively, Democratic senators at this stage of events were far more consistently procompromise than were Whigs.

Puzzling was Clay's absence when the 28-25 defeat was meted out to Pearce as he tried to restore the Bradbury measure. Whigs then accounted for 10, and Democrats for 15, of the total Pearce vote. The fact that 13 nay votes were of Whig origin also sheds light on the situation. Here Pearce was making a valiant effort to influence the direction of affairs, not as a sectional extremist but in the spirit of border-state adjustment. Four border-state Whigs rallied to his banner. Yet, even though Clay answered eight later roll calls, for the time being he disappeared. More under-

[24] *Congressional Globe*, 31 Cong., 1 Sess., *Appendix*, 1482-85; *Congressional Globe*, 31 Cong., 1 Sess., 1504; New York *Tribune*, August 2, 1850.

standable was his absence when the Utah measure came
up. Clay's vote then was not needed. Only three Democrats, thirteen Whigs, and the two Free Soilers were
ranged against the twenty-four Democrats and eight Whigs
supporting engrossment. Indeed, the Democrats were so
united that they could almost have carried the bill unaided.

For scholars inclined to equate the circumstances exclusively with sectionalism, a study of other statistics should
prove illuminating. If Pearce's motion to eliminate Dawson's amendment, Yulee's to do away with all consideration
of Texas, and Atchison's to drop California statehood may
be regarded as fair criteria, these figures are relevant: (1)
nineteen Northerners and fourteen Southerners were for
the 33-22 Pearce Amendment, and eight Northerners and
fourteen Southerners were against it; (2) sixteen Northerners and thirteen Southerners favored the Yulee motion,
which twelve Northerners and sixteen Southerners opposed;
(3) ten Northerners and twenty-four Southerners struck
out the California sections, with twenty Northerners and five
Southerners desiring retention. Now, breaking down the
totals into sectional-partisan categories (the abbreviations
"ND," "NW," "NFS," "SD," and "SW" representing northern
Democrats, northern Whigs, northern Free Soilers, southern
Democrats, and southern Whigs respectively), we find the
following:

	ND	NW	NFS	SD	SW	TOTAL
Pro-Pearce	5	12	2	9	5	33
Anti-Pearce	8			8	6	22
Not Voting	2	1		1	1	5
Pro-Yulee	3	12	1	12	1	29
Anti-Yulee	12			5	11	28
Not Voting		1	1	1		3
Pro-Atchison		10		16	8	34
Anti-Atchison	15	3	2	1	4	25
Not Voting				1		1

From the recapitulation, it is obvious that neither sectionalism alone nor partisanship alone can account for those

senatorial results. The largest partisan-sectional combination, that of the southern Democrats, was almost evenly divided on the first test, split two to one on the second, and nearly unanimous on the third. The northern Democrats were united once, and the northern Whigs twice, while the southern Whigs approached unanimity on a single occasion. More striking was the extent of the difference between northern Whigs and Democrats all three times. On these as on other tests, northern Democrats composed the most consistent procompromise group. If either northern Whigs or southern Whigs or southern Democrats as a whole had possessed equal ardor for adjustment, only a few additional votes from other quarters would have spelled victory for the Omnibus Bill.

In a biography of Millard Fillmore, the President and Pearce are credited with jointly making strategic plans for Pearce's moves on July 31.[25] There is a plausibility in this interpretation, especially in view of the danger represented by Dawson's amendment to the Bradbury commission "solution." It may be that solid support for such a view will turn up somewhere some day. But the totality of the evidence marshalled to date does not point to the cited conclusion. And when the sources listed by Fillmore's biographer are carefully examined, substantiation is found to be lacking.[26]

[25] Rayback, *Millard Fillmore*, 247-52.
[26] Rayback's basic sources appear to be: Albany *State Register*, July 15, 18, 20, 22, 27, 1850; New York *Express*, July 15, 17, 20, August 1, 2, 1850; Bernard C. Steiner, "James Alfred Pearce," *Maryland Historical Magazine*, XVI (Dec. 1921), 332. Rayback also says, "See Pearce's letter of August 5, 1850," giving no citation. There is a letter of that date in Steiner, "James Alfred Pearce," *Maryland Historical Magazine*, XVIII (Dec. 1923), 349-350, and it presents what may be the best case for the interpretation in question. The present writer has studied this material and has also examined the original August 5 Pearce letter at the Maryland Historical Society, Baltimore. While Pearce's testimony should not be peremptorily discarded, it must be evaluated in connection with other evidence including Atchison's version in the Liberty (Mo.) *Tribune*, December 13, 1850, and the Underwood version in the Louisville *Journal*, November 18, 1851.

Whatever other interpretative gloss may be placed upon the chain of events, the compromisers' basic 1850 error was contained in the "Omnibus" offering of Clay and the Committee of Thirteen. There simply were too many signs of sectionalism, of individualism, and of factional power to make the omnibus technique a logical one in the circumstances. Legislative instructions should not be discounted in the appraisal. Fourteen of the free states' general assemblies, at one time or another, had told their senators to uphold Wilmot Proviso positions. Most of the slave states were just as insistent that their congressmen should safeguard southern interests and institutions. Individual convictions, however, could be seen in the stands taken by such men as Benton, Cass, Dickinson, and Norris. The Iowans, George W. Jones and Augustus C. Dodge, were free to vote in accordance with their own judgment and never strayed from the compromisers' inner circle. Most border-state Whigs were independent, too, as Clay, Pearce, and Underwood demonstrated.

6

UNCERTAINTIES as to the probable outcome had been reflected in letters from April through July. On April 20, Seward had written Thurlow Weed: "I am quite well satisfied that the *extreme men* of the South will reject the Compromise." In the latter part of May, the New York senator reported that the Omnibus would be defeated by ten votes.[27] On June 1, the anticompromise John H. Clarke of Rhode Island told a member of the Taylor Cabinet that twelve Southerners and nineteen Northerners would "firmly

[27] Herman V. Ames (ed.), *State Documents on Federal Relations: The States and the United States* (Philadelphia, 1900-1906), 241-78; Louis Pelzer, *Augustus Caesar Dodge: A Study in American Politics* (Iowa City, 1909), 137-47; William H. Seward to Thurlow Weed, April 20, May 22, 1850, Thurlow Weed Papers, University of Rochester.

oppose" the Omnibus, and that five other Southerners might join them.[28] Twelve days later, the moderate Cass gave his son-in-law the "impression" that the committee's bill "will fail."[29] On June 25, Clay seemed desperate when he urged the absent Mangum to "come back to us forthwith, if you possibly can. We shall be hard run, if not defeated in the Senate without your vote."[30] On July 5, however, it was Seward's turn to be pessimistic. On July 26, he confided: "The Compromise Bill is now to pass." On July 27: "To day the friends of the bill give it up in despair. Their combination is broken, and they say irreparably." On July 31: "We have done our duty, and can do no more. The influences exerted are too much for weak Human Nature."[31]

These quotations or the letters from which they were culled show clearly how little apparently anyone knew of what was going on in the Senate. Clarke was absolutely wrong in supposing that Senator Turney of Tennessee favored Taylor's plan. Cass was every bit as mistaken about the Illinois Democrats. Seward had fretted over John Bell's course, and it is doubtful that Bell could have foretold what he would do. Bell "is so cautious a man," a southern Whig wrote on July 6, that "he advances a proposition, and then commences qualifying" until "there is scarcely any thing left of the original thought."[32] Though Clarke ranked King of Alabama with the anticompromisers, Supreme Court Justice John Catron the same day found King apprehensive that the bill might *not* pass.[33] Two traceable changes in the spring and summer were those of

[28] John II. Clarke to William M. Meredith, June 1, 1850, William M. Meredith Papers, Historical Society of Pennsylvania, Philadelphia.
[29] Lewis Cass to Henry Ledyard, June 13, 1850, Lewis Cass Papers, William L. Clements Library, Ann Arbor, Michigan.
[30] Henry Clay to Willie P. Mangum, June 25, 1850, Willie P. Mangum Papers, Duke University, Durham, North Carolina.
[31] Seward to Weed, July 5, 26, 27, 31, 1850, Weed Papers.
[32] David Outlaw to Mrs. Outlaw, July 6, 1850, David Outlaw Papers, Southern Historical Collection, University of North Carolina, Chapel Hill.
[33] John Catron to I. Thomas, June 1, 1850, Crittenden Papers.

Downs and Clemens. On May 22, the previously intransigent Downs announced his conversion to the compromise
creed. And on July 31, the once violent Clemens meekly
voted with Clay, Foote, and King on New Mexico and the
Texas boundary, resuming the Deep South position when
Atchison moved to eliminate California statehood.[34]

The reasons for Atchison's shift are peculiarly intriguing.
Personally preferring 36°30', he traveled with the Omnibus
but (after the Pearce-Clay confrontation) contributed to
wrecking it. "Although opposed to several features" in the
Omnibus Bill, the Missourian explained that autumn, "I
avowed myself in its favor, and supported it as it was
presented, voting however such amendments as in my
opinion were calculated to make it more acceptable to the
slaveholding States." When other amendments struck him
as twisting the spirit and substance of mutual concession,
Atchison felt justified in reverting to his former sectionalism.[35] Mangum returned to Washington from Mrs. Mangum's sick room in time to give Clay appreciable assistance.
The anticompromise Borland of Arkansas, whose wife was
also ill, was absent from the capital throughout this portion
of the struggle and thereby reduced the opposition by
one.[36] A Weed-Seward lieutenant, Orsamus B. Matteson,
said he was the first to tell Fillmore about the fate of the
Omnibus, encountering the President in a barbershop. The
head of state looked "blank enough" and exclaimed, "What
a pity!" Fillmore now "must 'face the music' and that is not
his policy," sneered the congressman from Utica. "His
friends had commenced their efforts to blacken every man
who did not support the bill. . . . Clay is indignant at his
Southern allies."[37]

[34] *Congressional Globe*, 31 Cong., 1 Sess., *Appendix*, 636-39,
1479-82.

[35] Liberty (Mo.) *Tribune*, December 13, 1850; Parrish, *David Rice
Atchison*, 105-106.

[36] Little Rock *Arkansas Gazette*, July 5, 19, 26, August 2, 9, September 20, 1850, April 22, 1853.

[37] Orsamus B. Matteson to Weed, August 1, 1850, Weed Papers.

The "Southern allies," who provoked Clay's wrath, are not easily identifiable. If the allusion was to southern Whigs, it must have been primarily directed at the lineup on Atchison's motion, as that was the sole one on which most of them did not vote as he did. It may have been that Clay's targets included all southern senators, Democrats as well as Whigs, who differed with him. After a review of all occurrences in the Senate over a four-month span, it is debatable that Clay was justified in indignation of that sort. For, at best, Clay's leadership had proven itself of dubious value in the Senate. As far as the Omnibus was concerned, the "followership" on which he counted may never have been his to command. Benton, Douglas, and Webster thought as much at the time. And Underwood admitted to a Kentucky audience in 1851 that it was a serious "error to attempt to unite . . . the various measures . . . in one bill. That course arrayed all the malcontents . . . into a formidable phalanx against the whole."[38]

[38] Louisville *Journal*, November 18, 1851.

CHAPTER VII

The Texas
Bond Lobby

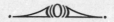

THERE NEVER was a time in American history, from the days of Alexander Hamilton's assumption bill down to the seventh decade of the twentieth century, when someone did not seek financial profit from pending legislation. The period between the Mexican War and the Civil War was no exception. For example, in Harrisburg, Pennsylvania, bribery was "extensively and habitually used." In Austin, a friend of Sam Houston's saw more "intrigue going on" than ever before in Texas history.[1] A Southeasterner characterized the national capital as a "theatre of heartless ambition and corruption." In May, 1850, a New Yorker in Washington warned of "vast moneyed interests" at work.[2] In June, a South Carolina representative condemned speculators who "infest the purlieus of the Capitol." In September, a journalist noted that "speculators and agents of all sorts of schemers crowd the lobbies to their utmost capacity."[3]

In this connection, it is surprising that more has not been written about official and unofficial pressures to obtain a new tariff law. "The iron masters mustered very strong in the lobby this morning," a newsman reported late in this session of Congress, and "another struggle for protection" was foreseen. Actually, manufacturers' spokesmen had been fairly vocal throughout the year, many supposing that higher duties could be linked with the compromise. In June, "Honest John" Davis told the Senate (among other things) that the Tariff of 1846 was "injurious." The same month a Rhode Island senator's son-in-law wrote that "everybody" in Providence was signing tariff petitions.[4] In July, Seward took seriously the idea of a tariff-compromise connection. In August, Francis P. Blair wrote Van Buren that "one of the means employed by Clay to command northern votes was his old make-weight—the tariff." According to Benton, it was not discovered until "very late" that Clay had the tariff "snugly stowed in the boot of his omnibus" in the hope that he could "smuggle" it through.[5]

If the tariff supporters ended the year unsatisfied, railroad promoters were heartened by a major enactment of 1850. Asa Whitney's persistent lobbying for a line to the Pacific met with another in a long series of Capitol Hill rebuffs.[6] But Stephen A. Douglas proved adroit in develop-

[1] Sidney G. Fisher, manuscript diary, January 23, 1850, Historical Society of Pennsylvania, Philadelphia; Washington D. Miller to Sam Houston, November 3, 1849, Thomas J. Rusk Papers, University of Texas, Austin.

[2] David Outlaw to Mrs. Outlaw, January 9, 1850, David Outlaw Papers, Southern Historical Collection, University of North Carolina, Chapel Hill; New York *Courier & Enquirer,* quoted in Washington *National Era,* June 20, 1850.

[3] Philadelphia *North American,* July 2, 1850; New York *Evening Post,* September 19, 1850.

[4] New York *Evening Post,* September 13, 1850; *Congressional Globe,* 31 Cong., 1 Sess., *Appendix,* 879-86; R. M. Larned to Albert C. Greene, June 27, 1850, Albert C. Greene Papers, Rhode Island Historical Society, Providence.

[5] William H. Seward to Thurlow Weed, July 14, 1850, Thurlow Weed Papers, University of Rochester; Francis P. Blair to Martin Van Buren, August 3, September 30, 1850, Martin Van Buren Papers, Library of Congress.

[6] Margaret L. Brown, "Asa Whitney and His Pacific Railroad Publicity Campaign," *Mississippi Valley Historical Review,* XX (Sept. 1933), 216-20; Asa Whitney, *A Project for a Railroad to the Pacific* (New York, 1849), 107-108 and *passim.*

ing the Illinois Central. Individually and through their
agents, both Whitney and Douglas sought large federal
land grants, which were essential to construction. Aware
that northwestern congressmen could not secure them without the enlistment of southern allies, Douglas bracketed
his state's interests with Alabama's and Mississippi's, seeking special benefits for the Mobile & Ohio as well as for
the Illinois Central.[7] Although the Douglas measure passed
the Senate in May, in the House it met nearly fatal opposition from Northeasterners and Southeasterners and on July
31 fell to the bottom of the House calendar. Extraordinarily
well handled from then on, the bill rose to the top on
September 17, when it commanded a favorable margin of
101-75.[8] Fillmore signed it, and the nation had a precedent
for even more significant railroad assistance in the 1860s and
after.

Tariff-slavery and railroad-tariff interests at times were
intertwined. Senator Badger told Blair that he, Berrien,
Dawson, and Mangum "entered into a solemn league &
covenant" to oppose tariff changes if the "northern manufacturing vote" did not sustain the Omnibus Bill.[9] A northern representative later said that the Illinois Central Bill
could not have passed the House if it had not been for a
mutual-aid compact between land-grant sponsors and some
tariff boosters.[10] Aside from the identities of men working
strenuously for both projects, no extremely close connection
between slavery and railroad legislation has yet come to

[7] George F. Milton, *The Eve of Conflict: Stephen A. Douglas and
the Needless War* (Boston, 1934), 10.

[8] *Congressional Globe,* 31 Cong., 1 Sess., 904, 1485, 1838.

[9] Blair to Van Buren, September 30, 1850, Van Buren Papers. See
also David D. Van Tassel, "Gentlemen of Property and Standing:
Compromise Sentiment in Boston in 1850," *New England Quarterly,*
XXIII (Sept. 1950), 317-19.

[10] John Wentworth, *Congressional Reminiscences* (Chicago, 1882),
40-42. *Cf.* Don E. Fehrenbacher, *Chicago Giant: A Biography of
"Long John" Wentworth* (Madison, Wis., 1957), 106-109, 249; Paul
W. Gates, *The Illinois Central Railroad and Its Colonization Work*
(Cambridge, Mass., 1934), 31-43.

light. These few men, however, were so ubiquitous in the whole Washington story of 1850 that their dual contributions must not be overlooked. Douglas stressed the importance of an Illinois Central "arrangement" between himself and a congressman from another section.[11] This was Chairman Bayly of the House Ways and Means Committee, a strangely slighted figure of the middle period and the same individual who had met with Clay and Ritchie at the National Hotel on February 10. Bayly manipulated the railroad proposition back to the top of the House calendar, which no other representative was in a position to do.[12] It may have been pure coincidence that the banker Corcoran, who was close to Douglas and had made Webster a $6,000 gift on the night of March 7, on August 16 ordered for Bayly $5,000 worth of Illinois state bonds and $12,000 in United States bonds.[13] No other part of the tantalizing record suggests an alternative to this acquisition other than as the *quid pro quo* to which Douglas alluded in his provocative "arrangement" reference.

2

AT LEAST TWO Southerners—Edmund Ruffin and Henry A. Wise—who did not emphasize Bayly's role in the situation, saw behind the compromisers' efforts a financial understanding between Ritchie and Clay. Congress had awarded

[11] J. Madison Cutts, *A Brief Treatise upon Constitutional and Party Questions* (New York, 1866), 195-99. *Cf.* John B. Sanborn, *Congressional Grants of Land in Aid of Railways* (Madison, Wis., 1899), 129-30.

[12] Sanborn's skepticism is reflected in Gates, *The Illinois Central Railroad*, 354, and in Milton, *The Eve of Conflict*, 10-11. I agree that the Cutts volume must be used with caution. But Sanborn's reasons for rejecting Bayly (whom he called "Bagly") as Cutts' mysterious "Mr. ———" should be compared with the general procedure recalled by Douglas and demonstrated in the *Globe, passim.*

[13] William W. Corcoran to Corcoran & Riggs, August 16, 1850, Riggs Family Papers, Library of Congress.

the proprietor of the *Union* a contract for the government printing. After the work was begun, it was found to entail far greater expenditures for materials and labor than had been anticipated. Ritchie then requested to be reimbursed for the unexpected costs. The charge was made that Clay promised that he and his congressional associates would do all in their power to help the editor, provided that Ritchie personally and journalistically would assist them along political lines.

As Ruffin's biographer points out, this prominent Virginian was convinced "that 'Old Ritchie' had accepted from Henry Clay a bribe of one hundred thousand dollars in government printing as the price of his support of the Compromise of 1850."[14] An authority on Senator Hunter's life declares: "The factor which the Compromise opponents thought the greatest barrier in their way was the interest of Thomas Ritchie in his public printing contract." "By it we were sold out to the Compromise," Wise told his friend Hunter.[15] It was not in 1850 but in 1852, however, that the venerable Ritchie was given what his own sympathetic biographer describes as "timely and deserved relief."[16] If there was indeed a financial feature in the National Hotel *rapprochement*, I have discovered no hint of it in the writings of either Clay or Ritchie.

Not all the maneuverings occurred in Capitol lobbies or even in Washington. Businessmen of New York, Boston, and Philadelphia associated prosperity with intersectional goodwill. Myndert Van Schaick, Manhattan dry goods merchant, had been a Wilmot Provisoist in 1849. In 1850, however, no mercantile competitor was more active in the adjustment cause. The extent to which "practical" Northerners were frightened by the crisis, and trimmed their

[14] Avery Craven, *Edmund Ruffin, Southerner: A Study in Secession* (New York, 1932), 119.

[15] Henry H. Simms, *Life of Robert M. T. Hunter: A Study in Sectionalism and Secession* (Richmond, 1935), 69.

[16] Charles H. Ambler, *Thomas Ritchie: A Study in Virginia Politics* (Richmond, 1913), 284-85, 296.

sails to suit the storm, is well exemplified by Van Schaick.[17]
In April, the abolitionist Lewis Tappan bore witness to the
applause lavished on Clay and Webster by merchants,
brokers, and stockholders. In May, the Washington stalemate was deplored in business circles where alarm was felt
because of British capitalists' diminished confidence in
American securities.[18] When Tammany Hall did its part in
mid-June, Senator Dickinson the Democrat singled out
Clay as "entitled to the gratitude and thanks of every friend
of his country, regardless of party considerations." "Who,"
Philip Hone mused, "would ever have expected to hear
such a sentiment" from such a man "uttered on such an
occasion and received with cheers by such a company."[19]

New Yorkers carried to Washington a petition bearing
thousands of signatures, impressing Congress and the nation at large. Speaker Cobb credited the 25,000 signers of
this document with serving the cause more effectively in
the South than Clay's and Webster's oft-quoted orations.[20]
In the South, too, economic overtones were audible. In
August, a Georgian wrote Senator Berrien that Southerners
should refuse to buy or use any fabric or article of labor
produced in the North, "until these states compel their
representatives to deal justly with us." On the assumption
that economic pressure would give the South an additional
bargaining point, Berrien later clearly and publicly advocated the same solution.[21] This "half-way stand between

[17] Philip S. Foner, *Business and Slavery: The New York Merchants
and the Irrepressible Conflict* (Chapel Hill, N.C., 1941), 23-24.

[18] "Correspondence of Lewis Tappan and Others with the British
and Foreign Anti-Slavery Society," *Journal of Negro History*, XII
(July 1927), 429; Frederick Wolcott, manuscript diary, May 11,
1850, New York Public Library; Prosper M. Wetmore to William L.
Marcy, May 19, 1850, New York State Library, Albany.

[19] Philip Hone, manuscript diary, June 18, 1850, New-York Historical Society, New York City.

[20] Foner, *Business and Slavery*, 29-32.

[21] Iverson L. Harris to John M. Berrien, August 2, 1850, John M.
Berrien Papers, Southern Historical Collection, University of North
Carolina, Chapel Hill; Raleigh *North Carolina Standard*, November
13, 1850.

Union and secession principles" has been described as
"bound to place" its proponents in an "unsatisfactory position."[22] In Berrien's case, that was true in the long run.
But, in the summer of 1850, it was anything but ineffectual.
There should be no discounting the impact of threatened
or actual retaliation against a region which, Southerners
thought, discriminated unfairly against the South.

3

MORE INTRIGUING than any other politicoeconomic relationship was the course of the Texas bondholder in and out of
Washington. From the first of January through torrid August and into climactic September, it was widely believed
that no compromise would pass unless provision were made
for the Texas debt. Texas' obligations were of two kinds.
One was unrelated to bonds or notes, the creditors being
people who had actively participated in the Texas Revolution or had supplied the Texas army when Mexico menaced
the republic. Nearly all the claims in this class were
modest, and an appropriation of $1,300,000 would have
wiped them off the books. The far more controversial
part of the debt consisted of principal and interest on
Republic of Texas securities, some of which had been issued
at face value but most at big discounts. Since the state
had lost the customs revenue formerly enjoyed by the
republic, both Texas and the bondholders held that it was
incumbent upon the United States to assume this "revenue
debt."[23]

Charles A. Beard and Mary R. Beard have a place among

[22] Richard H. Shryock, *Georgia and the Union in 1850* (Durham,
N.C., 1926), 268-69.
[23] "Register of Public Debts on Claims, 1835-1842," pp. 73-273,
Texas State Archives, Austin; Edmund T. Miller, *A Financial History
of Texas* (Austin, Texas, 1916), 117-24, 131-33; *Sen. Misc. Doc. 72*,
32 Cong., 1 Sess.; *Sen. Report 334*, 33 Cong., 1 Sess.; *House Misc.
Doc. 17*, 33 Cong., 2 Sess.

distinguished historians who have pondered the possible effects of speculation and lobbying on the events of 1850. Economic pressures were far-reaching, they concluded. "The very introduction of the indemnity project swept the price of Texas bonds upward from four or five cents on the dollar to fifty cents." When the House voted on the boundary bill, "lobbyists pressed around the desks of the Representatives in such force that one of the members asked for their removal from the floor, remarking drily that Texas bondholders could see and hear as well from the galleries." The Beards, however, also wrote: "How widespread was the influence of the speculators in the Texas paper cannot be estimated with any degree of exactness, for the distribution of the bonds and notes is not known."[24]

In one respect, it is necessary now to echo the candid admission of the Beards. Numerous investors never registered their holdings, and securities changed hands in Washington or Philadelphia without any accounting in Austin. While claims unseen by the Beards are currently filed at the National Archives, some are incomplete and others are missing. Thus there still seems to be no full record of the ownership of Texas securities on any given day in 1850, including those portentous days when the indemnity was debated in the Senate and the House. Happily, though precision cannot be attained, the searcher is blessed with a rich mine of primary source materials to help him approximate precision.[25] Those materials supply most of the long-sought facts respecting the bondholders. Among them were men of means or influence who came to Washington or lived there in 1850, enjoying personal friend-

[24] Charles A. Beard and Mary R. Beard, *The Rise of American Civilization* (2 vols., New York, 1930), I, 598-99.

[25] Texas Debt Claims and Warrants, Record Group 217, Records of the General Accounting Office; "Register of Texas Debt Warrants, 1856-1861," Record Group 39, Records of the Bureau of Accounts (Treasury); untitled "Workbook" pertaining to the Texas Debt of 1850, Record Group 56, General Records of the Department of the Treasury, National Archives, Washington.

ships with congressmen, dining at the messes or taking
rooms at the hotels of famous or forgotten politicians.[26]

Prominent among the lobbyists was James Hamilton, the
"nullification governor" of South Carolina who considered
himself adept as a lobbyist and who had access to the floor
of Congress as a former member of the House.[27] An
equally well-known holder of Texas paper was Leslie
Combs of Kentucky, a leading Whig and confidential
friend of Clay, who worked behind the scenes in the East
as well as in his own state.[28] As the star reporter in the
capital for the Philadelphia *Public Ledger* and the Baltimore *Sun,* the lobbyist Francis J. Grund dispatched hundreds of procompromise articles which reached homes and
offices of thousands of readers. Like Hamilton and Combs,
Grund was a holder of Texas bonds.[29] William W. Corcoran
of the Washington banking house of Corcoran & Riggs was
a bondholder, as was his associate and recent partner,
George W. Riggs, Jr.[30] Their bank had still more of the
Texas paper that appreciated so rapidly as a result of the
compromise potential. Contemporary bank and Corcoran
correspondence reveals an intense and unflagging interest

[26] In addition to annotated references on particular bondholders in
subsequent notes, see Allen Johnson *et al.* (eds.), *Dictionary of
American Biography* (22 vols. and index, New York, 1928-1958),
IV, 328, for Combs; IV, 440-41, for Corcoran; VIII, 187-88, for
Hamilton; XIV, 336-38, for Peabody; XXI, 362-64, for Grund.

[27] Austin *Texas State Gazette,* January 12, May 25, 1850, March
22, 1856; James Hamilton to Rusk, December 11, 1854, and Rusk
to Hamilton, January ——, 1857, Rusk Papers; Charles M. Wiltse,
John C. Calhoun: Sectionalist, 1840-1850 (Indianapolis, 1951), 460-
61.

[28] Newport *Daily News,* August 13, 1849; Louisville *Journal,* July
21, 1860; Philadelphia *Public Ledger,* June 5, 1850.

[29] Jay Cooke memoir, Baker Library, Harvard University, Cam-
bridge; Henry Clay to Thomas B. Stevenson, April 25, 1850, copy,
Historical and Philosophical Society of Ohio, Cincinnati; Claim 410,
Texas Debt Claims and Warrants, Record Group 217, National
Archives.

[30] New York *Evening Post,* September 7, 1850; Austin *Texas State
Gazette,* May 7, 1853; A. J. Glossbrenner to Corcoran & Riggs, September 27, 1850, Riggs Family Papers.

in the Texas indemnity and the progress of the debates. Ultimately, the biggest payment to any business institution in the country—over $400,000—would go to Corcoran's bank, with smaller sums in five and six figures to Corcoran and to Riggs.[31] The Drexels of Pennsylvania and the Milbanks of New York likewise held sizable portions of the Texas securities. Others were Thomas A. Biddle and Charles Macalester of Philadelphia, Gazaway Bugg Lamar of New York and Georgia, and Benjamin Tappan of Ohio. Also deeply interested were George Peabody of London and Peabody's erstwhile secret partners, William S. Wetmore and John Cryder of New York.[32]

The center of trading in Texas securities was the Philadelphia Stock Exchange, and its quotations shed much light on their rising value during 1850. As of February 1, Texas 10 percent bonds were making "a tremendous bound" to 29 cents on the dollar, the rise being over 20 percent. Those same bonds were being sold at 40 cents in April and 54 cents in May. In mid-June, the *Public Ledger* pointed out that Texas securities had advanced more than 100 percent in the expectation that the plan of the Committee of Thirteen would become law. But with President Taylor

[31] Charnley & Whelen to Corcoran & Riggs, February 23, 26, 1850, E. S. Whelen & Co. to Corcoran & Riggs, April 27, 1850, G. W. and P. E. Norton to Corcoran & Riggs, May 18, 1850, George H. Hickman to Corcoran & Riggs, June 20, 1850, W. W. Corcoran to Corcoran & Riggs, August 19, October 10, 11, 1850, Winslow, Lanier & Co. to Corcoran & Riggs, October 1, December 28, 1850, Riggs Family Papers; "Register of Texas Debt Warrants, 1856-1861," Record Group 39, *passim*, National Archives.

[32] Untitled "Workbook," pp. 9, 11-13, 16, 22-23, 26, 30, 32, 36, 52, 54-55, 57-58, 60, Record Group 56, National Archives; Muriel E. Hidy, "George Peabody, Merchant and Financier, 1829-1854" (Unpublished doctoral dissertation, Radcliffe College, 1939), 188-90; William S. Wetmore to George Peabody, June 21, 1844, June 17, 1846, November 13, 1848, John Cryder to Peabody, January 23, 1846, October 8, 23, November 7, 1849, Peabody to Wetmore & Cryder, July 30, 1850, George Peabody Papers, Essex Institute, Salem, Massachusetts; Wetmore to Corcoran, December 11, 1848, William W. Corcoran Papers, Library of Congress; New York *Herald*, August 12, 16, 20, 1849.

opposed to the compromise, and with the proceedings of Congress snarled and a veto a possibility, "there are no buyers . . . at prices anything like recent sales."[33] A fortnight before Taylor's death, those bonds "were offered . . . as low as 47½" with no takers, and ten days after Clay's failure on July 31 the selling price was down to 42½. Even this seems to have been an increase over the preceding two or three days, as it was the figure quoted the second week in August on the day after the Senate at last approved a bill for a $10 million indemnity. On August 17, the 10 percent bonds had advanced to 45. They reached 50 by the end of August; 55 by September 9; 60 by September 26; and 65½ by September 30, when Congress adjourned. The prices reflect proportionate gains in other Texas bonds and in Texas notes.[34] Thus the connection between the security prices and the August-September congressional action, which we shall observe, is a graphic one.

4

DEEPLY IN DEBT to Corcoran and others, James Hamilton acted on Wetmore's behalf as an agent at Austin in addition to the work he performed in Washington. For this service, as Wetmore explained to Peabody, Hamilton was paid 10 percent. But the record does not show whether it was 10 percent of Wetmore's profit, the scaled value of his bonds, the face value, or the return. Hamilton's position in 1850 was a far cry from that of 1832. Here was one of South Carolina's chief nullifiers acting as a leading compromise advocate! "The payment of the Debt of Texas," Hamilton predicted in March of 1850, "will enable me I trust to do a partial if not a total & plenary Justice to all my creditors."

[33] Philadelphia *Public Ledger*, February 1, April 2, May 10, June 14, 1850. Some of the large holdings at one time had been owned by the Bank of the United States of Pennsylvania.

[34] *Ibid.*, June 28, August 12, 19, September 10, 27, October 1, 1850.

Of course, "I would sacrifice every farthing of the Debt Texas owes me," he said, "and throw myself . . . on the Mercy of my Creditors rather than give up one principle[,] one security[,] one right to which the South is entitled.—In all my efforts & negotiations at Washington I kept this steadily in view and on my return from Texas early in May I shall take my Post again as a sort of Lobby Member until 'the great Question' shall find its solution under the guidance and influence of these opinions & feelings."[35]

There were Southerners who doubted Hamilton's sincerity. Beverley Tucker, professor of law at William and Mary College, was especially bitter. In Tucker's opinion, Hamilton's conduct was "disgraceful" and "a source of mortification." Working with Hamilton was Waddy Thompson, ex-congressman and ex-diplomat who was also a South Carolinian. In mid-August, when the compromisers were achieving success in the Senate, the perceptive Senator Robert W. Barnwell wrote: "The ten millions of money to be paid to the Texas creditors carried the day. I say it in strict confidence but I really do believe, that this whole difficulty about the boundary of Texas was gotten up by Hamilton, Thompson, & Clay[,] the Texas Senators & others interested in the Bonds of Texas. I can not else account for the whole proceeding." By October, Tucker had become convinced that "the ten millions to Texas were introduced into the scheme to supply a fund for bribing southern men both in and out of Congress. I know that one private man . . . receives a large sum, the only consideration of which was his mere *forbearance* to exert his influence against the measure. . . . For this forbearance he receives more than $10,000. This is the key to the *Compromise*. It did not offer a *quid pro quo* to the South, but only to men who were in a position to betray the South. . . . I defy the wit of man to see any thing but the foreshadowing of such operations

[35] Wetmore to Peabody, November 7, 1848, Peabody Papers; Hamilton to James H. Hammond, March 31, 1850, James H. Hammond Papers, Library of Congress.

to explain the mollifying influence of that Speech of
Webster."[36]

With the exception of Texas' David S. Kaufman, who
owned a very small amount, the name of no contemporary
representative or senator appears on lists of 1850 security
holders. A congressman or a congressman's wife, however,
sometimes gave friends or relatives a tip that an investment
in Texas bonds would be to their advantage. Mrs. Linn
Boyd, the beautiful bride of the second-ranking Democrat
in the House, had a letter from her brother in Pittsburgh
during April of the compromise year: "In reference to purchase of Texas Stocks, if it is as good a Speculation as you
say Mr. Boyd represents it to be, Geo[rge] could obtain
from 10 to 50 Thousand dollars to enter into any Such a
Speculation if there was an absolute certainty of making
by the operation. . . . When you next write[,] if Mr. Boyd
would be so kind as to give us a Statement of the real facts
of the case, Something might be done to advantage."[37]

Other communications of the period lead one to recognize
the reliance placed on the millionaire Corcoran by the millionaire Peabody and the millionaire Wetmore. In mid-
1849, Peabody counseled Corcoran & Riggs to "confer with
Wetmore & Cryder relative to the best Texas bonds." In
August of 1850, Cryder sent word across the Atlantic: "I
had a long talk with Corcoran a day or two since about the
Florida bonds. He thinks if they and the Texas ones could
be got hold of at fair rates, a good deal could be made by
them. He & Wetmore & myself are to consult about this
matter tomorrow."[38] The August consultation in New York
may have been a cause of Corcoran's buying additional

[36] Beverley Tucker to Hammond, February 4, 1851, Robert W.
Barnwell to Hammond, August 14, 1850, Tucker to Hammond,
October 9, 1850, Hammond Papers.

[37] Andrew J. Rhey to Mrs. Linn Boyd, April 20, 1850, Boyd Family
Papers, microfilm, University of Kentucky, Lexington.

[38] Jay Cooke memoir, Cambridge; Cryder to Peabody, March 26,
January 23, 1846, Peabody to Wetmore & Cryder, September 13,
1850, Peabody Papers.

Texas bonds in the name of Corcoran & Riggs or of some
other partnership or person. We know that Corcoran was
active in acquiring Texas securities both before and after
that third August week. Probably it was due to his aggressiveness that Texas bonds advanced so sharply. Corcoran
thought so, for on October 10 he told a Philadelphia
broker to suspend orders pending a decline in quotations,
"as I fear we have been putting up the market upon our-
selves." Later, when the value of the paper fell off a bit,
the Washington wizard removed the ban and resumed his
purchases.[39]

5

FROM THIS STUDY of speculation and pressure, William W.
Corcoran emerges as a vastly more important factor in
1850's convolutions than he has previously been considered.
It was Corcoran who lent thousands of dollars to that
indefatigable lobbyist, James Hamilton. It was Corcoran
to whom George Peabody turned for inside information
on Texas securities. When the Texas creditors were paid,
Corcoran appeared in the dual capacity of Combs' "as-
signee" and Wetmore's "attorney."[40] Corcoran was the principal sponsor, initiator, or guiding spirit in countless phases
of politico-financial enterprise connected with the compromise and compromisers. No wonder that he took it as a
matter of course that he could not visit Peabody in England, so long as Congress was in session.[41]

[39] Corcoran to Corcoran & Riggs, October 10, 11, November 9, 11,
1850, Winslow, Lanier & Co. to Corcoran & Riggs, December 18, 28,
1850, Riggs Family Papers.
[40] Corcoran to Hamilton, November 26, 1851, letterpress copy,
Stephen A. Douglas to Corcoran, September 10, 1850, Corcoran to
Francis J. Grund, March 25, May 8, July 21, September 4, 1851,
letterpress copies, Corcoran Papers; Warrants 146, 1046, 1068,
"Register of Texas Debt Warrants, 1856-1861," Record Group 39,
National Archives.
[41] Corcoran to Peabody, May 6, 1850, Peabody Papers.

Cancelling Webster's note in March, buying Illinois and United States bonds for Congressman Bayly in August, entertaining legislators in an expensive and tasteful manner, Corcoran had a finger in every Washington economic pie with the probable exception of the tariff. While there is no absolute proof that Texas bondholders influenced the vote of a single congressman, such contemporary witnesses as Senator Barnwell and Professor Tucker felt certain that the bondholders' lobby raised the boundary question in the first place and then proceeded to bribe Southerners in and out of Congress. With equal certainty we know that Hamilton considered himself extremely successful in his 1850 lobbying work, and that Grund excelled in some of the most clever and subtle propaganda of his generation; if Jay Cooke is to be believed, and circumstantial evidence heeded, Grund sat in on strategy sessions in addition to buying bonds and performing effective procompromise liaison work.

The activity and maneuvering of lobbyists like Grund, Hamilton, and Corcoran was matched on the Senate floor during August and September by Stephen A. Douglas. The older generation in the Senate had exhausted itself, and its best efforts had come to nothing with the defeat of the Omnibus Bill; now the younger men were to take over, and foremost among them was Douglas—sleepless, resilient, resourceful.

CHAPTER VIII

Douglas, the Maker
of Combinations

.———⋖((O))⋗———.

I T TOOK DOUGLAS only seven of the Senate's working days to demonstrate the quality of his aggressive
leadership. Clay was a sore trial to his friends on
Thursday, August 1. Not that they objected when he
declared: "I was willing to take the measures united. I am
willing now to see them pass separate and distinct." This
was fair enough. But what discouraged the moderates was
Clay's insistence on reviewing in detail his version of the
reasons for Wednesday's wreck of the Omnibus. More
aggravating was the undisguised bitterness with which he
blamed its collapse on Senator Pearce. The latter naturally
retaliated. Charges and countercharges flew. And Clay
served neither himself nor his cause in the acrimonious
exchange.[1]

After Clay's attack on Pearce, the nominal topic of
debate was Foote's amendment of Douglas' amendment
to the revived California statehood bill, which again was
before the chamber. As he had done earlier in the year,
Foote offered to divide California one degree below 36°30′;
a northern free state was to be created, while the southern
territory of "Colorado" would be subject to popular sov-

ereignty. Prompted by the discussion and by Clay's criticism of Pearce, several southern Democrats injected further
sectional opinion into the debate. Mason denounced Clay's
justification of employing force to oppose any "military
array against the Government of the Union." Then Butler
rushed in to attack Clay for allegedly holding that a
majority decision made for constitutionality. This was
untrue, said the South Carolinian, whose basic loyalty was
"to the State of my nativity and the State that gives me
protection, and her voice will always command my services."

Butler's speech gave Clay an opportunity for an eloquent
reply: Even if "my own State, lawlessly, contrary to her
duty, should raise the standard of disunion against a residue
of the Union, I would go against her. I would go against
Kentucky herself in that contingency, much as I love her."
As occurred so many times in 1850, Foote hastened to support Clay. Although Clay's words were chaste and even
memorable, Foote proved as bumptious as ever. Butler
soon attacked Foote, terming him an ex-Federalist (by
implication, an ex-Whig), and this the fiery Mississippian
denied. It was only after Dickinson had struck a sober note
that further consideration of the amended California bill
was postponed to Friday, and the Utah measure (carried
over from Wednesday) came up for its third reading and
was perfunctorily passed.[2]

On August 2, Atchison of Missouri released some of the
session's choicest invective. "Even the worm will turn and
sting when trodden on," he asserted in a tangle with Foote;
"and, sir, small as is the Senator from Mississippi in form,
we all know that he is a lion in heart." Here was ridicule,
here was sarcasm which must have been hard for Foote to
bear. As Atchison admitted, he had followed Foote's guidance for the last six or seven months. Now he was disillusioned. "Our northern friends" failed to "come to the
rescue" of moderate Southerners in late July. The Mis-

[1] *Congressional Globe,* 31 Cong., 1 Sess., *Appendix,* 1486-88.
[2] *Ibid.,* 1485, 1488-98. Foote's proposed "Colorado" was geo-
graphically unrelated to the later state of that name.

souri Democrat doubted the sincerity of the "veriest hypo-
crites that ever crawled upon the face of the earth."
Apologizing the same day, Atchison regretted his "strong
language," as "I did not intend to use my words in an
offensive sense to any portion of the northern Senators."
There was no apology, however, with respect to his former
leader—the "worm" was not unwormed, and, for once, the
"lion" failed to roar.

When a vote was taken, the Senate turned down an
altered form of the Foote amendment by a 33-23 margin,
with Benton, Clay, and the Delaware Whigs sustaining a
solid northern bloc. Douglas' own amendment, which was
intended to remove flaws from the California bill, then won
approval almost at once. But, before anything further was
done, Hunter of Virginia exclaimed: "We have been kept
here week after week, and we are worn out. I think, under
all the circumstances, we had better adjourn."[3] The adjournment was from Friday to Monday, and at this time
Clay left Washington for a rest on the New England sea-
shore. On August 5, he reached Philadelphia, where he
praised the Democratic party for its procompromise sentiment and tenacity. Thence he proceeded to Newport,
Rhode Island, where Leslie Combs and others met his boat.
Clay did not return until August 27.[4] In the interim,
Douglas directed virtually all of the successful senatorial
action that resulted in the Compromise of 1850.

2

SATURDAY, AUGUST 3, found Douglas supremely confident.
California statehood, he wrote, could be expected to obtain
the approval of the Senate very soon. New stipulations for

[3] *Ibid.*, 1499-1501, 1504-1505.
[4] Philip Hone, manuscript diary, August 6, 7, 1850, New-York Historical Society, New York City; Newport *Daily News*, August 8, 12,
26, 1850; George R. Poage, *Henry Clay and the Whig Party* (Chapel
Hill, N.C., 1936), 260-61.

the Texas boundary, which he and Pearce were preparing, would be next on the agenda. "We shall then take up the Bill for New Mexico & pass it just as I reported it four months ago." Thus would all the measures triumph in "the Senate & I believe the House also." When "all are passed . . . they will collectively be Mr. Clay's Compromise" and separately the recommendations of the Committee on Territories in March. There was, he added, every reason to think that "we will yet be able to settle the whole difficulty."[5] In the Baltimore *Sun,* Francis J. Grund was as well posted and almost as optimistic as Douglas. According to the journalist-bondholder, the success of Utah without the Proviso established a sufficient precedent for New Mexico. California was "capable of taking care of herself," while the "fugitive slave bill will also pass." Grund told his readers that the boundary legislation, to be introduced by Pearce on Monday, would give Texas one more degree of latitude than what had been claimed by her congressmen. The prophecy, however, contained a phrase of caution. For the boundary, Grund admitted, was the "difficulty in the whole arrangement."[6]

On Monday, August 5, Pearce came forward with his altered boundary. But the debaters returned to the bill for California, reaching no decision on its engrossment. Both chambers showed marked interest on Tuesday in Fillmore's special message on the New Mexico crisis and in the reply of Secretary of State Webster to a letter which Texas' governor had dispatched to Taylor in June. Both Fillmore and Webster stressed means of preserving peace, Fillmore strongly favoring a monetary payment to Texas in lieu of the Supreme Court and joint-commission alternatives. Senators departed, however, and remaining auditors were bored when Yulee of Florida launched a filibuster on the Cali-

[5] Stephen A. Douglas to Charles H. Lanphier and George Walker, August 3, 1850, in possession of Dr. Charles L. Patton, Springfield, Illinois.
[6] Baltimore *Sun,* August 5, 1850.

fornia question. Nor was the House particularly aroused by the accusation, flung by Representative Howard, that the President "draws the sword upon Texas." Grund whimsically reported that P. T. Barnum "expressed great curiosity to see that sword" and telegraphed for it for exhibition purposes.[7] Thus a touch of satire exposed the absurdity of the criticism.

On Wednesday, progress toward adjustment was made when the leaders turned the Senate floor over to Pearce, and the Marylander made a cogent appeal on behalf of his boundary proposal. Thursday witnessed the defeat of Ewing's move to table Pearce's offering in favor of bypassed California. On Friday, August 9, amendments introduced by Underwood and Mason were turned down. Other advocated changes were deferred or defeated or occasionally accepted by large or small majorities. Among the key decisions were those of Winthrop, who termed Pearce's boundary "less objectionable than I imagined"; of Clemens, who was willing to assume Texas' "whole debt without taking one foot of her territory"; and of Berrien, who emphasized "peace and harmony." These three senators had become waverers, and their growing amenability raised compromisers' hopes. The very fact that Pearce had been picked to promote the fresh boundary-and-debt combination also augured well for adjustment. Although Jefferson Davis and Andrew P. Butler desperately held out to the last, perceptibly less attention was paid them than before.

Pearce's bill contained, among other features, a section calling for the payment of $10,000,000 to Texas. Now he proposed the following as an amendment:

Provided, That no more than five millions of said stock shall be issued until the creditors of the State holding bonds and other certificates of stock of Texas for which duties on imports were specially pledged, shall first file at the Treasury of the United States releases of all claim against the United States

[7] *Congressional Globe,* 31 Cong., 1 Sess., 1520-21, 1525-29, 1531-33; *ibid., Appendix,* 1158-69, 1505-17; Baltimore *Sun,* August 8, 1850.

for or on account of said bonds or certificates, in such form as
shall be prescribed by the Secretary of the Treasury and approved by the President of the United States.

Rusk said it was "a matter of no great consequence"
whether the distribution of the five millions was left to
Washington or to Austin. In view of Texans' opinions in
and after 1850, one may safely conclude that Rusk was
mistaken and the issue was of "great consequence" indeed.

Interestingly, Senators Rusk and Houston were in the
minority when Pearce's amendment of his own measure
passed with no trouble at all by a vote of 35 to 12. There
was balloting on five other points, including the close
division in which—by a majority of three—the bill survived
its next-to-last test. Finally, the question of the bill's
passage was answered in the affirmative, with thirty senators
in favor and twenty opposed. Douglas' victory was made
possible by sixteen Democrats and fourteen Whigs (eighteen Northerners and twelve Southerners), while the opposition consisted of twelve Democrats, six Whigs, and two
Free Soilers (twelve Southerners and eight Northerners).
Five Democrats and five Whigs did not vote, most of them
being paired off. Berrien, Clemens, John Davis, and Winthrop stood alongside Douglas and Pearce.[8] The switch of
these and other men may be considered either as a tribute
to Douglas' leadership or as proof of the significance of
Taylor's demise.

3

SOME OF THE MOST impassioned words of the year were
delivered in the debates occurring between the night of
August 9 and the morning of August 24, notwithstanding
the relative concord symbolized by the recent boundary
achievement. On the 12th, certain differences involving

[8] *Congressional Globe,* 31 Cong., 1 Sess., 1540-45, 1551-52, 1554-
56; *ibid., Appendix,* 1517, 1561-81.

Soulé, Foote, and Douglas preceded a two-hour oration by Berrien and the briefer remarks of Cass and John Davis. On the 13th, Jefferson Davis, Clemens, Houston, and Barnwell extended the California discussion. The next day, nine senators commented on the New Mexico territorial program. On August 15, eight Southerners and four Northerners continued the verbal pyrotechnics touched off earlier in the week when nine southern Democrats and one southern Whig signed a protest against California's admission. On that evening the Senate adjourned for three days. But, beginning on August 19, there were no fewer than eighteen prominent participants in an exceedingly intricate debate on fugitive slave proposals.

Amid the crosscurrents of party and faction, Soulé of Louisiana cried: "Sir, I do not wish to heat, by any remarks of mine, the excitement which already prevails to such an alarming extent throughout the country." But God alone knew, he warned, the pitch it would reach with a victory for the "accursed" California bill, which, "in the madness of your impatience, you seem so eager to pass." "For the first time," declared Jefferson Davis, "we are about permanently to destroy the balance of power between the sections." The next step "may lead us to the point at which aggression will assume such a form as will require the minority to decide whether they will sink below the conditions to which they were born, or maintain it by forcible resistance." "I do not know what Alabama may do," declaimed Clemens, who had been rather docile about the boundary; but "if she determines to resist this [California] law by force, by secession, by any means, I am at her service. . . . If this be treason, I am a traitor—a traitor who glories in the name."[9]

One might assume that comparable shrillness would come from northern senators as the passage of the bill on runaways neared. Such, however, was not the case. Consider-

[9] *Ibid., Appendix,* 1519-61, 1581-1630. The Soulé, Davis, and Clemens quotations are from pp. 1520, 1533, and 1535 respectively.

ing the fury aroused in the North by the Fugitive Slave
Law in the years that followed, it is surprising how devoid
of emotion were many comments on the subject. A little
humor crept in now and then. Butler evoked chuckles and
smiles when he yawned audibly while Foote was speaking.
"I perceive," said Foote, "that my friend from South Carolina seems to suffer under my speech." "I was not thinking
about your speech at all," Butler replied as the Senate
rocked with laughter and President *Pro Tempore* King
called, "Order! order!" More typical were the technical,
legalistic analyses of proposed amendments and alternatives to the bills of Mason and others. Several radical
antislavery men were away from Washington, and this may
account in part for the tone in the chamber. Chase
sounded dry and matter-of-fact when he said: "If the most
ordinary controversy involving a contested claim to twenty
dollars must be decided by a jury, surely a controversy
which involves the right of a man to his liberty should
have a similar trial." "All laws depend for their execution
and efficiency, in no small degree, upon the opinion of the
community that they are just and responsible," Winthrop
asserted. Therefore, "principles of justice" should govern,
and anything that could be construed as "oppressive" ought
not to supervene. Yet Winthrop's realistic warning as to
probable northern attitudes was, for the most part, implicit
and subdued.[10]

Votes, indeed, seemed far more significant than anything
said in Congress that month. In contrast to the stalemate
lasting from the first of the year till the end of July, the
August decisions gratified the compromisers. As the new
trend had been apparent since the boundary verdict,
favorable decisions were no longer surprising. Still there
was rejoicing when, on August 13, California statehood won
approval by a majority of 16. Only two days later, the New

[10] *Ibid.*, 1581-1630. The Butler-Foote exchange and the quotations
from Chase and Winthrop appear on pp. 1615, 1587, and 1588
respectively.

Mexico bill succeeded overwhelmingly, 27 to 10. Neither the *Congressional Globe* nor the *Senate Journal* gives us a yea-and-nay breakdown of the final vote on the fugitive slave bill. What we do know is that, on August 23, only twelve senators opposed and twenty-seven assented to its engrossment for a third reading. This was tantamount to passage, which followed *viva voce* on August 26.[11]

The success of all four bills was quick work and impressive proof of Douglas' capabilities. As a maker of combinations, the Vermont-born Chicagoan surpassed his famous seniors in 1850—men whose names, in the minds of most Americans, are more closely associated with the outcome than his own. We have previously scrutinized the first of his majorities. When the California victory is studied, one finds seventeen Democrats, fifteen Whigs, and two Free Soilers (twenty-eight Northerners and six Southerners) ranged against fourteen Democrats and four Whigs (all Southerners). Two southern Democrats, four southern Whigs, and two northern Whigs did not vote. Nineteen Democrats and eight Whigs (eleven Northerners and sixteen Southerners) supplied the winning total for New Mexico; three Democrats, six Whigs, and one Free Soiler (all from the North) opposed; and this time there were twenty-three abstainers. The fugitive slave figures emphasize sectionalism. In favor of engrossing that bill were fifteen southern Democrats, nine southern Whigs, and three northern Democrats. Three northern Democrats, eight northern Whigs, and Chase of the Free Soilers stood in the tiny minority, while twenty-one senators were unavoidably absent or did not wish to be counted—or both.

After August 26 the center of importance became the House. On September 16, however, the Senate provided a very safe margin for the sixth part of the Compromise of 1850, the restriction of the slave trade in the District of Columbia. This was supported by sixteen northern Democrats, nine northern Whigs, two northern Free Soilers, two

11 *Ibid.*, 1573, 1589, 1647, 1660.

southern Democrats (Benton and Houston), and four
southern Whigs (from Kentucky and Delaware). Opposition to it came from twelve Democrats and seven Whigs,
Southerners all, while the roster of absentees comprised a
heterogeneous assortment of one northern Democrat, four
northern Whigs, four southern Democrats, and one southern
Whig.[12]

4

BEFORE TRACING the path of the Compromise in the House,
we should note some revealing or baffling senatorial decisions as well as partisan and sectional influences. Nothing
is more arresting than the enormous number of absentees,
particularly the nine who were present neither on August
15 nor on August 23. There can be no question that several
of these people had excellent reasons for being out of town.
That was true of Borland and Clay. Seward was said to be
sick; he probably had a pair with Dickinson. Still, the
wholesale exodus from the city or the floor when critical
roll calls could be anticipated seems mysterious at best.

One need not be a cynic to guess that Bright, Cass, and
Norris thought it better to dodge a showdown on fugitive
slaves. A similar suspicion is attached to Clarke of Rhode
Island and Truman Smith of Connecticut, whose procompromise votes on August 9 would have been beyond belief
a month earlier. Yet, assuredly, neither Jefferson Davis at
one extreme of the ideological line nor Hale at the other
was a person to avoid a statement or a stand. Their failure
to appear is harder to comprehend than the fact that
fifteen of the twenty-one senators unrecorded on the issue
of runaways were northern Democrats or northern Whigs.
If all fifteen had voted what probably was the sentiment of
their section, and if the six absent Southerners had not

[12] There were 112 affirmative Democratic and 67 affirmative Whig
votes on the six parts of the Compromise.

voted, the Fugitive Slave Law of 1850 would have died a-borning.

A tabulation of the roll calls on the various Compromise measures (see Appendix A) shows not only the absentees' indirect influence on the outcome but also the positive contribution made by the Democratic party and by individual Democrats. Many historians have given Whig leaders and the Whig party most of the credit for the result. Actually, more Democrats than Whigs voted for each of the component parts. Moreover, in the totality of affirmative ballots cast on the six tests, the numerical difference is 46 and the percentage difference 26. Both figures favor the Democrats quantitatively in the role of compromisers, vis-à-vis the Whigs.[13]

Four senators supported all six bills. These were Augustus C. Dodge, Democrat of Iowa; Sam Houston, Democrat of Texas; Daniel Sturgeon, Democrat of Pennsylvania, and John Wales, Whig of Delaware. Seven other senators voted "yea" on five occasions but abstained from casting ballots on a sixth. The seven were Jesse D. Bright, Democrat of Indiana; Lewis Cass, Democrat of Michigan; Stephen A. Douglas, Democrat of Illinois; Alpheus Felch, Democrat of Michigan; Moses Norris, Democrat of New Hampshire; James Shields, Democrat of Illinois, and Presley Spruance, Whig of Delaware. Thus, of the eleven senators who lent the cause of the moderates the greatest strength, nine were Democrats and two were Whigs.

In case these conclusions need further examination, it is well to recall what occurred when three sections of Clay's Omnibus Bill were defeated on July 31. Then only five of Clay's fellow Whigs sustained him on the New Mexico question (the major issue), while sixteen Democrats "fol-

[13] Ibid., 1485; Congressional Globe, 31 Cong., 1 Sess., 1504, 1555, 1573, 1589, 1647, 1830; Binghamton (N.Y.) Democrat, November 28, 1850. Two "yea" votes on the District bill were those of John C. Frémont and William M. Gwin, California Democrats, who took their seats September 10.

lowed" his lead. On the Texas boundary, at that time, Clay and ten other Whigs went down with seventeen Democrats in a very close vote. On the California statehood issue, Clay had only six Whigs in his camp together with sixteen Democrats and two Free Soilers. Of the nine men aligned with Clay on all three votes, eight were Democrats (see Appendix B). In defeat as in victory, under Clay's aegis as well as under Douglas', the Democrats aided the adjustment more consistently and more faithfully than did the Whigs.

5

THE CORE OF the Compromise of 1850 was composed of the territorial features and the boundary and debt arrangements. New Mexico was the issue which in July shattered the plan of the Committee of Thirteen, and it ought to be remembered that about three-fourths of the Senate Whigs contributed to its fate. When Douglas took control, he discovered that he dared not promote New Mexico until after the Texas boundary and California measures had been passed. Then, sensing that the situation was at least propitious, Douglas saw his sagacity sustained as only three members of his party spoiled the Democratic record at this point. The same three had likewise been the only Senate Democrats out of thirty-three to oppose the Utah bill of July 31.

This was no accident. For upwards of two years, the majority or national element of the Democratic party had supported the "nonintervention" or "popular sovereignty" doctrine embodied in the Douglas solution. In 1847, Dickinson, the New York Democrat, had introduced resolutions specifying that territorial legislatures should decide questions of domestic policy within the territories.[14] The same

---

[14] *Congressional Globe,* 31 Cong., 1 Sess., *Appendix,* 1479, 1481, 1483, 1485; *Congressional Globe,* 31 Cong., 1 Sess., 1589; *ibid.,* 30 Cong., 1 Sess., 21.

year, Lewis Cass addressed his controversial "Nicholson Letter" to Alfred O.P. Nicholson of Tennessee. "Leave to the people who will be affected" by the slavery issue "to adjust it upon their own responsibility and in their own manner," the Michigan Democrat urged. The Nicholson Letter became Cass's personal platform in his campaign for the 1848 Democratic presidential nomination. The Democratic national platform of that year was vague, but was capable of being interpreted along the lines of the Dickinson resolutions and the Nicholson Letter. In fact, it was thus interpreted by Jefferson Davis and by a host of northern Democrats loyal to Cass in his presidential race.[15]

Scholars have commented on the contrast between what Cass and Dickinson seemed to mean by nonintervention and what John C. Calhoun did mean. Before Cass wrote to Nicholson, Calhoun had employed the same label to mark a different doctrine. Calhoun's nonintervention disallowed either the federal or the territorial governments the authority to prevent slave-owners from taking their slaves into the western territories. During the Taylor-Cass-Van Buren struggle of 1848, many southern Democrats said that Cass's nonintervention was the same as Calhoun's. Davis suspected this was not the case at all. Cass himself in 1850, becoming more candid than in 1847 or 1848, verified the Davis suspicion. According to Cass's remarks in the "Great Debate," territorial legislatures could sanction or prohibit slavery as they preferred.[16]

Regardless of whether Cass's 1850 contention was justified or consistent, not a few of the southern Democratic senators went along with the New Mexico-Utah arrangement in

[15] William L. G. Smith, *Fifty Years of Public Life: The Life and Times of Lewis Cass* (New York, 1856), 607-16; Frank B. Woodford, *Lewis Cass: The Last Jeffersonian* (New Brunswick, N.J., 1950), 251-57; *Congressional Globe*, 36 Cong., 1 Sess., *Appendix*, 302, 456; Milo M. Quaife, *The Doctrine of Non-Intervention with Slavery in the Territories* (Chicago, 1910), 76.

[16] Richard K. Crallé (ed.), *The Works of John C. Calhoun* (6 vols., New York, 1853-1855), IV, 339-49; *Congressional Globe*, 31 Cong., 1 Sess., 398-99.

the Compromise of 1850, just as most northern Democratic
senators did. At various points, Foote, Houston, King, and
others joined Northerners on nonintervention. A single
phrase in the bills, "consistent with the Constitution,"[17]
made it possible for Southerners to put their own gloss on
the Compromise keystone. Hazy or anomalous as the provisions might appear, they were all Democratic provisions.
Created by Democrats and praised by Democrats from both
the sections, they were championed late and secondarily
by Henry Clay and Daniel Webster.

6

ONE OF THE MOST accurate contemporary summations of
the events of spring and early summer is contained in
Douglas' letter to Charles H. Lanphier and George Walker.
On August 3, he wrote:

You have doubtless heard of the defeat of the Compromise
of the Committee of thirteen. I regret it very much, altho I
must say that I never had very strong hopes of its passage. . . .
I declined being a member of the Committee of 13 for this
reason & for the same reasons opposed the appointment of the
Committee. . . . I had previously written & reported as Chmn
of the Com. on Territories two Bills—one for the admission of
California & the other providing territorial Governments for
Utah & New Mexico[,] also providing for the settlement of the
Texas Boundary. Before I reported these Bills I consulted Mr.
Clay & Gen'l Cass whether I should put them in one or separate
Bills. They both advised me to keep them separate & both
expressed the same opinions in debate about that time. I took
their advice & reported the measures in two Bills instead of one.
About two weeks afterward they changed their minds & con-
cluded to appoint a committee for the purpose of uniting them.
I opposed the movement as unwise & unnecessary as they
declared they did not intend to change any feature in my Bills.
The Committee was appointed & took my two printed Bills &
put a wafer between & reported them back without changing or

[17] Quaife, *The Doctrine of Non-Intervention*, 118.

writing a single word except one line. The one line inserted prohibited the Territorial Legislature from legislating upon the subject of slavery. This amendment was written in by the Com. in opposition to the wishes of Gen'l Cass & Mr. Clay, and they gave notice that they should move to strike it out in the Senate, & it was stricken out. So you see that the difference between Mr. Clay's Compromise Bill & my two Bills was a wafer & that he did not write one word of it & that I did write every word.

After the majority of the Senate decided that they would act upon the measures jointly instead of separately[,] I gave the Bill of Mr. Clay my active & unswerving support down to its final defeat. The same remark is true of my colleague Gen'l Shields. . . . The Compromise [Omnibus] Bill was defeated by a union between the Free Soilers & Disunionists & the administration of Gen'l Taylor. All the power & patronage of the Govt. was brought to bear against us & at the last the allied forces were able to beat us. The Utah Bill has passed the Senate in the precise words in which I wrote it. . . .[18]

Before the session ended, Douglas made a similar assertion in the Senate. He modestly pointed out that "no man and no party has acquired a triumph, except the party friendly to the Union triumphing over abolitionism and disunion." At the same time, however, he reminded his listeners that long before the Committee of Thirteen was formed, the Committee on Territories (which had a Democratic majority, and of which Douglas was the chairman) had considered and approved the component parts of the Omnibus. What Clay did was to connect old bills and to make the enactment of one dependent on the enactment of all. Therefore, Clay was less the originator and more the improviser or rather the adopter of Foote's improvisation. Incorporated in his recommendations (as in Douglas'), indeed the epitome of them, was the nonintervention theory of Dickinson and Cass.

Several persons claimed the honor of having originated the compromise settlement. One, on the Senate floor, was

[18] Douglas to Lanphier and Walker, August 3, 1850, Springfield. The quotation from Douglas' fairly long letter has been divided into three paragraphs for the reader's sake.

Foote, who said "without egotism" that "the report of the
Committee on Territories was based upon bills introduced
by myself." Jefferson Davis' response to this sally was a
relaxed "Oh, yes, I am willing to give you all the credit for
that." Referring to the Compromise itself, however, Davis
added: "If any man has a right to be proud of the success
of these measures, it is the Senator from Illinois."[19] Years
afterward, Foote traced popular sovereignty's inception
back past his own contribution and Cass's Nicholson Letter
to Dickinson's resolutions. Without subtracting at all from
Douglas' part in the settlement, we must also give credit
to Cass, Foote, and Dickinson—Democrats all—as well as to
Douglas.

Incidentally, it must be acknowledged that, if Democrats
originated most of the compromise, and if Douglas deserves
the greater share of whatever honor accrues to the principal
contributors, Democrats should be saddled with part of the
blame for the Omnibus expedient. In the light of the May-
June-July occurrences, Foote cannot escape culpability.
For it was he, probably assisted by Thomas Ritchie, who
prevailed on Clay to desert Douglas' tactics and to adopt
those of Foote instead. It has been explained that Clay
came around reluctantly in the late winter, and that Webster
followed suit with protestations.[20] Clay erred, but Foote
erred before he did, and Clay might never have made his
fundamental mistake if Foote had not enticed him down
the path to failure.

7

DICKINSON'S RESOLUTIONS of 1847, Cass's Nicholson Letter
of 1848, the territorial portion of Cass's candidacy in 1848,

[19] *Congressional Globe,* 31 Cong., 1 Sess., 1830.
[20] Henry S. Foote, *War of the Rebellion; or, Scylla and Charybdis*
(New York, 1866), 71-74; *Congressional Globe,* 31 Cong., 1 Sess.,
367-69; *The Writings and Speeches of Daniel Webster* (18 vols.,
Boston, 1903), XVIII, 369-70.

and Foote's proposals in the latter part of 1849 were Democratic contributions. The majority of Douglas' Committee on Territories was Democratic, as were most of the compromise leaders. If Douglas the Democrat guided the compromise through to success, if Democrats supplied most of the votes, and if Democrats were far more consistent than Whigs in underwriting component parts, small wonder that in 1852 the Democrats ran a procompromise nominee —and that the Whigs went down to party defeat and party death.

Two other observations merit attention. One is the likelihood that the Whig party was hopelessly split on the sectional question in 1850 and even before. Unable to elect one of their seasoned statesmen to the Presidency, the Whigs had to rally their faltering forces behind the glamour of a military hero. During Zachary Taylor's lifetime, the bulk of the Whig senators stoutly resisted the efforts of the compromisers. After Taylor's death, Clay's Omnibus was halted and abandoned despite the push Democrats gave it. Even under Millard Fillmore, and with Douglas in command in the Senate, the piecemeal measures could not have passed if many Whigs had not absented themselves. Thus opposition, followed by negation, should be highlighted in accounts of the crisis and in the decline of Whiggery.

The other key point, related to the first, is that the prominence of Webster and Clay in version after version of the debates seems undeserved. Why the exaggerated emphasis on what they are presumed to have contributed? True, Clay returned to the Senate from retirement and for months did take charge of the compromise in the public gaze. Webster delivered one of the most brilliant speeches in American history. These facts are incontrovertible. Yet from the standpoint of strength, of votes, of origins, and of practical influence on Capitol Hill, the Clay-Webster contribution was secondary to the primary Democratic direction of the adjustment forces.

Years ago, a scholar of another generation stressed the need of reexploring the Compromise of 1850.[21] Discoveries in old manuscripts and a more extensive reading of the *Congressional Globe,* newspapers, and kindred sources, make it possible to come closer now to the realities of 1850 —and to view the true structure behind the facade.

[21] St. George L. Sioussat, "Tennessee, the Compromise of 1850, and the Nashville Convention," *Mississippi Valley Historical Review,* II (Dec. 1915), 347.

CHAPTER IX

Allegro Whistles and Cannon Salutes

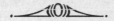

WHILE DOUGLAS and his allies were engaged in hammering out a compromise, the crisis seemed to grow more acute south of the Red River and west of the Sabine. Communication delays deepened misunderstandings. On August 13, a Nacogdoches Democrat warned Senator Rusk: "A Telegraphic rumor . . . of the failure of the Compromise Bill fills your friends here with grief and terror." Even "the moderation men among us must look for a *military promenade*" to Santa Fe, "if not actual Civil War . . . North vs. South. What *are* we to do?"[1] A less excitable correspondent thought on August 16 that "the Legislature will not act precipately." A week later, however, the same man wrote that a select joint committee "agreed on yesterday to report in favor of war measures—to raise and equip three thousand rangers, with a large reserve —and to appropriate all the means of the State to that object."[2]

The relatively conservative Rusk, whose term would expire the following year, overwhelmingly won reelection on August 26. Yet one of his friends, who sent him the good news, "was told this morning that Governor Bell said

He would not Sell a Bit of land as large as a handkerchief
for a million of Dollars. . . . A Dissolution of the Union is
evidently wished for, and contemplated by many persons in
this State."[3] Bell was being encouraged by Southerners
beyond Texas' borders. Governor John A. Quitman of Mississippi is said to have promised Bell 5,000 picked men in
the event of a clash of arms between United States and
Texas troops. In the Kershaw district of South Carolina,
it was resolved "that the course which the General Government is pursuing towards the sovereign State of Texas is
. . . insulting and degrading to the South, and should be
resisted 'at all hazards and to the last extremity.'" Excitement prevailed in other public meetings in Alabama, Mississippi, and elsewhere. "These," a Mississippi leader assured Bell, "speak the voice of the South, now upheaving
& in commotion; and thank God! it is so."[4]

The obduracy of Texas feeling on the New Mexico
question was epitomized in resolutions adopted in Austin,
San Antonio, LaGrange, Marshall, Crockett, and other Texas
communities endorsing the militant Governor Bell. The
Clarksville *Northern Standard,* the Galveston *News,* and
the Houston *Gazette* were three of the many newspapers
which likewise upheld the Texas claim upon New Mexico.
In Austin, the *Texas State Gazette* quoted the New York
Tribune as saying: "If Texas wants to get out of the Union,
let her go without a struggle or a murmur; but that she
should remain in it and bully it by military force is not
tolerable." To such criticism, the Texas editor replied in
kind: "If any one of Mr. Greeley's friends in Congress will
move to repeal the act of annexation, he will meet with

[1] Thomas J. Jennings to Thomas J. Rusk, August 13, 1850, Thomas
J. Rusk Papers, University of Texas, Austin.
[2] Washington D. Miller to Rusk, August 16, 23, 1850, Rusk Papers.
[3] John H. Moffitt to Rusk, August 28, 1850, Rusk Papers.
[4] New York *Tribune,* September 7, 1850; New York *Herald,* Sep-
tember 6, 1850; P. H. Brittan and Thomas F. Leonard to P. H. Bell,
August 19, 1850, Anderson Hutchinson to Bell, September 6, 1850,
Governor's Letters, Texas State Archives, Austin; Cleo Hearon,
"Mississippi and the Compromise of 1850," Mississippi Historical
Society *Publications,* XIV, 67, 175.

no opposition from Texas. She has had quite enough of
the tender mercies of the 'paternal' government at Washington."[5]

"There are many here," State Senator John H. Moffitt
informed Rusk near the end of August, "who in times past
either belonged to, or were appendages of the army." These
men "deprecate the quiet, and peaceable life, by which our
countrys [sic] best interests are subserved. Their Main purpose is to fan the flames of discord."[6] One warlike spirit
was Jacob Roberts of Plum Creek, whose response to the
call for military manpower was at once arresting and
memorably human. The shades of Jim Bowie and Davy
Crockett must have hovered over this untutored Texan as,
with the utmost frontier formality, his unfamiliar pen
scratched the following:

> August the 27 1850   Goveneor P H Bell
> Sir I tak this oppertunity of riting to you informing you that
> I have about got my company rased for Santafee and will note
> your order I seen Capt McCullock the other day and he tolde
> me that he wood not go and I ask him his reason for not going
> and his anser was to me that he thought you did not treate him
> rite in given me an order and told sum others pursons that he
> exspected to git an order to rase men for the frunt teers survis
> as for my part I am perfectley willing to surve my contry
> Goveneor if the Santafee expadision dos not go on and the is a
> chance to git in to the Survis on the frunt teers and you think
> me worthey of a companey and wood give me an order it wood
> be a favor thankfulley recieved so nothing moor at present but
> remandes your true frende and brother Solder
>   Jacob Roberts[7]

2

WHILE THE TEXAS-New Mexico situation was indeed
serious, some journalists and politicians in the East tended

[5] Austin *Texas State Gazette*, June 15, July 6, 13, August 10, 17,
24, 31, 1850.
[6] Moffitt to Rusk, August 28, 1850, Rusk Papers.
[7] Jacob Roberts to Bell, August 27, 1850, Governor's Letters,
Texas State Archives.

to ignore it. Certainly this was the case with abolitionists, Free Soilers, and other northern extremists. The Washington *National Era*, for example, had long considered the crisis artificial. Gamaliel Bailey associated it with Sam Houston's trip home the preceding winter and accused Houston of instigating make-believe hostility in Texas.[8] Despite the anxieties of the nation a certain levity invaded Congress in the midst of the grimness of 1850. Senator Chase rhapsodized a rinse that turned gray hair brown and about which Washington was "agog." During dull speeches, members of the House snapped the little dried paste wafers used for sealing letters through the air in such numbers that they resembled "an inverted snow-storm."[9] In early September, a southern Whig grieved that the House was "apparently reckless of consequences," while another Southerner branded proceedings "childish," "wicked," and unsteady.[10] Yet with Douglas' bills approved by the Senate, the House now became the center of events in the Capitol.

The optimistic felt that, with the Senate example before it, the House would give the compromise approval. "Light is dawning," one of Fillmore's Cabinet members had written on August 25. He and his confreres concluded "last night" that the compromise measures would go through the House "without amendment, and by handsome majorities."[11] Nineteen of New York's House delegation were ready to side with Fillmore and Webster, a newsman noted on August 29. The same day, Chase thought an Omnibus possible. The "passengers" would be "carried" somehow,

8 Washington *National Era*, June 20, 1850.
9 Salmon P. Chase to Mrs. Chase, August 13, 1850, Salmon P. Chase Papers, Library of Congress; Madison (Ind.) *Courier*, August 23, 1850.
10 David Outlaw to Mrs. Outlaw, September 4, 1850, David Outlaw Papers, Southern Historical Collection, University of North Carolina, Chapel Hill; John P. Kennedy, manuscript diary, September 7, 1850, John P. Kennedy Papers, Peabody Institute, Baltimore.
11 William A. Graham to James Graham, August 25, 1850, Graham Papers, Southern Historical Collection, University of North Carolina, Chapel Hill.

the lobbyist Grund asserted, no matter whether in "omni-buses, coaches, buggies, sulkies or wheelbarrows."[12] Al-though Speaker Cobb professed "an abiding faith that in the end we shall do what is right & proper," he was sorry to say that "the prospect of getting through, shortly, is not very flattering at this time."[13] Conditions "look more gloomy than at any time since this Congress assembled," Congress-man Outlaw thought on September 5. "Things are in great confusion," agreed John P. Kennedy, whose forebodings were not dissipated by the "great anxiety expressed in the papers."[14]

It was accepted that the Texas boundary and Texas debt constituted the crux of the controversy. Here the most serious objections were to the Texas bonds and the bond-holders' lobby. Men were reminded that payment of the $10 million grant would "make splendid fortunes in little time," taking money from "the pockets of the people" and giving it to "stock-jobbers" and "gamblers in Texas scrip."[15] The prophetic word to New York *Herald* subscribers was: "Texas scrip is rising. Holders are not willing to sell. Good sign."[16] A Washington correspondent thought it would be hard to convince Texans "that the ten millions paid to speculators in Wall street, and borers in Washington, will be to them of any benefit. Not a copper of the sum will touch their palms; and, for fear some of the stuff might stick to their fingers, they are not to be trusted with the handling of the five millions, provided for creditors whom the Government chooses to prefer."[17] To the public there was a slightly unsavory odor about the affair.

Despite contradictions in the press, August 28 and 29

[12] New York *Herald,* September 1, 1850; Chase to Mrs. Chase, August 29, 1850, Chase Papers; Baltimore *Sun,* August 30, 1850.

[13] Howell Cobb to Mrs. Cobb, August 28, 1850, Howell Cobb Papers, University of Georgia, Athens.

[14] Outlaw to Mrs. Outlaw, September 5, 1850, Outlaw Papers; Ken-nedy, manuscript diary, September 6, 1850, Kennedy Papers.

[15] *Congressional Globe,* 31 Cong., 1 Sess., 1562.

[16] New York *Herald,* September 2, 1850.

[17] Baltimore *Sun,* August 26, 1850.

marked progress out of the House impasse. The stage was
set for Boyd of Kentucky and McClernand of Illinois, who
joined in a demand for speedy action. On August 28, Boyd
offered an amendment combining the bill for the Texas
boundary and debt with the one for New Mexico Territory. The next day, Cobb peremptorily overruled a Virginia obstructionist's point of order that this "little omnibus"
of Boyd's should not be accorded priority. Boyd and a
South Carolinian simultaneously jumped to their feet, the
latter seeking to let the bill languish in the Committee of
the Whole. Again Cobb ruled in favor of the compromisers.

At this juncture, the House heard very effective remarks
from the lips of the usually silent Boyd. Acknowledging
doubt whether the bills should be considered in a connected
or separate form, the Kentucky Democrat hoped to "test
the sense of the House in relation to the establishment of
territorial governments upon the non-intervention principle." "I want to see that principle carried out—I want to
see it carried out in good faith," Boyd proceeded. "I wish
to see peace restored to the country. . . . I am astonished
at the patience with which our constituents have borne our
procrastination. I think we have talked enough—in God's
name let us act. If the result of our action should be, that
we cannot settle these questions upon the only principles
on which . . . I believe they can be settled, then I, for one,
shall be . . . pleased . . . to see every man of this House
resign his commission into the hands of the people. . . .
Leave it to them to send here Representatives better disposed to do their duty and to save the Union. I have not
another word to say."[18]

3

ON MONDAY, September 2, Boyd maneuvered to have the
"little omnibus" made the special order for Tuesday and

[18] *Congressional Globe*, 31 Cong., 1 Sess., 1682-87, 1695-704.

every subsequent working day until disposed of. During
the next afternoon's protracted speeches, Cobb asked Boyd
to preside temporarily—whereupon Boyd ruled on parliamentary points directly affecting his own bill. On Wednesday, the combat was resumed. In spite of "constant disorder" and "great confusion in the Hall," Cobb controlled
the situation. Perilously close votes were recorded, and
the roll was called eleven times. The Compromise appeared
in difficulty when Boyd's bill was referred to the Committee
of the Whole. Then a move for reconsideration resulted in
a tie until the Speaker cast his ballot and gave a majority
of 104-103 to the Compromise. This vote of September 4
indicated the thin line separating triumph from disaster,
for Cobb and Boyd scored a 104-101 victory on the very
next vote. They also were cheered when, by 103 to 101,
the House refused to send the bill back to the Committee
of the Whole.[19]

These were Wednesday's most important votes. They are
easy to overlook because, before the day was over, Boyd's
New Mexico amendment was summarily rejected and a
lopsided 126-60 majority turned thumbs down on engrossing
the boundary-debt measure alone.[20] Trained observers,
however, did not despond—W. W. Corcoran writing privately that, "notwithstanding the vote . . . on the slavery
bills, I feel entire confidence in their passage."[21] Corcoran
was "in and about the House . . . continually" during the
critical week. Nearly half the senators were "spectators,
and, to some extent, operators in the House";[22] among these
were Douglas, Foote, Cass, and Clay. There were reports
that on Wednesday night Whig congressmen met with

[19] *Ibid.*, 1727, 1736-38, 1746-50; *Journal of the House of Representatives of the United States: Being the First Session of the Thirty-
first Congress* (Washington, 1849-1850), 1358, 1363-65, 1367-78.
[20] *Congressional Globe,* 31 Cong., 1 Sess., 1750; *Journal of the
House of Representatives,* 1378-87.
[21] William W. Corcoran to Joshua Bates, September 5, 1850, Baring
Brothers Papers, Public Archives of Canada, Ottawa.
[22] New York *Evening Post,* September 9, 1850; New York *Herald,*
September 8, 1850.

Fillmore. What he told them is open to conjecture, but no one doubted the President's endorsement of the Boyd-Cobb strategy. After inconclusive developments Thursday on the House floor, there were additional conferences Thursday night.[23] While there is no proof that patronage plums were dangled in front of jobseekers at this time, it cannot be doubted that the Executive arm was using every means at its disposal to secure passage of the Compromise bills.

On Friday, September 6, came the moment when the decisions of leaders and followers alike would become known. Swagger, bluster, resignation, and cool planning all were in evidence. Cobb, "perfectly worn out and exhausted," was somehow equal to "another hard days work."[24] The House galleries and lobbies were filled. Onto the floor, as obvious as the swish of skirts in the Senate when Clay and Webster had delivered their orations, tramped Texas-bond lobbyists, who were there for serious business when the fortunes of speculators were at stake. After preliminaries were brushed aside, reconsideration of Thursday's antiadjustment vote was overwhelmingly approved. The question of engrossment then recurred. Before the tallying could begin, however, an Ohio representative drew attention to the lobbyists on the floor and demanded their expulsion. Cobb replied that the seventeenth rule of the House (keeping lobbyists off the floor) "would be enforced." But, as a Mississippian later reminded him, this simply was not done.[25]

"It was an exciting time, and much confusion prevailed," a journalist informed his readers; ". . . as the Clerk commenced calling the roll, the noise ceased, and seldom have we known so much quiet as then. When the roll call was concluded, there was a movement all over the hall. Votes

[23] New York *Herald*, September 5, 1850; New York *Evening Post*, September 9, 1850.
[24] Cobb to Mrs. Cobb, September 6, 1850, Cobb Papers.
[25] *Congressional Globe*, 31 Cong., 1 Sess., 1762-64.

were changed, and every proceeding watched with the utmost anxiety."[26] Howard of Texas, who for months had spoken against his state's dismemberment, was wildly acclaimed when he voted aye. Cobb silenced the outburst. Few members stayed in their assigned seats. Many were milling around the area in front of the clerk's table, and disorder had broken out afresh when Cobb rapped again for quiet and started to announce the result. "Ayes 107," he intoned. Then, pausing to let a latecomer vote, he loudly and firmly corrected the total—"Yeas 108, nays 98." So the long-contested legislation at last went forward to its third reading.

"The announcement of the result was received with manifestations of applause of various kinds," reported the *Globe* for September 6, "the most peculiar and attractive of which was a sort of unpremeditated *allegro* whistle, which the Reporter does not remember to have heard before (certainly never in the House of Representatives). The other tokens of glorification were of a less musical order. It was evident that the greater portion of the applause, especially at the outset, was on the floor of the Hall itself." Cobb now interposed "vigorously" to check the demonstrators. Cries of "Order!" were met with shouts of "Let them stamp!" and "It is all right!" The chamber was in an uproar. After the cheering had subsided, it seemed anticlimactic when the "little omnibus" formally passed, 108 to 97.[27]

4

ELEMENTS OF dilemma and suspense were absent from the House on Saturday, September 7, and in a quiet fashion a great deal was accomplished. Although diehards made

[26] New York *Herald*, September 7, 1850.
[27] New York *Tribune*, September 9, 1850; *Congressional Globe*, 31 Cong., 1 Sess., 1764.

stabs at blocking California statehood, it won adoption handsomely by 150-56 after remarkably little debate. Later, when the final vote on Utah was taken, the result showed 97 yeas and only 85 nays. Thus two more parts were added to the Compromise during a single afternoon. Saturday evening was festive. A salute of a hundred guns was fired in honor of California and Utah. When darkness fell, the entire front of the National Hotel was beautifully illuminated. As a throng of people came to admire, skyrockets shot into the air and the Marine Band appeared on Pennsylvania Avenue playing "The Star-Spangled Banner," "Yankee Doodle," and "Hail Columbia."

Now the serenaders took over. The crowd and the red-coated musicians went about the city, from boardinghouses to taverns and on to private residences, to honor the men who had worked for compromise. Clay was not on hand at the National, but the bandsmen played an air or two under his windows. Foote, Cass, and Cobb responded to acclaim. Douglas "spoke with a glow of enthusiasm." The marchers applauded Houston, Rusk, Dickinson, Boyd, and Webster—the latter emerging from a dinner party to misquote Shakespeare in an amusing way. Beneath the clear sky, bonfires and bells signaled joy and jubilee.[28] The next day a naval surgeon in Washington wrote to his old friend, James Buchanan: "This morg. Mr. Foote has diarrhoa [sic] from 'fruit' he ate—Douglas has headache from 'cold' &c. No one is willing to attribute his illness to drinking or frolicking—Yet only last evg. all declared it was 'a night on which it was the duty of every patriot to get drunk.' I have never before known so much excitement upon the passage of any law."[29]

While revelers recovered over the weekend, they realized that some of their work lay unfinished. Passage of the rest

[28] *Ibid.*, 1768-76; New York *Herald*, September 8, 10, 1850; New York *Tribune*, September 10, 1850; New York *Evening Post*, September 10, 1850.
[29] Jonathan M. Foltz to James Buchanan, September 8, 1850, James Buchanan Papers, Historical Society of Pennsylvania, Philadelphia.

of the Compromise, however, was regarded as a foregone conclusion. On Monday, senators acquiesced in the House's "little omnibus" solution. Three days later, a House majority of 109-76 sent the fugitive slave bill to the President for his signature. On September 16, as we have seen, the District's slave-trade legislation slipped smoothly through the Senate. Then, the following afternoon, the same measure won favor in the House, 124 to 59. On September 9, 18, and 20, Fillmore signed the various bills which went to the statute books.[30] The Compromise of 1850 was law.

5

No ASSESSMENT of the struggle can be complete without a detailed evaluation of House results. In a review of the record, it is instructive to discover more Democrats than Whigs aiding the Texas-New Mexico, Utah, and fugitive-slave portions of the compromise by respective margins of 9, 26, and 52. Twenty-seven fewer Democrats than Whigs voted affirmatively on California, and 18 fewer on the District bill. On all five measures taken together, there were 305 Democratic and 262 Whig "yea" votes. Not only were Democrats mainly responsible for the enactment of three of the five bills, but a larger proportion of Democrats than Whigs cast "yea" ballots in the aggregate. It is equally true that 176 Democratic "nay" votes outweighed the 168 cast by Whigs. Here, however, the Democratic percentage of the major-party total was only 51.2 as against 53.8 in the affirmative category.

The single area in which the Whigs' comprehensive contribution in the House appreciably surpassed the Democrats' was that of the absentees. Six Democrats and nine Whigs failed to vote on Texas-New Mexico; five Democrats

[30] *Congressional Globe,* 31 Cong., 1 Sess., 1784, 1806-807, 1829-30, 1837; *The Public Statutes at Large and Treaties of the United States of America* (76 vols., Boston, 1845-1963), IX, 446-58, 462-65, 467-68.

and nine Whigs on California; seventeen Democrats and twenty-one Whigs on Utah; eleven Democrats and twenty-four Whigs on fugitive slaves, and fifteen Democrats and twenty Whigs on the District trade. Although some of the missing congressmen were away from Washington when the tallies were taken, most of them were in town. Thaddeus Stevens, in fact, called attention to the departure of northern Whigs from the floor just before one of the most consequential votes was taken. The Pennsylvanian ironically suggested sending a page to notify the brethren "that the fugitive slave bill has been disposed of, and that they may now come back into the Hall."[31] Three parts of the legislation would have fared very differently if large numbers of the absentees had been present and voted in the negative.

Perhaps those figures are less significant than a study on the basis of sections. Fifty-six northern representatives and 52 Southerners voted with the majority on Texas; 123 Northerners and 27 Southerners on California; 41 Northerners and 56 Southerners on Utah; 31 Northerners and 78 Southerners on rendition of fugitives, and 120 Northerners and 4 Southerners on the District bill. Respecting Texas, 67 "nay" votes were northern and 30 southern; California, 56 southern; Utah, 70 northern and 15 southern; the fugitive-slave proposition, 76 northern; and the District measure, 60 southern. The aggregate northern division affecting all five bills was 371-213 (63.5 percent favorable), while the Southerners split 217-161 (57.4 percent favorable). Northern nonvoters numbered eighty-eight and southern nonvoters fifty-three.[32] There was not a single negative vote from the South on the fugitive bill, and not one from the North on either the California or the District legislation.

The 1850 North-South antagonism and the nature of

[31] *Congressional Globe,* 31 Cong., 1 Sess., 1807.
[32] This and preceding tabulations of nonvoters exclude two men who were dying, one who was extremely sick, and four others who probably had valid reasons for not being recorded.

future sectional differences thus are mirrored. It is scarcely a surprise to anyone familiar with House speeches that southern representatives provided most of the votes for the fugitive slave bill, or that Northerners strongly endorsed a free California and the District slave pen's elimination. Perhaps unexpected by the nonspecialist are (a) the nearly equal South-North strength behind the touchy Texas-New Mexico plan, and (b) the slightly less even backing for Utah. It is likewise revealing that twenty-eight members cast their ballots for every one of the bills. Twenty-five of the twenty-eight were Democrats, and three were Whigs. Twenty-five were Northerners, and three Southerners. Only two were southern Whigs. Only one was a southern Democrat, and only one a northern Whig. Such statistics demonstrate that wholehearted backing of the adjustment was predominately Democratic, almost exclusively northern, and exceptional. It was rooted principally in the Northwest, the Maine-New Hampshire fringe, and Pennsylvania.

Further analysis shows how the Whigs came influentially into the picture. Nine representatives supported the first four bills but absented themselves on the District test; all nine hailed from the slave states of Kentucky, Missouri, Tennessee, North Carolina, or Delaware—and two-thirds of them were Whigs. All eight who voted affirmatively four times but were not recorded on the fugitive bill represented New York, Pennsylvania, or Ohio districts—four Whigs, three Democrats, and one Native American. Sixteen members answered "yea" four times and "nay" once. Of the thirty-five congressmen who cast affirmative ballots in four instances and either opposed or abstained in the fifth, twenty were Whigs, fourteen Democrats, and one was a Native. Nineteen were Southerners, sixteen Northerners.

At this point, it becomes obvious that members from the border states in general were willing to move along adjustment lines, provided they did not have to endorse District slave-trade reform; that a number of compromise-minded Northerners refused to underwrite the fugitive bill; and

that even some moderate representatives sidestepped em-
barrassing showdowns. Of the sixty-three men who backed
at least four of the bills, thirty-nine were Democrats,
twenty-three Whigs, and one was a Native. Forty-one were
Northerners, and twenty-two Southerners. The contrast between Democrats and Whigs on one hand, and between
Northerners and Southerners on the other, is less distinctly
marked in this larger grouping than where only the twenty-
eight consistent yea-voters were studied. Still, the fact that
the Compromise was primarily Democratic- and North-
supported is borne out by both sets of figures.

6

As IMPORTANT to an understanding of the Compromise
victory as the distribution of the votes on the five bills were
the shifts that occurred in the voting on September 4, 5, and
6, preceding the passage of the Texas measure (see Appendix C). On the 104-103 test of September 4, twenty-
eight representatives took positions different from those
they held on the subsequent 108-98 vote of September 6,
which inspired the whistles and cheers. Such shifting
support must have challenged the leadership of Cobb,
Boyd, McClernand, and other compromisers to the utmost.
    One of several difficulties on September 4 was the
absence of two northern Democrats, on whose help the
compromise forces had depended. Under the circumstances,
it was necessary to find compensating aid in unpromising
places. As a result of their search, there occurred a development of which posterity has tended to lose sight. Such
unlikely prospects as Jacob Thompson of Mississippi,
Joseph W. Jackson of Georgia, and "Long John" Wentworth
of Illinois voted with the Cobbs and the Boyds! It is
possible that their personal regard for the Speaker influenced the anticompromise Jackson and Thompson to become compromisers for a few minutes. Who persuaded

Wentworth even his highly competent biographer has been unable to ascertain, for Long John's free-soil ideas made Democratic regularity offensive to him in 1850.[33] But there stood Wentworth with men of the Deep South saving the day for moderation under the guidon of Howell Cobb!

The compromisers' 107-99 defeat on September 5 saw Wentworth and other momentary moderates back on familiar extremist ground. There they remained the next afternoon. Meanwhile the Administration's "missionary" work had been performed so efficiently that three northwestern Whigs, seemingly intransigent on Wednesday, joined the compromisers on Friday. Two others assisted Cobb by not voting, while several southern Democrats and one from the North filled out the Cobb-Boyd ranks.[34] It is perfectly clear that, in the House as in the Senate, Democratic leadership and Democratic followership were mainly responsible for the Compromise of 1850. Northern moderates and southern moderates worked well in harness. The dominant Senate leader, his House counterpart, most adjustment votes in both chambers, and the origin of most measures were Democratic. The Whig contribution should not be minimized, but it was supplemental.

[33] Don E. Fehrenbacher wrote the author: "I think that Long John wanted above all to get a roll call vote on the House floor on the Proviso. . . . I think he had some faint hope that, on a naked vote, certain Northern compromisers would not dare to vote against it. . . . Why he indulged in the generosity that trapped him I do not know, unless he was looking ahead to the Illinois Central Bill. . . . Wentworth's strange behavior on September 4 and again on September 6 was in no way representative. He had no following and stood alone."

[34] *Journal of the House of Representatives*, 1372-73, 1402-403, 1409-11.

CHAPTER X

The Compromise
in Operation

WHEN THE Compromise of 1850 was enacted into law, its proponents exulted in the achievement. The Boston *Evening Traveller* hailed the boundary-bill victory as snuffing out "disunion and treason in Congress and the country." The Philadelphia *Pennsylvanian* felt confident that "peace and tranquility" would be secured. Out in Springfield, the *Illinois State Journal* called for "national jubilation."[1] Many Southerners agreed with the Louisville *Journal* that a weight seemed to be lifted from the heart of America. The Nashville *Republican Banner* urged friends of free government to congratulate each other. "We hope that the question is now definitely settled," the New Orleans *Picayune* asserted, and that "contentions and bickerings will cease, and harmony be again restored."[2] Many political leaders held similar views. Fillmore the Whig and Douglas the Democrat acknowledged their happiness and relief. Senators Berrien of Georgia and Clemens of Alabama penned letters to constituents indicating that the adjustment would strengthen the South. Recent accomplishments, Webster declared, surpassed in importance "any acts of legislation which I have known for thirty years."[3]

Not all papers and people were equally certain. "We are not among those who rejoice," announced the Albany *Evening Journal.* "They have fired cannons in Washington," the Charleston *Mercury* commented, "and displayed lights as if for a great victory. Well, it is a victory . . . over justice and all sound statesmanship. The burning of powder may not stop with Washington."[4] The Columbus (Georgia) *Sentinel* was for "open, unqualified, naked *secession.*" The Cleveland *Plain Dealer* hoped that New Mexico "will insist on her State Government and resist by force of arms all encroachments. . . . We should glory in being a humble volunteer in such a war."[5] Charles Francis Adams of Massachusetts wrote George W. Julian of Indiana: "The consummation of the iniquities of this most disgraceful session of Congress is now reached—I know not how much the people will bear." A young Kentuckian, familiar with Deep South reactions, opined in October that the Compromise "has proven more like oil poured upon the flames than upon the waves."[6] "If the fugitive slave bill is not enforced in the north," a Tennessee Democrat warned, "the moderate men

---

[1] Boston *Traveller,* September 9, 1850; Philadelphia *Pennsylvanian,* September 10, 1850; Springfield *Illinois State Journal,* September 25, 1850.

[2] Louisville *Journal,* September 16, 1850; Nashville *Republican Banner,* September 16, 1850; New Orleans *Picayune,* September 15, 1850.

[3] Millard Fillmore to Hamilton Fish, September 9, 1850, Hamilton Fish Papers, Library of Congress; George F. Milton, *The Eve of Conflict: Stephen A. Douglas and the Needless War* (Boston, 1934), 77-78; Albany *Evening Journal,* September 23, 1850; Washington *National Intelligencer,* September 9, 1850.

[4] Albany *Evening Journal,* September 9, 1850; Charleston *Mercury,* September 10, 1850.

[5] Columbus (Ga.) *Sentinel,* September 12, 1850; Cleveland *Plain Dealer,* September 18, 1850.

[6] Charles F. Adams to George W. Julian, September 14, 1850, Giddings-Julian Papers, Library of Congress; R. S. Holt to Joseph Holt, October 27, 1850, Holt Papers, Library of Congress.

of the South . . . will be overwhelmed by the *'fire-eaters.'*"
And over in England the London *Times* predicted: "This
measure, whilst an apparent gain to the South, will ultimately, like the others, prove a real gain to the North."[7]

In analyzing the Compromise of 1850 as a whole, we see
that moderate congressmen and influential noncongressional
leaders of similar persuasion had supplied answers (correct
or incorrect) to the questions of 1848 and 1849. California
was now a state of the Union. Territorial governments had
been provided for New Mexico and Utah. The Texas
boundary and debt issues had been resolved. A new Fugitive Slave Law supplanted the old one. And while slavery
was retained in the District of Columbia, the slave trade
was restricted there. It is tempting to declare dogmatically
that the Compromise of 1850 represented a victory for the
North and a defeat for the South. Viewed with the hindsight available to post-Civil War generations, such an
assertion has much to support it. But we find it vital, too,
to examine the decade before the war in order to ascertain
how the Compromise operated before the election of Abraham Lincoln, and in order to examine similarities and differences between actual and suppositious accomplishments.
The Compromise should thus be scrutinized both in terms
of its Civil War links and from the standpoint of American
society in the 1850-1860 decade.

2

THE FUGITIVE Slave Law was decidely the most explosive
part of the Compromise. Summary arrangements for de-
termining title to Negroes aroused cries that civil rights
were being violated. Doubling the fines formerly assessed
against rescuers of runaways was attacked as harsh by vocal

[7] Cave Johnson to James Buchanan, November 10, 1850, James
Buchanan Papers, Historical Society of Pennsylvania, Philadelphia;
London *Times*, October 18, 1850.

critics. The addition of United States commissioners to aid judges in executing the law was assailed with equal ardor. The knowledge that these commissioners received ten dollars for issuing a warrant, but only five for discharging a Negro, was termed a travesty of just procedure. Provocation, too, came from the stipulation that any citizen of the United States was expected to assist officials in apprehending fugitives. As early as September 25, 1850, an Ohio editor prophesied with pleasure that the law "will be a dead letter upon the statute book." In November, another was shocked to hear "men advising their fellow-men to treat a law of Congress as a nullity, and trample its provisions under foot."[8] An editorial in a Maine newspaper, typical of dozens, advocated resistance to the will of Congress and the President. Southern journalists naturally complained. "No sooner has this Fugitive Slave Law gone into effect," wrote a disillusioned Floridian, than "the cry of repeal . . . resounds from one end of the Northern States to the other."[9]

Enforced for the first time when only one week old, the law led to a succession of lurid incidents involving desperate runaways, grim agents, fanatical Northerners, and disenchanted Southerners. In February 1851 an escaped slave made his way to a Canadian refuge after a mob bristling with weapons enabled him to flee from a Massachusetts courtroom. Later the same year, the outcome was reversed when a brig from Boston harbor delivered a luckless Georgia Negro to his owner at Savannah.[10] From the eastern seaboard to the Great Lakes region, similar episodes heated the blood. Sometimes bondsmen were dragged back to plantations they hoped never to see again. It was possible— as at Christiana, Pennsylvania, in the dawn of a September morning—for a kindly if credulous Marylander to be killed

[8] Cleveland *Plain Dealer*, September 25, 1850; Columbus *Ohio State Journal*, November 2, 1850.

[9] Augusta (Me.) *Kennebec Journal*, October 10, 1850; St. Augustine *Ancient City*, November 9, 1850.

[10] Harold Schwartz, "Fugitive Slave Days in Boston," *New England Quarterly*, XXVII (June 1954), 195-201.

and mutilated by black men when he tried to regain his property. It was also possible—as at Syracuse in the 1851 "Jerry Rescue"—for New York judges to be defied and sympathizers to chortle and cheer, while fugitives were hidden in private houses and then spirited across the international border.[11]

The American who today reads closely the commentary of the *Liberator*, or peruses the *Anti-Slavery Standard* and the *Anti-Slavery Bugle*, can hardly avoid the conclusion that here we have a preeminent model for the pressure politics of the twentieth century. A scholar has truly written that to the abolitionists the Fugitive Slave Law of 1850 "afforded a common rallying point for all the schisms by which the movement was plagued. Political action men, disunionists, anti-Constitutionalists, non-voters, and non-resistant pacifists found it an issue upon which all could agree."[12] The Jerry Rescue was a *cause célèbre*. As a participant said after it was over, "men that I supposed cared not at all for the enslavement of our colored countrymen, have taken pains to express to me their detestation of the attempt to rob Jerry of his liberty."[13] On this question many a Whig and Democrat who never had sought identification with a Garrison or a Gerrit Smith would react in the same way. Not only did the Fugitive Slave Law intensify extremism, but it broadened the antislavery base as well.

There is no doubt that *Uncle Tom's Cabin*, whose serial publication began in 1851, was inspired by what Harriet Beecher Stowe regarded as an evil law. Ultimately this novel became the most widely read book of the 1850s and one of the century's most influential. The reminder that Mrs. Stowe had little firsthand knowledge of southern life

[11] W. U. Hensel, *The Christiana Riot and the Treason Trials of 1851* (Lancaster, Pa., 1911), 20-24, 32-33; Samuel J. May, *Some Recollections of Our Antislavery Conflict* (Boston, 1869), 374-84.

[12] Russel B. Nye, *Fettered Freedom: Civil Liberties and the Slavery Controversy* (East Lansing, Mich., 1949), 206.

[13] Samuel J. May to Charlotte G. Coffin, October 15, 1851, William Lloyd Garrison Papers, Boston Public Library.

made no difference whatever to uncritical admirers. Just as the Fugitive Slave Law (plus maternal loss, religious commitment, and literary ambition) had induced her to venture into novel-writing, so the same law created an emotional climate that led her readers to an unquestioning acceptance of her melodramatic tale. It would be presumptuous to argue that characters like Little Eva, Simon Legree, Mas'r Haley, and Uncle Tom could not have appeared in print, had not the Compromise of 1850 and its Fugitive Slave Law been adopted. But it is indisputable that the book gave a dramatic form and focus to the passions aroused by the legislation, and the legislation in turn gave an obvious significance to Mrs. Stowe's fable.[14]

The Fugitive Slave Law was not repealed until June 1864. In the decade following its enactment—and in after years—allegations were made that it was unconstitutional as well as immoral, inhuman, and unchristian.[15] Whatever its other faults, subsequent judgments have agreed on its constitutionality. Although James Schouler characterized it as "scarcely within the full shelter of the Federal constitution," the single word "scarcely" was his protecting hedge.[16] The Illinois attorney, Abraham Lincoln, recognized the law's constitutionality and risked his political future in opposing Salmon P. Chase's desire to nail an anti-Fugitive Slave Law plank in the 1860 Republican platform. In 1899, Albert Bushnell Hart acknowledged: "To-day it is clear that the federal authorities, in their insistence on the superiority of federal law, were on the side of orderly national life."[17] In 1921, Allen Johnson discussed the pros

[14] Charles H. Foster, *The Rungless Ladder: Harriet Beecher Stowe and New England Puritanism* (Durham, N.C., 1954), 6, 18-66.

[15] Theodore C. Smith, *Parties and Slavery, 1850-1859* (New York, 1906), 15-16.

[16] James Schouler, *History of the United States under the Constitution* (6 vols., New York, 1880-1889), V, 205-206.

[17] Roy P. Basler *et al.* (eds.), *The Collected Works of Abraham Lincoln* (8 vols. and index, New Brunswick, N.J., 1953-1955), II, 227, 233, 260, III, 317, 384, 386, 435, IV, 150; Albert B. Hart, *Salmon Portland Chase* (Boston, 1899), 166.

and cons in great detail and then summarized his findings
with the statement that the law "must be declared constitutional in every particular."[18]

Propagandists of abolition underscored both pity and
mercy, castigating vile "slave-catchers," making the most
of Negro virtues, and minimizing owners' rights. Occasionally, they sponsored "rescues" when there was no one to
be rescued and initiated hunts for "slavers" when the so-
called slavers were rescuers or bystanders. While many
were sincere, many found martyrdom appealing. To go to
jail, to stay in jail, and to refuse the payment of fines
attracted idealists or sentimentalists whom fervor or notoriety thrust into prominence. Perhaps the most accurate
brief conclusion ever offered on the subject is that "after
1850, the pursuit of fugitive slaves became, like the Fugitive
Slave Law itself, more a symbolic than a practical matter."
Both the issue and the law were of "enormous value in
winning sympathy for a once unpopular movement."[19]
Anticipation of that development probably would have
amazed most congressmen in 1850. Only a tiny portion of
their debates was devoted to the question of fugitive slaves.
Indeed, there was no suggestion then that many of them
foresaw the fury of the ensuing tempest.

3

THE TERRITORIAL settlements, which so much of the "Great
Debate" had concerned, proved generally acceptable to the
American people in late 1850 and immediately thereafter.
Scholars, however, have been astonishingly confused as to
some of the laws' most important contents, particularly with
regard to slavery.

The nature of these regulations has been delineated and

[18] Allen Johnson, "The Constitutionality of the Fugitive Slave Acts,"
Yale Law Journal, XXXI (Dec. 1921), 161-82.
[19] Larry Gara, *The Liberty Line: The Legend of the Underground
Railroad* (Lexington, Ky., 1961), 141.

clarified by Robert R. Russel. As he points out, the New Mexico and Utah "legislatures were left entirely free to legislate on slavery as well as on all other 'rightful' subjects not expressly removed from their province. . . . When informed people of the day used the term 'squatter sovereignty' or 'popular sovereignty' they meant the right of a *territory* (not of a *state*) to decide for itself what to do with regard to slavery during the *territorial stage*. Congress in the Utah and New Mexico acts gave the power to make that decision to the legislatures of the respective territories." Therefore, "*first and principally,* the territorial legislatures were given full power to legislate on slavery subject to a possible veto by the governor or a possible disallowance by Congress. That was squatter or popular sovereignty." A second feature of the 1850 territorial regulations was the provision that appeals in cases involving title to slaves could be taken from territorial courts to the United States Supreme Court, though it never resulted in a suit taken to the highest tribunal. Far less significant were the statehood sections, which frequently and improperly have been underscored, as the Constitution rather than the Compromise accorded to "new states the right to decide . . . whether they should be slave or free."[20]

Surveying the historiography of the Compromise of 1850, Russel finds tangible evidence of the confusion which exists among scholars concerning territorial matters. Twenty-two college textbooks, he notes, give at least twelve "substantially different descriptions" of the provisions respecting slavery.[21] This becomes comprehensible when one realizes that supposed experts, to whom textbook writers look for what should be clarification, also committed several sorts of errors in their own "authoritative" volumes. Among inadequate phrases is the declaration that arrangements were made for territorial governments "without prohibiting slavery, under the so-called 'principle of Congressional non-

---

[20] Robert R. Russel, "What Was the Compromise of 1850?", *Journal of Southern History,* XXII (Aug. 1956), 295-308.
[21] Russel, "What Was the Compromise of 1850?", 292-94.

interference.' "[22] Another is the statement that "the territories of Utah and New Mexico were formally organized —thus rejecting the Wilmot Proviso without guaranteeing the extension of slavery."[23] Numerous authors were aware that Congress promised New Mexico and Utah (or fractions thereof) subsequent entry into the Union under precisely defined conditions. Others noted the Supreme Court feature. But rare was the historian who carefully scrutinized the wording of the laws or the debates pertaining to them; and the world of scholarship is indebted to Russel for brushing away long-accumulated cobwebs from this important aspect of the Compromise of 1850.

4

IN UTAH, FILLMORE pleased the Church of Jesus Christ of Latter-day Saints by naming its leader, Brigham Young, as territorial governor. Lesser posts were divided, Mormons getting about half and Gentiles the rest. Although Young took the oath of office in February 1851, the general assembly of Deseret was not dissolved until April, and the legislature of Utah Territory did not convene until September.[24] Slavery was legally recognized in 1852 and was subsequently reaffirmed three times prior to 1863.[25] The Census of 1860 listed twenty-nine slaves in Utah. "If slaves are brought here by those who owned them in the states," Young told Horace Greeley, "we do not favor their escape from the service of those owners."[26] Friction developed

[22] Smith, *Parties and Slavery*, 8-9.
[23] Charles A. Beard and Mary R. Beard, *The Rise of American Civilization* (2 vols., New York, 1930), I, 716.
[24] Dale L. Morgan, "The State of Deseret," *Utah Historical Quarterly*, VIII (April-July-October 1940), 129-31.
[25] Richard D. Poll, "The Mormon Question Enters National Politics, 1850-1856," *Utah Historical Quarterly*, XXV (April 1957), 126.
[26] *Population of the United States in 1860; Compiled from the Original Returns of the Eighth Census* (Washington, 1864), 574-76; Horace Greeley, *An Overland Journey from New York to San Francisco, in the Summer of 1859* (Washington, 1860), 211-12.

between Gentile and Mormon officeholders, but polygamy rather than slavery was the principal cause of dissension. Repeatedly frustrated in their struggle to make their Zion one of the United States, Young and his followers bitterly resented the American military force which was sent to Utah in 1857. In fact, they teetered on the brink of war. A curious civil development was the revival of the "State of Deseret" as a ghost government from 1862 to 1870. Young delivered gubernatorial messages at a time when he held no federal commission, and a "shadow" Deseret legislature approved laws originally passed by the territorial assembly. Slavery faded from Utah around 1862. The idea of the State of Deseret gradually passed out of mind. Plural marriages were officially prohibited in the early 1890s. Then, in 1896, Utah at last gained admission to the Union after almost half a century of controversy.[27]

Less in the public eye than Utah during its territorial stage, New Mexico contained certain features that must not be minimized. Indian depredations were a constant threat to its small population. New Mexico had no adequate soldiery, no Mormon discipline, no Brigham Young. In some ways, the most effective of its governors in the 1850s was William Carr Lane, a St. Louis physician who reduced chaos on the frontier and won the respect of responsible citizens.[28] In the course of the decade, a major issue was the disposition of that part of the region which in 1863 became Arizona Territory. Even more significant was the desire of Washington authorities to acquire additional land from Mexico, which was obtained in 1853-1854 as a result of James Gadsden's diplomacy. Governor Lane bought two Negro slaves at Santa Fe in 1852.[29] Seven years later, the

[27] Morgan, "The State of Deseret," 132-55; Poll, "The Mormon Question Enters National Politics," 117-31.

[28] William A. Keleher, *Turmoil in New Mexico, 1846-1868* (Santa Fe, N.M., 1952), 57-65, 79-92; Allen Johnson *et al.* (eds.), *Dictionary of American Biography* (22 vols. and index, New York, 1928-1958), X, 583-84.

[29] Aurora Hunt, *Major General James Henry Carleton* (Glendale, Calif., 1958), 120-22.

legislature passed "An Act Providing for the Protection of Slave Property in this Territory." Though the Negro problem was minor, the number of Indian slaves was probably between 1,500 and 3,000. Moreover, peonage was widespread long after the passage of the Compromise. Neither slavery nor peonage, however, deterred most able New Mexicans from siding with the North in the Civil War. This was partially an outgrowth of their traditional fear and hatred of Texas and Texans, intensified in 1850.[30] New Mexico's social development was slow, and it was not until 1912 that it became the forty-seventh state.

Slavery was legal in California for several years after 1850, according to rulings of its supreme court.[31] The number of California slaves cannot be ascertained, and they were not so important as the roles of the state's congressmen in the period between the Compromise and the Civil War. William M. Gwin, another versatile physician, was one of California's two senators from 1850 to 1861. His Tennessee-Mississippi-Louisiana background, his well-advertised association with Andrew Jackson, and his friendly attitude toward the South gave this ambitious and fluent Democrat a seat in his party's inner circle. John B. Weller, a native of Ohio but very southern in his sentiments, served for five years as Gwin's colleague and then was chosen governor. David C. Broderick, who belonged to the anti-Gwin and anti-Weller faction, had his hour as a senator but was slain in a duel and supplanted in Washington by Democrats with southern orientations. Thus the Senate "equilibrium," a familiar topic in the Great Debate, was not altered at once in favor of the North. The California members of the House likewise tended to be Democrats and

[30] Keleher, *Turmoil in New Mexico*, 163-277, 482-83; *The Works of Hubert Howe Bancroft* (39 vols., San Francisco, 1883-1890), XVII, 261-63; Loomis M. Ganaway, *New Mexico and the Sectional Controversy, 1846-1861* (Albuquerque, N.M., 1944), 77-125.

[31] Clyde A. Duniway, "Slavery in California after 1848," American Historical Association *Annual Report . . . for the Year 1905* (Washington, 1906), I, 243-48.

southern sympathizers. On the basis of the history of the 1850s, the South—not the North—profited in Congress from the admission of California.[32]

Hardly more predictable was the confusion which compromisers bequeathed to generations of Americans with respect to western boundaries. The adjusters' inexact language regarding what they thought was the Sierra Madre Range caused part of the San Luis Valley to "belong" to New Mexico in 1860 and to Colorado Territory in 1861. A series of contradictory surveys resulted in legal conflicts over Los Conejos until recent years.[33] Congress created no government at all for an expanse greater than Connecticut's, now the rich farming area of the Oklahoma Panhandle but prior to 1890 variously denominated as "No-Man's-Land," the "Neutral Strip," the "Public Land Strip," or the "Territory of Cimarron."[34] For more than a century, misunderstandings stemmed from California's eastern boundary, unsurveyed when it was approved at Monterey in 1849 and adopted as Utah Territory's western boundary at Washington in 1850. Nevada relinquished 415 square miles to California before 1900, but a controversy of sorts persisted into the 1960s.[35] The Compromise figured in an 1896 Supreme Court ruling, as a result of which a huge Texas county was transferred to the United States and later as-

[32] John W. Caughey, *California* (New York, 1953), 281-83, 285; Johnson *et al.* (eds.), *Dictionary of American Biography*, VIII, 64-65, XIX, 628-29.

[33] LeRoy R. Hafen, "Status of the San Luis Valley, 1850-1861," *Colorado Magazine*, III (May 1926), 46-49.

[34] Morris L. Wardell, "The History of No-Man's-Land or Old Beaver County," *Chronicles of Oklahoma*, XXXV (Spring 1957), 11-33; Carl C. Rister, *No Man's Land* (Norman, Okla., 1948), 3-43, 67-70, 96-102, 140-67.

[35] W. N. Davis, Jr., "The Territory of Nataqua: An Episode in Pioneer Government East of the Sierra," California Historical Society *Quarterly*, XXI (Sept. 1942), 225-38; Effie M. Mack, *Nevada: A History of the State from the Earliest Times through the Civil War* (Glendale, Calif., 1936), 173-85, 383-409; San Francisco *Chronicle*, Feb. 24-26, 1959; Reno *Nevada State Journal*, Feb. 12, 19, 21, 22, 1959; Sacramento *Bee*, Oct. 18, 1959.

similated by Oklahoma.[36] New Mexico lost to Texas a zone
310 miles long and from 2½ to 4 miles wide. Subsequently,
over 7,100 acres were exchanged between Texas and New
Mexico following a judicial decision that, while the Rio
Grande had moved physically, it could not move legally.
Today's visitors to El Paso find mixed drinks served in the
3600 block of Doniphan Drive because, in 1850, the river
flowed east of the site of the present cocktail lounges.[37]

These, in time, are far-ranging echoes of the Compromise
—some significant, some trivial. Several of them affected
infinitely more people than the District of Columbia slave
trade law. It is erroneous to assume that the buying and
selling of Negroes came to a halt at the nation's capital.
Item: "A Negro slave named Emma about eleven years old"
was sold for $150 on May 29, 1851. Item: "Received Wash-
ington August the 30th 1852 of Joseph Walsh Six hundred
dollars for Negro servant George Washington aged about
twenty seven years." Item: Bill of sale on April 6, 1853,
for one Negro (Robert Dix), bought by Anthony Bowen
from Charles Wallach.[38] Phrases like "designed to suppress
all slave trade in the District"[39] are misleading if one's
definition of "trade" is comprehensive. The law did eliminate a "slave pen" or "depot," the notorious yellow house
which stood between Capitol Hill and the Smithsonian. It
also ended the transportation of slaves into the District
for purposes of sale and transfer out of it. That was
something. But that was all.[40]

[36] Berlin B. Chapman, "The Claim of Texas to Greer County,"
Southwestern Historical Quarterly, LIII (April 1950), 404-10, 420-21.

[37] J. J. Bowden, "The Texas-New Mexico Boundary Dispute along
the Rio Grande," *Southwestern Historical Quarterly*, LXIII (Oct.
1959), 221-37.

[38] Book J.A.S. 26, Folio 421; Book 44, Folio 257; Book 53, Folio
129, Land and Chattel Records, Recorder of Deeds Office, Washington.

[39] Schouler, *History of the United States*, V, 197.

[40] Walter C. Clephane, "The Local Aspect of Slavery in the District of Columbia," Columbia Historical Society *Records*, III (1900),
224-25; Boston *Liberator*, October 25, 1850.

5

THE CONGRESSIONAL solution of the Texas boundary problem was accepted by the Texas General Assembly in November 1850. That Texas obtained approximately 33,000 square miles more than had been planned by the Committee of Thirteen may have been the decisive factor. The state received $5 million from the federal government—slightly over a quarter of the sum being paid out to cancel the unbonded debt, while the remainder was kept by Texas and gradually expended for schools and other purposes.[41] As Austin and Washington could not agree on a basis for scaling the revenue debt, bondholders went unpaid from 1850 through 1855. In 1852, a group of them—including James Hamilton, Leslie Combs, and John F. May (father-in-law of Representative Bayly)—memorialized Congress to the effect that "the United States are liable for every dollar." No action was taken. Two years later, another creditors' committee referred plaintively to "hope deferred."[42] Finally, in 1856, when the ostensible value of the bonds amounted to $10,078,703.21 and Texas wished the investors to get only $4,467,756.41, Congress added $2,750,000 to the five millions originally retained in Washington. Texas reluctantly sanctioning the new arrangement, nearly the whole of the available $7,750,000 was expended. Revenue debt creditors were paid at 76.895 cents on the dollar, regardless of purchase prices or dates of issue of the securities. In June 1856 Secretary of the Treasury James Guthrie commenced the distribution of drafts to the bondholders.[43]

One thousand seventy payments were made, most of

[41] Edmund T. Miller, A Financial History of Texas (Austin, Texas, 1916), 82, 118-33.
[42] Sen. Misc. Doc. 72, 32 Cong., 1 Sess.; Sen. Report 334, 33 Cong., 1 Sess.
[43] Miller, A Financial History of Texas, 125-29.

them in 1856. Payees were 647 in number. More bondholders lived in Pennsylvania than in any other state, more
in Philadelphia than in any other city. They included stove-
makers, umbrella makers, grocers, and "gentlewomen" as
well as lawyers, brokers, and physicians. Sixteen men,
banks, and estates drew over $100,000 apiece. In this
relatively limited category were United States Senator
James A. Bayard of Delaware; the Washington bank of
Corcoran & Riggs; Drexel & Company of Philadelphia;
Milbank & Company of New York, and George W. Riggs,
Jr., of Washington. Excluding District of Columbia and
foreign residents, the geographical distribution of the 174
individuals, estates, pools, and institutions receiving more
than $5,000 was 60 percent northern and 40 percent south-
ern. The largest payment to a business enterprise was the
$426,631.67 collected by Corcoran & Riggs. Milbank &
Company led the New York firms with $408,631.67.[44] For
many investors, the sums were enormous by the standards
of that era. And the fact that not a few of the certificates
were acquired in 1850 (when they were rising in value)
or in 1849 (just before the rapid rise began) spelled
impressive gains for those who had purchased the Texas
bonds on speculation.

There is a relationship between the Compromise of 1850,
the payments of 1856, and political events of 1857-1861.
Four men were mainly responsible for James Buchanan's
nomination for the Presidency by the Democratic party.
The quartet was composed of Senators Bayard of Delaware,
Jesse D. Bright of Indiana, and Judah P. Benjamin and
John Slidell of Louisiana. Bayard was a major bondholder.
Bright, chairman of the senatorial committee setting up the
payment procedure, benefited financially from the disburse-
ment; intimately connected with Riggs, whose son was
married to Bright's daughter, he also "had the confidence"

[44] "Register of Texas Debt Warrants, 1856-1861," *passim*, Record
Group 39, Records of the Bureau of Accounts (Treasury), National
Archives, Washington.

of Corcoran.[45] Slidell obtained $7,689.50 for his Texas bonds, and the substantial amount of $62,887.20 was endorsed over to him by Manuel de la Quintana.[46] Benjamin was directly identified with Slidell in the leadership of the Louisiana Democracy, and they were collaborating colleagues in the Senate.[47]

Two weeks before the 1856 Democratic convention opened in Cincinnati, Slidell, Bright, and Corcoran "hired a spacious suite at the Burnet House for lavish entertainment of incoming delegates and other politicians."[48] Bayard, who headed the committee on credentials, made sure that the rivalry between the contesting New York delegations was resolved so as to help Buchanan. Bright swung Indiana out of Douglas' camp and into Buchanan's. Slidell appears to have masterminded the Cincinnati strategy. The convention was called to order on June 2. The Texas bondholders were paid on June 1. Money was spent freely on Buchanan's behalf both at Cincinnati that fateful June and in the ensuing campaign.[49] Was some of it Texas-bond money? At least it is certain that the men who spent it were Texas bondholders, whose fortunes appreciated as a result of the Compromise of 1850. It may be sensible to suggest that they constituted the pivot on which Buchanan's election turned, and that therefore their activities aided in postponing the Civil War. With John C. Frémont in the White House, main currents of American history undoubtedly would have been different from the 1857-1861 record.

[45] Table of Disbursements, Letterbook XII, 182-83, William W. Corcoran Papers, Library of Congress; Roy F. Nichols, *The Disruption of American Democracy* (New York, 1948), 3-5, 12-17.

[46] Warrants 3 and 28, "Register of Texas Debt Warrants, 1856-1861," Record Group 39; Claim 23, Texas Debt Claims and Warrants, Record Group 217, Records of the General Accounting Office, National Archives.

[47] Robert D. Meade, *Judah P. Benjamin: Confederate Statesman* (New York, 1943), 51, 79, 105-106.

[48] Allan Nevins, *Ordeal of the Union* (2 vols., New York, 1947), II, 456-57.

[49] Nichols, *The Disruption of American Democracy*, 4, 13-17.

6

ANOTHER LINK connecting 1850 with the future was the emphasis Douglas put on the territorial settlements of the Compromise in defending his Nebraska bill, and its amended revision, in 1854.[50] Politicians and historians have disagreed about the existence of a "vital difference"[51] between the constitutional principles governing (a) popular sovereignty in Utah and New Mexico and (b) popular sovereignty in Nebraska and Kansas. Douglas, however, thought them identical. He also believed that the Missouri Compromise was "inconsistent with the principle of non-intervention" recognized by the Compromise of 1850 and thus was "inoperative and void."[52]

Actually, the chief distinction between pertinent parts of the Compromise of 1850 and the Kansas-Nebraska Law lay rather in the practical politics and the fervent emotions involved in the issue than in any legalistic differences. New Mexico and Utah had not been defined as free soil by the Missouri Compromise or any other American legislation. Therefore, the application of popular sovereignty to the problems of 1850 did not evoke the sectional turbulence so disruptive in 1854. The telling argument in 1854 was that land solemnly guaranteed to freedom might be lost to slavery. Accusations of "an atrocious plot" and a "criminal betrayal," committed on the basis of "meditated bad faith," convinced numerous Northerners and led tens of thousands of erstwhile moderates to abandon their moderation.[53]

Though the Kansas-Nebraska question is not under scrutiny here, it is important in viewing the Compromise of 1850 in connection with later events to note that Douglas,

[50] *Congressional Globe*, 33 Cong., 1 Sess., 275-81.

[51] Allen Johnson, "The Genesis of Popular Sovereignty," *Iowa Journal of History and Politics*, III (Jan. 1905), 14, 18.

[52] *The Public Statutes at Large and Treaties of the United States of America* (76 vols., Boston, 1845-1963), X, 283, 289.

[53] Milton, *The Eve of Conflict*, 120-41; Washington *National Era*, January 24, 1854.

its principal architect, stressed its prominence in the historical sequence. He did this again when he debated with Lincoln at Galesburg in 1858 and when he published an elaborate policy paper in *Harper's Magazine* in 1859.[54] Important, too, is the realization that Douglas was consistently railroad-minded and that he wished to eliminate the Indian barrier blocking his preferred rail route from Illinois to California. To create a Territory of Nebraska, which the tracks of his dreams could traverse, was a means to the end he sought.[55] Nowhere in his statesmanship, from the 1840s until his death, is there convincing proof that he was a southern agent, a traitor to his section, or an amoral schemer who supposed that the result of popular sovereignty would be the extension of chattel slavery. As Albert J. Beveridge wrote, "Douglas was a great man, and he grows bigger all the time."[56] Douglas thought in terms of the West and of the nation as a whole instead of permitting himself to be constricted by narrow contemporaries of South or North.

The 1850 part of Douglas' record did not fit into the context of earlier historians with a Federalist-Whig-Republican bias. Seeing in him an 1854 villain, they, however, could not ascribe villainies to him in the 1850 setting—as one of their heroes, Henry Clay, had the same aims, albeit not the same methods. They played up Clay and the Whigs, therefore, and they played down Douglas and the Democrats. Thus the vital Douglas-Democratic contributions were relegated to a secondary status, until Frank H. Hodder began revising the work of the original revisionists.[57]

[54] Basler *et al.* (eds.), *The Collected Works of Abraham Lincoln*, III, 207-208; Stephen A. Douglas, "The Dividing Line between Federal and Local Authority; Popular Sovereignty in the Territories," *Harper's Magazine* (New York), XIX (Sept. 1859), 533-36.

[55] Frank H. Hodder, "The Railroad Background of the Kansas-Nebraska Act," *Mississippi Valley Historical Review*, XII (June 1925), 3-22.

[56] Benjamin P. Thomas, *Portrait for Posterity: Lincoln and His Biographers* (New Brunswick, N.J., 1947), 262.

[57] Frank H. Hodder, "Stephen A. Douglas," *The Chautauquan*, XXIX (Aug. 1899), 432-37, reprinted with some changes in *Kansas Historical Quarterly*, VIII (Aug. 1939), 227-37.

Even today, despite the corrections of Hodder and of post-Hodder historians, the "Clay's Compromise" label persists in many books and many minds. The enactment of the Illinois Central bill, also under Douglas' aegis, should be restored to the same frame of reference as the passage of the Compromise of 1850. It should likewise be related to his later hopes, broached and blasted in the larger sense in 1854. Douglas' *annus mirabilis* was 1850, when he was equally responsible for both major actions of the Thirty-first Congress. The dual accomplishment showed that he, transcending all of the old masters, was a personage of the first magnitude before his thirty-eighth birthday.

7

THE COMPROMISE of 1850 was a temporary success in securing tranquillity for the country. Delegates to the second session of the Nashville Convention, held two months after the congressional adjustment, created little stir when they met and less when they adjourned.[58] The Texas cauldron simmered down. The adoption of the moderate "Georgia Platform" at Milledgeville in late 1850 was followed in 1851 by Benton's defeat for reelection in Missouri and by the gubernatorial triumphs of Cobb and Foote in Georgia and Mississippi.[59] In Alabama and even South Carolina, the tide of extremist sentiment receded.[60] In the North, though much was made of Charles Sumner's elevation to the Senate, neither the Massachusetts radical

[58] Dallas T. Herndon, "The Nashville Convention of 1850," Alabama Historical Society *Transactions*, V (1906), 227-37.

[59] Richard H. Shryock, *Georgia and the Union in 1850* (Durham, N.C., 1926), 222-27, 303-42; William N. Chambers, *Old Bullion Benton: Senator from the New West* (Boston, 1956), 374-76; Cleo Hearon, "Mississippi and the Compromise of 1850," Mississippi Historical Society *Publications*, XIV (1914), 200-215.

[60] Lewy Dorman, *Party Politics in Alabama from 1850 through 1860* (Wetumpka, Ala., 1935), 48-60; Harold S. Schultz, *Nationalism and Sectionalism in South Carolina, 1852-1860* (Durham, N.C., 1950), 13, 16, 28-41.

nor Ohio's Benjamin F. Wade typified senatorial newcomers. Conservatism and the Democratic party dominated the House of Representatives,[61] and the "Cave of the Winds" proved unusually placid from 1851 through 1853. In February 1852 Edwin M. Stanton observed that "besides the Presidential agitation there is nothing of any interest in Washington." And in July 1853 the Richmond *Enquirer* reported "a calm, comparatively, in the political world."[62]

That moderation was the rule, rather than the exception, is indicated by the inclusion of pro-Compromise planks by both Democrats and Whigs in their 1852 national platforms. The leading Democratic preconvention aspirants—Cass, Douglas, Buchanan, and William L. Marcy—were, or posed as, Compromise champions. The three hopeful Whigs— Fillmore, Webster, and Winfield Scott—had been proadjustment in the critical days of 1850 and now subscribed to the Compromise stand of the Baltimore delegates. The Democratic nomination went to a dark horse, Franklin Pierce, who was acceptable to competing factions and whose endorsement of the Compromise probably clinched his victory. Scott, defeating Fillmore and Webster, opposed Pierce in November. Even before his nomination, however, the ranking American soldier was regarded as being under Seward's domination. In 1852, this was fatal, and Pierce was the natural beneficiary of antiextremist feeling.[63]

In a 1922 article, Herbert D. Foster summarized the argument that the Compromise of 1850 delayed the Civil War ten years and therefore served an invaluable purpose.[64]

[61] Nevins, *Ordeal of the Union*, I, 391-96; James F. Rhodes, *History of the United States from the Compromise of 1850* (7 vols., New York, 1893-1906), I, 226-30.

[62] Edwin M. Stanton to Benjamin Tappan, February 9, 1852, Benjamin Tappan Papers, Library of Congress; Richmond *Enquirer*, July 6, 1853.

[63] Roy F. Nichols, *Franklin Pierce: Young Hickory of the Granite Hills* (Philadelphia, 1958), 201-16; Charles W. Elliott, *Winfield Scott: The Soldier and the Man* (New York, 1937), 608-47.

[64] Herbert D. Foster, "Webster's Seventh of March Speech and the Secession Movement, 1850," *American Historical Review*, XXVII (Jan. 1922), 261, 267-70.

Maybe so, but it is just as possible that a golden opportunity
was lost when Fillmore and Congress failed to confront
disunionists with the bluntest sort of nationalism in the
Jackson-Taylor tradition. James Schouler believed that, in
1850, Zachary Taylor "saw more clearly the bold headlands
of national policy through the mists that were gathering,
than the wisest and world-renowned of our statesmen."
Edward Channing wrote: "It seems not impossible that . . .
Taylor . . . really had more political prescience than the
most veteran political war horses of them all." George Fort
Milton declared: "The stern determined character of 'Old
Rough and Ready' made it more than likely that the revolt
would not have gotten so far and taken so long as the Civil
War itself. And this despite the fact that the North grew
more than the South did in the ensuing decade."[65] Disagreeing with these authors on certain other points, I subscribe to their quoted opinions. I think that the resolution
of Taylor either would have called the Texas bluff or
would have defeated secession, rebellion, civil war, or challenges to federal authority under any other name.

The Compromise formula demanded statesmanship, and
especially presidential statesmanship, of a different sort
from what might have sufficed if Taylor's attitude had
prevailed. It is doubtful that, after 1850, Jacksonian stern-
ness would have been equal to the altered situation; the
Compromise solution depended on an unusual degree of
sustained skill, anticipation, delicacy, and elevation of outlook in the White House. Unfortunately, those qualities
were not forthcoming. Enormous psychological strains
challenged the resources of limited leaders. And Douglas,
the one man apparently endowed with the vigor and intel-
lect needed to cope with sectionalistic threats under the
new order, never was clothed with the presidential power.

In the period from September 1850 to March 1861, the

[65] Schouler, *History of the United States*, V, 186-87; Edward Channing, *A History of the United States* (6 vols., New York, 1905-1925),
VI, 138; George F. Milton to author, April 27, 1937.

President who had the best opportunity to keep the Union permanently intact without war was neither Fillmore nor Buchanan but the genial and pathetic Pierce. Committed to upholding the "finality" of the Compromise and having carried all but four states in the election, Pierce started out with big majorities in Congress.[66] The time for him to act effectively along constructive lines was during the half-year from March through August of 1853. Imagination should have suggested reasons for anticipating difficulties which might soon become dilemmas. If railroad legislation was needed to connect the East Coast and the heartland with the Pacific Ocean, then a dynamic executive might have led the way in securing it. This is not to say that all trouble could have been avoided. But what was necessary might well have been accomplished with minimal vituperation, if a special session of Congress had been called and if action had been taken before the patronage was distributed or factionalists could turn on Pierce and sting him.

Another serious weakness lay in Pierce's failure to make a Jeffersonian-Jacksonian appeal to the common man. In 1862 homestead legislation and a land-grant college bill were enacted. How unfortunate it was, from the standpoint of long-range primacy of moderates as well as improvement of the underdog's lot, that these measures were not given a presidential push in 1853 or soon thereafter. A Department of Agriculture, headed by a commissioner, was to be formed in 1862. Might its creation not have occurred eight or nine years earlier? Even if one grants that many southern spokesmen of the 1850s were opposed to most reforms, and that Pierce was acutely aware of the southern influence in the Democratic party, our greatest Presidents from George Washington on have been effective makers of combinations. A really great leader in 1853, armed with the advantages Pierce first possessed, might have effected another and more comprehensive compromise. This positive program might have encompassed railroads, homesteads,

[66] Nichols, *Franklin Pierce*, 216, 302.

land-grant colleges, tariff revision, and scientific agriculture
—with something in the legislative package for every congressman whose vote he needed and for every region and
class on which his dominance depended.

Roy F. Nichols has written that in the 1850s "democratic
ideas were embalmed in platforms," their remains "exhibited to the faithful at election times and on patriotic
anniversaries." Members of the Democratic hierarchy "had
lost the spirit of the doctrines they preached." Progressive
principles became a cult's mumbo-jumbo, and the "priest-
hood of the cult . . . went through the forms and ceremonies
seemingly without comprehension of their meaning."[67] The
federal government, says Bray Hammond, was now a "cave-
dwelling affair." Withdrawing into the "modest performance of minor routines"[68] or resorting to foreign adventures
of dubious popularity or merit, Democrats rejected domestic
procedures which common sense might have recommended.
Blocking, vetoing, retreating, standing still, the once militant
Democracy created a political and psychological vacuum
of dangerous magnitude. Thereupon a new variety of northern politicians, appealing to a strengthened sectionalism,
marched into the vacuum and in seven years filled it, even
as strident sectionalists of the South tried to do the same
thing but failed for want of numbers.

8

CRITICISM OF Pierce and other Democratic officeholders
contains no implication whatever that Whigs, Know Noth-
ings, or Republicans were guiltless as Armageddon neared.
The prominence of Democrats in this procession of failures
is due to the larger part which their party played in produc-

[67] Roy F. Nichols, *The Democratic Machine, 1850-1854* (New
York, 1923), 223-26.
[68] Bray Hammond, *Banks and Politics in America from the Revolution to the Civil War* (Princeton, N.J., 1957), 719-20.

ing the adjustment and hence their responsibility for carrying through its spirit. If the Civil War was a needless tragedy (as I think it was), the biggest share of blame must be borne not by moderate men of good will but by firebrands of North and South who never thought themselves culpable for four years of brutal bloodletting. That, however, is another story—one less directly associated with the aftermath of the Compromise.

A study of the Compromise in operation shows that not one of its component parts did all that many people thought it did, or expected it to do. The California senators of the 1850s were mostly southern sympathizers. Slavery existed, to some extent, in Utah and New Mexico during part or all of the pre-Sumter decade. The Texas creditors were not paid at once. The Texas government at Austin did not receive $10 million. Negroes continued to be bought and sold in the District of Columbia. The Fugitive Slave Law further irritated sectional relations, instead of allaying southern discontent. Important locally, and more than locally, have been the curious boundary tangles identified with lines which compromisers scanned only at a distance and through opaque glasses. Popular sovereignty did give the territories power to legislate on slavery. All these things are true of the Compromise in operation. And behind them are the complicated maneuvers around the Omnibus Bill and proposals before and after it, the parts played by Douglas, Clay, Webster, and numerous lesser men, by the Democratic party, by the Texas bondholders, and by Presidents Taylor and Fillmore. All these and the place of the Compromise as a body of laws and a precedent go to make up the complex whole which is the Compromise of 1850.

The coming of the Civil War has been subjected to countless interpretations. Hate, zeal, intolerance, pride, the slavery institution, slavery plus race, race alone, and the errors committed by a "blundering generation" have all been thought of as causes of the conflict. The breakdown of democratic processes from 1861 to 1865 has been attributed to cultural, economic, moral, constitutional, philosophical, political, and psychological considerations.[69] To these should be added the tendency of democratic government to procrastinate, to adopt makeshift measures, in the hope that a problem will go away or work itself out if simply let alone. Germane, too, is the traditional unwillingness of Americans, gallant and self-immolating when wars come, to make minor sacrifices of thought and time and convenience and conduct in order to prevent those wars. As undeniable in 1850 as in any later year was the fact that residents of major sections were appallingly ignorant about each other. The most fateful forms of this ignorance consisted of (a) a fantastic caricature of the slave labor system which won wide acceptance in northern minds, and (b) the conviction on the part of many Southerners that the North would not fight successfully—if at all—in the event of secession.

Distortion thus supplanted truth. The intellectual and ideological underpinnings, which the average citizen neglected to give himself, should have been supplied by the citizen's leaders. What are we to think of all the fictions, the frictions, the fumblings, the failures? As a British scholar expressed it, "the failures of statesmen are not ordinarily due to treason, felony, or misdemeanour . . . but to errors of judgment, of temper, and of calculation."[70] It is equally correct to conclude that applauded "solutions" of imposing governmental problems are not always of permanent benefit to "the last best, hope of earth."[71]

[69] Thomas J. Pressly, *Americans Interpret Their Civil War* (Princeton, N.J., 1954), 129-323; Howard K. Beale, "What Historians Have Said about the Causes of the Civil War," Social Science Research Council *Bulletin 54* (New York, 1946), 53-102.

[70] H.A.L. Fisher, *A History of Europe* (London, 1939), 660.

[71] Basler *et al.* (eds.), *The Collected Works of Abraham Lincoln*, V, 537.

APPENDIX A

SENATE ROLLCALLS ON COMPROMISE MEASURES

Senator	Section & Party	Utah (July 31)	Texas (Aug. 9)	Calif. (Aug. 13)	N. Mex. (Aug. 15)	Fug. Sl. (Aug. 23)	District (Sept. 16)
Atchison	SD	Yea	Nay	Nay	Yea	Yea	Nay
Badger	SW	Yea	Yea	NV	Yea	Yea	Nay
Baldwin	NW	Nay	Nay	Yea	NV	Nay	Yea
Barnwell	SD	NV	Nay	Nay	NV	Yea	Nay
Bell	SW	Nay	Yea	Yea	NV	Yea	Nay
Benton	SD	Yea	Nay	Yea	Yea	NV	Yea
Berrien	SW	Yea	Yea	Nay	Yea	Yea	Nay
Borland	SD	NV	NV	NV	NV	NV	NV
Bradbury	ND	Yea	Yea	Yea	Yea	Nay	NV
Bright	ND	Yea	Yea	Yea	Yea	NV	Yea
Butler	SD	Yea	Nay	Nay	NV	Yea	Nay
Cass	ND	Yea	Yea	Yea	Yea	NV	Yea
Chase	NFS	Nay	Nay	Yea	Nay	Nay	Yea
Clarke	NW	Nay	Yea	NV	NV	NV	Yea
Clay	SW	NV	NV	NV	NV	NV	Yea
Clemens	SD	NV	Yea	Nay	NV	NV	NV
Cooper	NW	NV	Yea	Yea	Yea	Nay	Yea
Jeff Davis	SD	Yea	Nay	Nay	NV	Yea	Nay
John Davis	NW	Nay	Yea	Yea	Nay	Nay	Yea
Dawson	SW	Yea	Yea	Nay	Yea	Yea	Nay
Dayton	NW	Nay	NV	NV	NV	Nay	Yea
Dickinson	ND	Yea	Yea	Yea	NV	NV	Yea
A. C. Dodge	ND	Yea	Yea	Yea	Yea	Yea	Yea
H. Dodge	ND	Nay	Nay	Yea	Nay	Nay	Yea
Douglas	ND	Yea	Yea	Yea	Yea	NV	Yea
Downs	SD	Yea	NV	NV	Yea	Yea	Nay
Ewing	NW	Nay	Nay	Yea	NV	NV	Yea
Felch	ND	Yea	Yea	Yea	Yea	NV	Yea
Foote	SD	NV	Yea	Nay	NV	Yea	NV
Frémont	ND						Yea

Senator	Section & Party	Utah (July 31)	Texas (Aug. 9)	Calif. (Aug. 13)	N. Mex. (Aug. 15)	Fug. Sl. (Aug. 23)	District (Sept. 16)
Greene	NW	Nay	Yea	Yea	Nay	Nay	Yea
Gwin	ND						Yea
Hale	NFS	Nay	Nay	Yea	NV	NV	Yea
Hamlin	ND	Nay	NV	Yea	Nay	NV	Yea
Houston	SD	Yea	Yea	Yea	Yea	Yea	Yea
Hunter	SD	Yea	Nay	Nay	Yea	Yea	Nay
Jones	ND	Yea	NV	Yea	NV	Yea	Yea
King	SD	Yea	Yea	Nay	Yea	Yea	Nay
Mangum	SW	NV	NV	NV	Yea	Yea	Nay
Mason	SD	Yea	Nay	Nay	Yea	Yea	Nay
Miller	NW	Nay	NV	Yea	Nay	NV	NV
Morton	SW	Yea	Nay	Nay	NV	NV	Nay
Norris	ND	Yea	Yea	Yea	Yea	NV	Yea
Pearce	SW	Nay	Yea	NV	NV	Yea	NV
Phelps	NW	NV	Yea	Yea	Nay	NV	NV
Pratt	SW	Yea	NV	Nay	Yea	NV	Nay
Rusk	SD	NV	Yea	Nay	Yea	Yea	NV
Sebastian	SD	Yea	NV	Nay	Yea	Yea	Nay
Seward	NW	Nay	Nay	Yea	NV	NV	Yea
Shields	ND	Yea	Yea	Yea	Yea	NV	Yea
Smith	NW	Nay	Yea	Yea	NV	Nay	NV
Soulé	SD	Yea	Nay	Nay	NV	Yea	Nay
Spruance	SW	Yea	Yea	Yea	NV	Yea	Yea
Sturgeon	ND	Yea	Yea	Yea	Yea	Yea	Yea
Turney	SD	Yea	Nay	Nay	NV	Yea	Nay
Underwood	SW	Yea	Nay	Yea	Yea	Yea	Yea
Upham	NW	Nay	Nay	Yea	Nay	Nay	NV
Wales	SW	Yea	Yea	Yea	Yea	Yea	Yea
Walker	ND	Nay	Nay	Yea	Nay	Nay	Yea
Whitcomb	ND	NV	Yea	Yea	Yea	NV	Yea
Winthrop	NW	Nay	Yea	Yea	Nay	Nay	Yea
Yulee	SD	Yea	Nay	Nay	NV	Yea	Nay
TOTALS	Yea	32	30	34	27	27	33
	Nay	18	20	18	10	12	19
	NV	10	10	8	23	21	10

ND—northern Democrat; NFS—northern Free Soiler; NV—not voting; NW—northern Whig; SD—southern Democrat; SW—southern Whig. Frémont and Gwin, the California senators, were sworn in September 10.

APPENDIX B

Senator	Section & Party	N. Mex.	Texas	Calif.
Atchison	SD	Nay	Nay	Yea
Badger	SW	Nay	Nay	Yea
Baldwin	NW	Yea	Yea	Yea
Barnwell	SD	Yea	Yea	Yea
Bell	SW	NV	Nay	Yea
Benton	SD	Yea	Yea	Yea
Berrien	SW	Yea	Nay	Yea
Borland	SD	NV	NV	NV
Bradbury	ND	NV	Nay	Nay
Bright	ND	Nay	Nay	Nay
Butler	SD	Yea	Yea	Yea
Cass	ND	Nay	Nay	Nay
Chase	NFS	Yea	Yea	Nay
Clarke	NW	Yea	Yea	Yea
Clay	SW	Nay	Nay	Nay
Clemens	SD	Nay	Nay	Yea
Cooper	NW	NV	NV	Nay
Jeff Davis	SD	Yea	Yea	Yea
John Davis	NW	Yea	Yea	Yea
Dawson	SW	Nay	Nay	Yea
Dayton	NW	Yea	Yea	Nay
Dickinson	ND	Nay	Nay	Nay
A. C. Dodge	ND	Nay	Nay	Nay
H. Dodge	ND	Yea	Yea	Nay
Douglas	ND	Yea	Nay	Nay
Downs	SD	Nay	Nay	Yea
Ewing	NW	Yea	Yea	Yea
Felch	ND	NV	Nay	Nay
Foote	SD	Nay	Nay	Yea

Senator	Section & Party	N. Mex.	Texas	Calif.
Greene	NW	Yea	Yea	Yea
Hale	NFS	Yea	NV	Nay
Hamlin	ND	Yea	Yea	Nay
Houston	SD	Nay	Yea	Nay
Hunter	SD	Yea	Yea	Yea
Jones	ND	Nay	Nay	Nay
King	SD	Nay	Nay	Yea
Mangum	SW	Nay	Nay	Yea
Mason	SD	Yea	Yea	Yea
Miller	NW	Yea	Yea	Nay
Morton	SW	Yea	Yea	Yea
Norris	ND	Nay	Nay	Nay
Pearce	SW	Yea	Nay	Yea
Phelps	NW	Yea	Yea	Yea
Pratt	SW	Nay	Nay	Yea
Rusk	SD	Nay	Yea	Yea
Sebastian	SD	Nay	Yea	Yea
Seward	NW	Yea	Yea	Yea
Shields	ND	Yea	Nay	Nay
Smith	NW	Yea	Yea	Yea
Soulé	SD	Yea	Yea	Yea
Spruance	SW	Nay	Nay	Nay
Sturgeon	ND	Nay	Nay	Nay
Turney	SD	Yea	Yea	Yea
Underwood	SW	Yea	Nay	Nay
Upham	NW	Yea	Yea	Yea
Wales	SW	Yea	Nay	Nay
Walker	ND	Yea	Yea	Nay
Whitcomb	ND	Nay	Nay	Nay
Winthrop	NW	Yea	Yea	Yea
Yulee	SD	Yea	Yea	Yea
TOTALS	Yea	33	29	34
	Nay	22	28	25
	NV	5	3	1

ND—northern Democrat; NFS—northern Free Soiler; NV—not voting; NW—northern Whig; SD—southern Democrat; SW—southern Whig. Yea—against Omnibus; Nay—for Omnibus.

APPENDIX C

HOUSE ROLLCALLS ON COMPROMISE MEASURES AND SELECTED ·PROCEDURAL VOTES

Representative			Compromise Measures					Procedural Votes		
Name	State	Section & Party	Tex-NM (Sept. 6)	Calif. (Sept. 7)	Utah (Sept. 7)	Fug. Sl. (Sept. 12)	Dist. (Sept. 17)	Sept. 4 104-103	Sept. 5 99-107	Sept. 6 108-98
Albertson	Ind.	ND	Yea	Yea	Yea	Yea	Yea	Pro	Yea	Yea
Alexander	N.Y.	NW	Nay	Yea	Nay	Nay	Yea	Anti	Nay	Nay
Allen	Mass.	NFS	Nay	Yea	Nay	Nay	NV	Anti	Nay	Nay
Alston	Ala.	SW	Yea	Nay	Yea	Yea	Nay	Pro	Yea	Yea
Anderson	Tenn.	SW	Yea	Yea	Yea	Yea	Nay	Pro	Yea	Yea
Andrews	N.Y.	NW	Yea	Yea	NV	NV	Yea	Pro	Yea	Yea
Ashe	N.C.	SD	NV	Nay	Yea	Yea	Nay	Anti	Nay	Nay
Ashmun	Mass.	NW	NV	NV	NV	NV	Yea	NV	NV	NV
Averett	Va.	SD	Nay	Nay	Yea	Yea	Nay	Anti	NV	Nay
Baker	Ill.	NW	Nay	Yea	NV	Nay	NV	Anti	Nay	Nay
Bay	Mo.	SD	Yea	Yea	Yea	Yea	NV	Pro	Yea	Yea
Bayly	Va.	SD	Yea	Nay	Yea	Yea	Nay	Pro	Yea	Yea
Beale	Va.	SD	Yea	Nay	Yea	Yea	Yea	Pro	Yea	Yea
Bennett	N.Y.	NW	Nay	Yea	Nay	Nay	NV	Anti	Nay	Nay
Bingham	Mich.	ND	Nay	Yea	Nay	Nay	Yea	Anti	Nay	Nay
Bissell	Ill.	ND	NV	Yea	Yea	Yea	Yea	NV	NV	NV
Bokee	N.Y.	NW	Yea	Yea	Yea	NV	NV	Pro	Yea	Yea
Booth	Conn.	NFS	Nay	Yea	Nay	Nay	Yea	Anti	Nay	Nay
Bowdon	Ala.	SD	Nay	Nay	Nay	Yea	Nay	Anti	NV	Nay
Bowie	Md.	SW	Yea	Yea	NV	Yea	Nay	Pro	Yea	Yea
Bowlin	Mo.	SD	Yea	Yea	Yea	Yea	NV	Pro	Yea	Yea
Boyd	Ky.	SD	Yea	Nay	Yea	Yea	NV	Pro	Yea	Yea
Breck	Ky.	SW	Yea	Yea	Yea	Yea	NV	Pro	Yea	Yea
Briggs	N.Y.	NW	Yea	Yea	Yea	Nay	Yea	Pro	Yea	Yea
Brooks	N.Y.	NW	Yea	Yea	Yea	NV	Yea	Pro	Yea	Yea
Brown, A. G.	Miss.	SD	Nay	Nay	Nay	Yea	Nay	Anti	Nay	Nay
Brown, W. J.	Ind.	ND	Yea	Yea	Yea	Yea	Yea	Pro	Yea	Yea
Buel	Mich.	ND	Yea	Yea	NV	Yea	Yea	Pro	Yea	Yea

Name	State	Section & Party	Tex-NM (Sept. 6)	Calif. (Sept. 7)	Utah (Sept. 7)	Fug. Sl. (Sept. 12)	Dist. (Sept. 17)	Sept. 4 104-103	Sept. 5 99-107	Sept. 6 108-98
Burrows	N.Y.	NW	Nay	Yea	Nay	Nay	Yea	Anti	Nay	Nay
Burt	S.C.	SD	Nay	Nay	Nay	Yea	Nay	Anti	Nay	Nay
Butler, C.	Pa.	NW	Yea	Yea	Yea	NV	Yea	Pro	Yea	Yea
Butler, T. B.	Conn.	NW	Nay	Yea	Nay	Nay	Yea	Anti	Nay	Nay
Cabell, E. C.	Fla.	SW	Yea	Nay	NV	NV	Nay	Pro	Yea	Yea
Cable, J.	Ohio	ND	Nay	Yea	Nay	Nay	Yea	Anti	Nay	Nay
Caldwell, G. A.	Ky.	SD	Yea	Nay	Yea	Yea	Nay	Pro	Yea	Yea
Caldwell, J. P.	N.C.	SW	Yea	Yea	Yea	Yea	Nay	Pro	Yea	Yea
Calvin	Pa.	NW	Nay	Yea	Nay	Nay	Yea	Anti	Nay	Nay
Campbell	Ohio	NW	Nay	Yea	Nay	Nay	Yea	Anti	Nay	Nay
Cartter	Ohio	ND	Nay	Yea	NV	Nay	Yea	Pro	Nay	Nay
Casey	Pa.	NW	Yea	Yea	Yea	NV	Yea	Pro	Yea	Yea
Chandler	Pa.	NW	Yea	Yea	Nay	Nay	Yea	Anti	Yea	Yea
Clarke	N.Y.	NW	Nay	Yea	Nay	Nay	Yea	Anti	Nay	Nay
Cleveland	Conn.	ND	NV	NV	NV	NV	Yea	NV	NV	NV
Clingman	N.C.	SW	Nay	Nay	NV	Yea	Nay	Pro	Nay	Nay
Cobb, H.	Ga.	SD	NV	NV	NV	NV	NV	Pro	NV	NV
Cobb, W. R. W.	Ala.	SD	Yea	Nay	Yea	Yea	Nay	Pro	Yea	Yea
Colcock	S.C.	SD	Nay	Nay	Nay	Yea	Nay	Anti	Nay	Nay
Cole	Wis.	NW	Nay	Yea	Nay	Nay	Yea	Anti	Nay	Nay
Conger	N.Y.	NW	Nay	NV	NV	NV	NV	Anti	Nay	Nay
Corwin	Ohio	NW	Nay	Yea	Nay	Nay	Yea	Anti	Nay	Nay
Crowell	Ohio	NW	Nay	Yea	Nay	Nay	Yea	Anti	Nay	Nay
Daniel	N.C.	SD	Nay	Nay	Yea	Yea	NV	Anti	Nay	Nay
Deberry	N.C.	SW	Yea	Nay	Yea	Yea	Nay	Pro	Yea	Yea
Dickey	Pa.	NW	Nay	Yea	Nay	Nay	Yea	Anti	Nay	Nay
Dimmick	Pa.	ND	Yea	Yea	Yea	Yea	Yea	Pro	Yea	Yea
Disney	Ohio	ND	Yea	Yea	Yea	Nay	Yea	Anti	Yea	Yea
Dixon	R.I.	NW	Nay	Yea	Nay	Nay	Yea	Anti	Nay	Nay
Doty	Wis.	ND	Nay	Yea	Nay	Nay	Yea	Anti	Nay	Nay
Duer	N.Y.	NW	Yea	Yea	Nay	NV	Yea	Pro	Yea	Yea
Duncan	Mass.	NW	Yea	Yea	Nay	Nay	Yea	Anti	Yea	Yea
Dunham	Ind.	ND	Yea	Yea	Yea	Yea	Yea	Pro	Yea	Yea
Durkee	Wis.	NFS	Nay	Yea	Nay	Nay	Yea	Anti	Nay	Nay
Edmundson	Va.	SD	Yea	Nay	Yea	Yea	Nay	Anti	Yea	Yea
Eliot	Mass.	NW	Yea	Yea	Yea	Yea	Yea	Pro	Yea	Yea
Evans, A.	Md.	SW	NV	Yea	Yea	NV	Nay	NV	NV	NV
Evans, N.	Ohio	NW	Nay	Yea	Nay	Nay	Yea	Anti	Nay	Nay
Ewing	Tenn.	SD	Yea	Yea	Yea	Yea	Nay	Pro	Yea	Yea
Featherston	Miss.	SD	Nay	Nay	Nay	Yea	Nay	Anti	Nay	Nay

Name	State	Section & Party	Tex-NM (Sept. 6)	Calif. (Sept. 7)	Utah (Sept. 7)	Fug. Sl. (Sept. 12)	Dist. (Sept. 17)	Sept. 4 104-103	Sept. 5 99-107	Sept. 6 108-98
Fitch	Ind.	ND	Yea	Yea	Nay	Nay	Yea	Anti	Yea	Yea
Fowler	Mass.	NW	Nay	Yea	Nay	Nay	Yea	Anti	Nay	Nay
Freedley	Pa.	NW	NV	Yea	NV	Nay	Yea	Anti	Nay	NV
Fuller	Me.	ND	Yea	Yea	Yea	Yea	Yea	Pro	Yea	Yea
Gentry	Tenn.	SW	Yea	Yea	Yea	Yea	Yea	Pro	Yea	Yea
Gerry	Me.	ND	Yea	Yea	Yea	Yea	Yea	Pro	Yea	Yea
Giddings	Ohio	NFS	Nay	Yea	Nay	Nay	NV	Anti	Nay	Nay
Gilbert	Cal.	ND				Yea	Yea			
Gilmore	Pa.	ND	Yea	Yea	Yea	NV	Yea	Pro	Yea	Yea
Gorman	Ind.	ND	Yea	Yea	Yea	Yea	Yea	Pro	Yea	Yea
Gott	N.Y.	NW	Nay	Yea	Nay	Nay	Yea	Anti	Nay	Nay
Gould	N.Y.	NW	NV	Yea	Nay	Nay	Yea	Anti	Nay	NV
Green	Mo.	SD	Yea	Nay	NV	Yea	Nay	Pro	Yea	Yea
Grinnell	Mass	NW	Yea	Yea	NV	NV	Yea	Pro	Yea	Yea
Hall	Mo.	SD	Yea	Yea	Yea	Yea	Yea	Pro	Yea	Yea
Halloway	N.Y.	NW	Nay	Yea	Nay	Nay	Yea	Anti	Nay	Nay
Hamilton	Md.	SD	NV	Yea	NV	Yea	Nay	NV	NV	NV
Hammond	Md.	SD	Yea	NV	NV	NV	NV	Pro	Yea	Yea
Hampton	Pa.	NW	NV	NV	NV	Nay	Yea	NV	NV	NV
Haralson	Ga.	SD	Nay	Nay	Yea	Yea	Nay	Pro	Nay	Nay
Harlan	Ind.	ND	Nay	Yea	Nay	Nay	Yea	Anti	Nay	Nay
Harris, I. G.	Tenn.	SD	Yea	Nay	Yea	Yea	Nay	Pro	Yea	Yea
Harris, S. W.	Ala.	SW	Nay	Nay	Nay	Yea	Nay	Anti	Nay	Nay
Harris, T. L.	Ill.	ND	Yea	Yea	Yea	Yea	Yea	Pro	Yea	Yea
Hay	N.J.	NW	NV	NV	NV	Nay	Yea	NV	NV	NV
Haymond	Va.	SW	Yea	Yea	Yea	Yea	Yea	Pro	Yea	Yea
Hebard	Vt.	NW	Nay	NV	Nay	Nay	Yea	Anti	Nay	Nay
Henry	Vt.	NW	Nay	Yea	Nay	Nay	Yea	Anti	Nay	Nay
Hibbard	N.H.	ND	Yea	Yea	Yea	Yea	Yea	Pro	Yea	Yea
Hilliard	Ala.	SW	Yea	Nay	Yea	Yea	NV	Pro	Yea	Yea
Hoagland	Ohio	ND	Yea	Yea	Yea	Yea	Yea	Pro	Yea	Yea
Holladay	Va.	SD	Nay	Nay	Nay	Yea	Nay	Anti	Nay	Nay
Holmes	S.C.	SD	Nay	NV	Nay	Yea	NV	Anti	Nay	Nay
Houston	Del.	SW	Yea	Yea	Yea	Yea	NV	Pro	Yea	Yea
Howard	Tex.	SD	Yea	Nay	Yea	Yea	Nay	Pro	Nay	Yea
Howe	Pa.	NFS	Nay	Yea	Nay	Nay	Yea	Anti	Nay	Nay
Hubbard	Ala.	SD	Nay	Nay	Nay	Yea	Nay	Anti	Nay	Nay
Hunter	Ohio	NW	Nay	Yea	Nay	Nay	Yea	Anti	Nay	Nay
Inge	Ala.	SD	Nay	Nay	Nay	Yea	Nay	Anti	Nay	Nay
Jackson, J. W.	Ga.	SD	Nay	Nay	Yea	Yea	Nay	Pro	Nay	Nay

Name	State	Section & Party	Tex-NM (Sept. 6)	Calif. (Sept. 7)	Utah (Sept. 7)	Fug. Sl. (Sept. 12)	Dist. (Sept. 17)	Sept. 4 104-103	Sept. 5 99-107	Sept. 6 108-98
Jackson, W. T.	N.Y.	NW	Nay	Yea	Nay	Nay	Yea	Anti	Nay	Nay
Johnson, A.	Tenn.	SD	Yea	Yea	Yea	Yea	Nay	Pro	Yea	Yea
Johnson, J. L.	Ky.	SW	Yea	Yea	Yea	Yea	NV	Pro	Yea	Yea
Johnson, R. W.	Ark.	SD	Nay	Nay	NV	Yea	NV	Pro	Nay	Nay
Jones	Tenn.	SD	Yea	Yea	Yea	Yea	Nay	Pro	Yea	Yea
Julian	Ind.	NFS	Nay	Yea	Nay	Nay	Yea	Anti	Nay	Nay
Kaufman	Tex.	SD	Yea	Nay	Yea	Yea	Nay	Pro	Yea	Yea
Kerr	Md.	SW	Yea	Yea	Yea	Yea	Nay	Pro	Yea	Yea
King, G. G.	R.I.	NW	Yea	Yea	Nay	Nay	Yea	Anti	Nay	Yea
King, J. G.	N.J.	NW	Nay	Yea	Nay	Nay	Yea	Anti	Nay	Nay
King, J. A.	N.Y.	NW	Nay	Yea	Nay	Nay	Yea	Anti	Nay	Nay
King, P.	N.Y.	NFS	Nay	Yea	Nay	Nay	Yea	Anti	Nay	Nay
La Sere	La.	SD	Nay	Nay	Yea	Yea	Nay	Anti	Nay	Nay
Leffler	Iowa	ND	Yea	Yea	Yea	Yea	Yea	Pro	Yea	Yea
Levin	Pa.	NNA	Yea	Yea	Yea	NV	Yea	Pro	Yea	Yea
Littlefield	Me.	ND	Yea	Yea	Yea	Yea	Yea	Pro	Yea	Yea
Mann, H.	Mass.	NW	Nay	Yea	Nay	Nay	Yea	Anti	Nay	Nay
Mann, J.	Pa.	ND	Yea	Yea	Yea	Yea	Yea	Pro	Yea	Yea
Marshall	Ky.	SW	Yea	Yea	Yea	Yea	Nay	Pro	Yea	Yea
Mason	Ky.	SD	Yea	Yea	Yea	Yea	NV	Anti	Nay	Yea
Matteson	N.Y.	NW	Nay	Yea	Nay	Nay	Yea	Anti	Nay	Nay
McClernand	Ill.	ND	Yea	Yea	Yea	Yea	Yea	Pro	Yea	Yea
McDonald	Ind.	ND	Yea	Yea	Yea	Yea	Yea	Pro	Yea	Yea
McDowell	Va.	SD	Yea	Nay	Yea	NV	Nay	Pro	Yea	Yea
McGaughey	Ind.	NW	Nay	Yea	NV	Yea	Yea	Pro	Nay	Nay
McKissock	N.Y.	NW	Yea	Yea	Nay	Nay	Yea	Anti	Yea	Yea
McLanahan	Pa.	ND	Yea	Yea	Yea	Yea	Yea	NV	Yea	Yea
McLane, R. M.	Md.	SD	Yea	Yea	Yea	NV	Nay	Pro	Yea	Yea
McLean, F. E.	Ky.	SW	Yea	Yea	Yea	Yea	NV	Pro	Yea	Yea
McMullen	Va.	SD	Yea	Nay	Yea	Yea	Nay	Pro	Yea	Yea
McQueen	S.C.	SD	Nay	Nay	Nay	Yea	Nay	Anti	Nay	Nay
McWillie	Miss.	SD	Nay	Nay	Yea	Yea	NV	Anti	Nay	Nay
Meacham	Vt.	NW	Nay	Yea	Nay	Nay	Yea	Pro	Nay	Nay
Meade	Va.	SD	Nay	Nay	Nay	Yea	NV	Anti	Nay	Nay
Miller	Ohio	ND	NV	NV	NV	Yea	Yea	NV	NV	NV
Millson	Va.	SD	Nay	Nay	NV	Yea	Nay	Anti	Nay	Nay
Moore	Pa.	NW	Nay	Yea	Nay	Nay	Yea	Anti	Nay	Nay
Morehead	Ky.	SW	Yea	Yea	Yea	NV	NV	Pro	Yea	Yea
Morris	Ohio	ND	Nay	Yea	Nay	Nay	Yea	Anti	Nay	Nay
Morse	La.	SD	Nay	Nay	NV	NV	Nay	Anti	Nay	Nay
Morton	Va.	NV	Pro	Yea	Yea	SW	Yea	Nay	Yea	Yea

Name	State	Section & Party	Tex-NM (Sept. 6)	Calif. (Sept. 7)	Utah (Sept. 7)	Fug. Sl. (Sept. 12)	Dist. (Sept. 17)	Sept. 4 104-103	Sept. 5 99-107	Sept. 6 108-98
Nelson	N.Y.	NW	Yea	Yea	Nay	Nay	Yea	Pro	Yea	Yea
Newell	N.J.	NW	Nay	Yea	Nay	NV	NV	Anti	Nay	Nay
Ogle	Pa.	NW	Nay	Yea	Nay	NV	Yea	Anti	Nay	Nay
Olds	Ohio	ND	Nay	Yea	Nay	NV	NV	Anti	Nay	Nay
Orr	S.C.	SD	Nay	Nay	NV	Yea	Nay	Anti	Nay	Nay
Otis	Me.	NW	Nay	Yea	Nay	Nay	Yea	Anti	Nay	Nay
Outlaw	N.C.	SW	Yea	Nay	Yea	Yea	Nay	Pro	Yea	Yea
Owen	Ga.	SW	Yea	Nay	Yea	Yea	NV	Pro	Yea	Yea
Parker	Va.	SD	Yea	Nay	Yea	Yea	Nay	Pro	Yea	Yea
Peaslee	N.H.	ND	Yea	Yea	Yea	Yea	Yea	Pro	Yea	Yea
Peck	Vt.	ND	Nay	Yea	Nay	NV	NV	Anti	Nay	Nay
Phelps	Mo.	SD	Nay	Yea	NV	Yea	Nay	Anti	Nay	Nay
Phoenix	N.Y.	NW	Yea	Yea	NV	NV	Yea	Pro	Yea	Yea
Pitman	Pa.	NW	Yea	Yea	Yea	Nay	Yoa	Pro	Yoa	Yoa
Potter	Ohio	ND	Yea	Yea	Yea	NV	Yea	NV	Yea	Yea
Powell	Va.	SD	Nay	Nay	NV	Yea	Nay	Anti	Nay	Nay
Putnam	N.Y.	NW	Nay	Yea	NV	Nay	Yea	Anti	Nay	Nay
Reed	Pa.	NW	Nay	Yea	Nay	Nay	Yea	Anti	Nay	Nay
Reynolds	N.Y.	NW	Nay	Yea	Nay	NV	NV	Pro	Nay	Nay
Richardson	Ill.	ND	Yea	Yea	Yea	Yea	Yea	Pro	Yea	Yea
Risley	N.Y.	NW	NV	NV	NV	NV	Yea	NV	NV	NV
Robbins	Pa.	ND	Yea	Yea	Yea	Yea	Yea	Pro	Yea	Yea
Robinson	Ind.	ND	Yea	Yea	Yea	Nay	Yea	Pro	Yea	Yea
Rockwell	Mass.	NW	Nay	NV	NV	NV	NV	Anti	Nay	Nay
Root	Ohio	NFS	Nay	Yea	Nay	Nay	NV	Anti	Nay	Nay
Rose	N.Y.	NW	Yea	Yea	Yea	NV	Yea	Pro	Yea	Yea
Ross	Pa.	ND	Yea	Yea	Yea	Yea	Yea	Pro	Yea	Yea
Rumsey	N.Y.	NW	Nay	Yea	Nay	Nay	Yea	Anti	Nay	Nay
Sackett	N.Y.	NW	Nay	Yea	Nay	Nay	Yea	Anti	Nay	Nay
Savage	Tenn.	SW	Yea	Nay	Yea	Yea	Nay	Pro	Yea	Yea
Sawtelle	Me.	ND	Nay	Yea	Nay	Nay	Yea	Anti	Nay	Nay
Schenck	Ohio	NW	Nay	Yea	Nay	NV	Yea	Anti	Nay	Nay
Schermerhorn	N.Y.	NW	Yea	Yea	NV	Nay	Yea	Anti	Nay	Yea
Schoolcraft	N.Y.	NW	Nay	Yea	Nay	Nay	Yea	Anti	Nay	Nay
Seddon	Va.	SD	Nay	Nay	Nay	Yea	Nay	Anti	Nay	Nay
Shepperd	N.C.	SW	Yea	Nay	Yea	Yea	NV	Pro	Yea	Yea
Silvester	N.Y.	NW	Nay	Yea	Nay	Nay	Yea	Anti	Nay	Nay
Spaulding	N.Y.	NW	NV	NV	NV	NV	Yea	NV	NV	NV
Sprague	Mich.	NFS	Nay	Yea	Nay	Nay	Yea	Anti	Nay	Nay
Stanly	N.C.	SW	Yea	Yea	Yea	Yea	NV	Pro	Yea	Yea
Stanton, F. P.	Tenn.	SD	Yea	Nay	Yea	Yea	Nay	Pro	Nay	Yea

Name	State	Section & Party	Tex-NM (Sept. 6)	Calif. (Sept. 7)	Utah (Sept. 7)	Fug. Sl. (Sept. 12)	Dist. (Sept. 17)	Sept. 4 104-103	Sept. 5 99-107	Sept. 6 108-98
Stanton, R. H.	Ky.	SD	Yea	Nay	Yea	Yea	Nay	Anti	Nay	Yea
Stephens, A. H.	Ga.	SW	NV	NV	NV	NV	Nay	NV	NV	NV
Stetson	Me.	ND	Nay	Yea	Nay	Nay	Yea	Anti	Nay	Nay
Stevens, T.	Pa.	NW	Nay	Yea	Nay	Nay	Yea	Anti	Nay	Nay
Strong	Pa.	ND	Yea	Yea	Yea	NV	Yea	Pro	Yea	Yea
Sweetser	Ohio	ND	Nay	Yea	Nay	NV	NV	Anti	Nay	Nay
Taylor	Ohio	NW	Yea	Yea	Nay	Yea	Yea	Anti	Yea	Yea
Thomas	Tenn.	SD	Yea	Nay	NV	Yea	Nay	Pro	Nay	Yea
Thompson, Jacob	Miss.	SD	Nay	Nay	Yea	Yea	Nay	Pro	Nay	Nay
Thompson, James	Pa.	ND	Yea	Yea	Yea	Yea	Yea	Pro	Yea	Yea
Thompson, John B.	Ky.	SW	Yea	Yea	Yea	Yea	NV	Pro	Yea	Yea
Thurman	N.Y.	NW	Yea	Yea	Yea	Nay	Yea	Pro	Yea	Yea
Toombs	Ga.	SW	Yea	Nay	Yea	Yea	NV	Pro	Yea	Yea
Tuck	N.H.	NFS	Nay	Yea	Nay	Nay	Yea	Anti	Nay	Nay
Underhill	N.Y.	NW	Yea	Yea	NV	Nay	Yea	Anti	Nay	Yea
Van Dyke	N.J.	NW	Nay	Yea	Nay	NV	NV	Anti	Nay	Nay
Venable	N.C.	SD	Nay	Nay	NV	Yea	Nay	Anti	Nay	Nay
Vinton	Ohio	NW	Nay	Yea	Nay	Nay	Yea	Anti	Nay	Nay
Walden	N.Y.	ND	Yea	Yea	Yea	Yea	Yea	Pro	Yea	Yea
Waldo	Conn.	ND	Nay	Yea	Nay	Nay	Yea	Anti	Nay	Nay
Wallace	S.C.	SD	Nay	Nay	Nay	Yea	Nay	Anti	Nay	Nay
Watkins	Tenn.	SW	Yea	Yea	Yea	Yea	Nay	Pro	Yea	Yea
Wellborn	Ga.	SD	Yea	Nay	Yea	Yea	NV	Pro	Yea	Yea
Wentworth	Ill.	ND	Nay	Yea	Nay	Nay	Yea	Pro	Nay	Nay
White	N.Y.	NW	Yea	Yea	NV	NV	Yea	Anti	Yea	Yea
Whittlesey	Ohio	ND	Yea	Yea	NV	Nay	Yea	Pro	Nay	Yea
Wildrick	N.J.	ND	Yea	Yea	Yea	Yea	Yea	Pro	Yea	Yea
Williams	Tenn.	SW	Yea	Yea	Yea	Yea	Nay	Pro	Yea	Yea
Wilson	N.H.	NW	Yea	Yea	Yea			Pro	Yea	Yea
Wood	Ohio	ND	NV	NV	NV	Nay	Yea	NV	NV	NV
Woodward	S.C.	SD	Nay	Nay	Nay	Yea	Nay	Anti	Nay	Nay
Wright	Cal.	ND				Nay	NV			
Young	Ill.	ND	Yea	Yea	Yea	Yea	Yea	Pro	Yea	Yea
TOTALS Yea (Pro)			108	150	97	109	124	104	99	108
Nay (Anti)			97	56	85	76	59	103	107	98
NV			16	15	39	36	39	14	15	15

ND—northern Democrat; NFS—northern Free Soiler; NNA—northern Native American; NV—not voting; NW—northern Whig; SD—southern Democrat; SW—southern Whig. On the vote to table of September 4 those in favor of the Compromise are indicated by Pro; those opposed, by Anti. In this instance the compromisers voted nay, against tabling, while the opposition voted yea, for tabling. Gilbert and Wright were sworn in September 11. Wilson resigned September 9.

APPENDIX D

THE COMPROMISE OF 1850: FIVE LAWS[1]

An Act proposing to the State of Texas the Establishment of her Northern and Western Boundaries, the Relinquishment by the said State of all Territory claimed by her exterior to said Boundaries, and of all her Claims upon the United States, and to establish a territorial Government for New Mexico.

Be it enacted by the Senate and House of Representatives of the United States of America in Congress assembled, That the following propositions shall be, and the same hereby are, offered to the State of Texas, which, when agreed to by the said State, in an act passed by the general assembly, shall be binding and obligatory upon the United States, and upon the said State of Texas: *Provided,* The said agreement by the said general assembly shall be given on or before the first day of December, eighteen hundred and fifty:

FIRST. The State of Texas will agree that her boundary on the north shall commence at the point at which the meridian of one hundred degrees west from Greenwich is intersected by the parallel of thirty-six degrees thirty minutes north latitude, and shall run from said point due west to the meridian of one hundred and three degrees west from Greenwich; thence her boundary shall run due south to the thirty-second degree of north latitude; thence on the said parallel of thirty-two degrees of north latitude to the Rio Bravo del Norte [Rio Grande], and thence with the channel of said river to the Gulf of Mexico.

SECOND. The State of Texas cedes to the United States all her claim to territory exterior to the limits and boundaries which she agrees to establish by the first article of this agreement.

THIRD. The State of Texas relinquishes all claim upon the United States for liability of the debts of Texas, and for compensation or indemnity for the surrender to the United States of her ships, forts, arsenals, custom-houses, custom-house revenue, arms and munitions of war, and public buildings with their sites, which became the property of the United States at the time of the annexation.

FOURTH. The United States, in consideration of said establishment of boundaries, cession of claim to territory, and relinquishment of claims, will pay to the State of Texas the sum of ten millions of dollars in a stock bearing five per cent. interest, and redeemable at the end of fourteen years, the interest payable half-yearly at the treasury of the United States.

FIFTH. Immediately after the President of the United States shall have been furnished with an authentic copy of the act of the general assembly of Texas accepting these propositions, he shall cause the stock to be issued in favor of the State of Texas, as provided for in the fourth article of this agreement: *Provided, also,* That no more than five millions of said stock shall be issued until the creditors of the State holding bonds and other certificates of stock of Texas for which duties on imports were specially pledged, shall first file at the treasury of the United States releases of all claim against the United States for or on account of said bonds or certificates in such form as shall be prescribed by the Secretary of the Treasury and approved by the President of the United States: *Provided,* That nothing herein contained shall be construed to impair or qualify any thing contained in the third article of the second section of the "joint resolution for annexing Texas to the United States," approved March first, eighteen hundred and forty-five, either as regards the number of States that may hereafter be formed out of Texas, or otherwise.

SEC. 2. *And be it further enacted,* That all that portion of the Territory of the United States bounded as follows: Beginning at a point in the Colorado River where the boundary line with the republic of Mexico crosses the same; thence eastwardly with the said boundary line to the Rio Grande; thence following the main channel of said river to the parallel of the thirty-second degree of north latitude; thence east with said degree to its intersection with the one hundred and third degree of longitude west of Greenwich; thence north with said degree of longitude to the parallel of thirty-eighth degree of north latitude; thence west with said parallel to the summit of the Sierra Madre; thence south with the crest of said mountains to the thirty-seventh parallel of north latitude; thence west with said parallel to its

---

[1] *The Public Statutes at Large and Treaties of the United States of America* (76 vols., Boston, 1845-1963), IX, 446-58, 462-65, 467-68. Nonessentials have been excised from the first four laws.

intersection with the boundary line of the State of California; thence with said boundary line to the place of beginning—be, and the said is hereby, erected into a temporary government, by the name of the Territory of New Mexico: *Provided,* . . . That, when admitted as a State, the said Territory, or any portion of the same, shall be received into the Union, with or without slavery, as their constitution may prescribe at the time of their admission. . . .

Sec. 7. *And be it further enacted,* That the legislative power of the Territory shall extend to all rightful subjects of legislation, consistent with the Constitution of the United States and the provisions of this act; but . . . all the laws passed by the legislative assembly and governor shall be submitted to the Congress of the United States, and, if disapproved, shall be null and of no effect. . . .

Sec. 10. *And be it further enacted,* That the judicial power of said Territory shall be vested in a Supreme Court, District Courts, Probate Courts, and in justices of the peace. . . . Writs of error and appeals from the final decisions of said Supreme Court shall be allowed, and may be taken to the Supreme Court of the United States. . . .

Sec. 17. *And be it further enacted,* That the Constitution, and all laws of the United States which are not locally inapplicable, shall have the same force and effect within the said Territory of New Mexico as elsewhere within the United States.

Sec. 18. *And be it further enacted,* That the provisions of this act be, and they are hereby, suspended until the boundary between the United States and the State of Texas shall be adjusted; and when such adjustment shall have been effected, the President of the United States shall issue his proclamation, declaring this act to be in full force and operation. . . .

An Act for the Admission of the State of California into the Union.

Whereas the people of California have presented a constitution and asked admission into the Union, which constitution was submitted to Congress by the President of the United States, by message dated February thirteenth, eighteen hundred and fifty, and which, on due examination, is found to be republican in its form of government:

Be it enacted by the Senate and House of Representatives of the United States of America in Congress assembled, That the

State of California shall be one, and is hereby declared to be one, of the United States of America, and admitted into the Union on an equal footing with the original States in all respects whatever. . . .

An Act to Establish a Territorial Government for Utah.

Be it enacted by the Senate and House of Representatives of the United States of America in Congress assembled, That all that part of the territory of the United States included within the following limits, to wit: bounded on the west by the State of California, on the north by the Territory of Oregon, and on the east by the summit of the Rocky Mountains, and on the south by the thirty-seventh parallel of north latitude, be, and the same is hereby, created into a temporary government, by the name of the Territory of Utah; and, when admitted as a State, the said Territory, or any portion of the same, shall be received into the Union, with or without slavery, as their constitution may prescribe at the time of their admission. . . .

Sec. 6. *And be it further enacted,* That the legislative power of said Territory shall extend to all rightful subjects of legislation, consistent with the Constitution of the United States and the provisions of this act; but . . . all the laws passed by the legislative assembly and governor shall be submitted to the Congress of the United States, and, if disapproved, shall be null and of no effect. . . .

Sec. 9. *And be it further enacted,* That the judicial power of said Territory shall be vested in a Supreme Court, District Courts, Probate Courts, and in justices of the peace. . . . Writs of error, and appeals from the final decisions of said Supreme Court, shall be allowed, and may be taken to the Supreme Court of the United States. . . .

Sec. 17. *And be it further enacted,* That the Constitution and laws of the United States are hereby extended over and declared to be in force in said Territory of Utah, so far as the same, or any provision thereof, may be applicable. . . .

An Act to amend, and supplementary to, the Act entitled "An Act respecting Fugitives from Justice, and Persons escaping from the Service of their Masters," approved February twelfth, one thousand seven hundred and ninety-three.

Be it enacted by the Senate and House of Representatives of the United States of America in Congress assembled, That the

persons who have been, or may hereafter be, appointed commissioners, in virtue of any act of Congress, by the Circuit
Courts of the United States, and who, in consequence of such
appointment, are authorized to exercise the powers that any
justice of the peace, or other magistrate of any of the United
States, may exercise in respect to offenders for any crime or
offence against the United States, by arresting, imprisoning, or
bailing the same under and by virtue of the thirty-third section
of the act of the twenty-fourth of September seventeen hundred
and eighty-nine, entitled "An Act to establish the judicial courts
of the United States," shall be, and are hereby, authorized and
required to exercise and discharge all the powers and duties conferred by this act.

Sec. 2. *And be it further enacted,* That the Superior Court of
each organized Territory of the United States shall have the
same power to appoint commissioners . . . who . . . shall moreover exercise and discharge all the powers and duties conferred
by this act.

Sec. 3. *And be it further enacted,* That the Circuit Courts of
the United States, and the Superior Courts of each organized
Territory of the United States, shall from time to time enlarge
the number of commissioners, with a view to afford reasonable
facilities to reclaim fugitives from labor, and to the prompt
discharge of the duties imposed by this act.

Sec. 4. *And be it further enacted,* That the commissioners
above named shall have concurrent jurisdiction with . . . judges
. . . and shall grant certificates to such claimants, upon satisfactory proof being made, with authority to take and remove
such fugitives from service or labor, under the restrictions herein
contained, to the State or Territory from which such persons may
have escaped or fled.

Sec. 5. *And be it further enacted,* That it shall be the duty
of all marshals and deputy marshals to obey and execute all
warrants and precepts issued under the provisions of this act,
when to them directed; and should any marshal or deputy
marshal refuse to receive such warrant, or other process, when
tendered, or to use all proper means diligently to execute the
same, he shall, on conviction thereof, be fined in the sum of one
thousand dollars, to the use of such claimant, on the motion of
such claimant, by the Circuit or District Court for the district
of such marshal; and after arrest of such fugitive, by such
marshal or his deputy, or whilst at any time in his custody under
the provisions of this act, should such fugitive escape, whether
with or without the assent of such marshal or his deputy, such
marshal shall be liable, on his official bond, to be prosecuted

for the benefit of such claimant, for the full value of the service
or labor of said fugitive in the State, Territory, or District
whence he escaped; and the better to enable the said commissioners, when thus appointed, to execute their duties faithfully
and efficiently, in conformity with the requirements of the Constitution of the United States and of this act, they are hereby
authorized and empowered, within their counties respectively, to
appoint, in writing under their hands, any one or more suitable
persons . . . to execute all such warrants and other process as
may be issued by them in the lawful performance of their
respective duties; with authority to such commissioners, or the
persons to be appointed by them, to execute process as aforesaid,
to summon and call to their aid the bystanders, or *posse
comitatus* of the proper county, when necessary to ensure a
faithful observance of the clause of the Constitution referred to,
in conformity with the provisions of this act; and all good citizens
are hereby commanded to aid and assist in the prompt and
efficient execution of this law, whenever their services may be
required, as aforesaid, for that purpose; and said warrants shall
run, and be executed by said officers, any where in the State
within which they are issued.

SEC. 6. *And be it further enacted,* That when a person held
to service or labor in any State or Territory of the United States,
has heretofore or shall hereafter escape into another State or
Territory of the United States, the person or persons to whom
such service or labor may be due, or his, her, or their agent or
attorney, duly authorized, by power of attorney, in writing,
acknowledged and certified under the seal of some legal officer
or court of the State or Territory in which the same may be
executed, may pursue and reclaim such fugitive person, either
by procuring a warrant from some one of the courts, judges, or
commissioners aforesaid, of the proper circuit, district or county,
for the apprehension of such fugitive from service or labor, or
by seizing and arresting such fugitive, where the same can be
done without process, and by taking, or causing such person
to be taken, forthwith before such court, judge, or commissioner,
whose duty it shall be to hear and determine the case of such
claimant in a summary manner; and upon satisfactory proof
being made . . . , to use such reasonable force and restraint as
may be necessary, under the circumstances of the case, to take
and remove such fugitive person back to the State or Territory
whence he or she may have escaped as aforesaid. In no trial
or hearing under this act shall the testimony of such alleged
fugitive be admitted in evidence. . . .

SEC. 7. *And be it further enacted,* That any person who shall knowingly and willingly obstruct, hinder, or prevent such claimant, his agent or attorney, or any person or persons lawfully assisting him, her, or them, from arresting such a fugitive from service or labor, either with or without process as aforesaid, or shall rescue, or attempt to rescue, such fugitive from service or labor, from the custody of such claimant, his or her agent or attorney, or other person or persons lawfully assisting as aforesaid, when so arrested, pursuant to the authority herein given and declared; or shall aid, abet, or assist such person . . . to escape from such claimant, his agent or attorney, or other person or persons legally authorized as aforesaid; or shall harbor or conceal such fugitive, so as to prevent the discovery and arrest of such person, after notice or knowledge of the fact that such person was a fugitive from service or labor as aforesaid, shall, for either of said offences, be subject to a fine not exceeding one thousand dollars, and imprisonment not exceeding six months . . . ; and shall moreover forfeit and pay, by way of civil damages to the party injured by such illegal conduct, the sum of one thousand dollars, for each fugitive so lost as aforesaid, to be recovered by action of debt. . . .

SEC. 8. *And be it further enacted,* That the marshals, their deputies, and the clerks of the said District and Territorial Courts, shall be paid, for their services, the like fees as may be allowed to them for similar services in other cases; and where such services are rendered exclusively in the arrest, custody, and delivery of the fugitive to the claimant, his or her agent or attorney, or where such supposed fugitive may be discharged out of custody for the want of sufficient proof as aforesaid, then such fees are to be paid in the whole by such claimant, his agent or attorney; and in all cases where the proceedings are before a commissioner, he shall be entitled to a fee of ten dollars . . . upon the delivery of the said certificate to the claimant, his or her agent or attorney; or a fee of five dollars in cases where the proof shall not, in the opinion of such commissioner, warrant such certificate and delivery. . . . The person or persons authorized to execute the process . . . shall also be entitled to a fee of five dollars each for each person he or they may arrest and take before any such commissioner. . . .

SEC. 9. *And be it further enacted,* That, upon affidavit made by the claimant of such fugitive, his agent or attorney, after such certificate has been issued, that he has reason to apprehend that such fugitive will be rescued by force from his or their possession before he can be taken beyond the limits of the State in which the arrest is made, it shall be the duty of the officer making the arrest to retain such fugitive in his custody, and to remove him to the State whence he fled, and there to deliver him to said claimant, his agent, or attorney. And to this end, the officer aforesaid is hereby authorized and required to employ so many persons as he may deem necessary to overcome such force, and to retain them in his service so long as circumstances may require. . . .

An Act to suppress the Slave Trade in the District of Columbia.

Be it enacted by the Senate and House of Representatives of the United States of America in Congress assembled, That from and after the first day of January, eighteen hundred and fifty-one, it shall not be lawful to bring into the District of Columbia any slave whatever, for the purpose of being sold, or for the purpose of being placed in depot, to be subsequently transferred to any other State or place to be sold as merchandize. And if any slave shall be brought into the said District by its owner, or by the authority or consent of its owner, contrary to the provisions of this act, such slave shall thereupon become liberated and free.

SEC. 2. *And be it further enacted,* That it shall and may be lawful for each of the corporations of the cities of Washington and Georgetown, from time to time, and as often as may be necessary, to abate, break up, and abolish any depot or place of confinement of slaves brought into the said District as merchandize, contrary to the provisions of this act, by such appropriate means as may appear to either of the said corporations expedient and proper. And the same power is hereby vested in the Levy Court of Washington county, if any attempt shall be made, within its jurisdictional limits, to establish a depot or place of confinement for slaves brought into the said District as merchandize for sale contrary to this act.

BIBLIOGRAPHICAL ESSAY

READERS DEEPLY interested in American political developments of the 1840s and 1850s cannot afford to ignore the many books composed by historical writers of past generations. Among the older works—each containing its share of defects, but worthy of consideration—are Hermann E. von Holst, *The Constitutional and Political History of the United States* (7 vols. and index, Chicago, 1876-1892); James Schouler, *History of the United States under the Constitution* (6 vols., New York, 1880-1899); James Ford Rhodes, *History of the United States from the Compromise of 1850* (7 vols., New York, 1893-1906); John Bach McMaster, *A History of the People of the United States from the Revolution to the Civil War* (8 vols., New York, 1883-1913); and Edward Channing, *A History of the United States* (6 vols., New York, 1905-1925).

More recent and generally more satisfactory are Allan Nevins, *Ordeal of the Union* (2 vols., New York, 1947) and its sequel, *The Emergence of Lincoln* (2 vols., New York, 1950); George Fort Milton, *The Eve of Conflict: Stephen A. Douglas and the Needless War* (Boston, 1934); Avery O. Craven, *The Growth of Southern Nationalism, 1848-1861* (Baton Rouge, La., 1953); and three books by Roy F. Nichols—*The Democratic Machine, 1850-1854* (New York, 1923), *Franklin Pierce: Young Hickory of the Granite Hills* (Philadelphia, 1958), and *The Disruption of American Democracy* (New York, 1948). Although the scope of the

Nichols volumes is almost wholly post-1850, they are helpful in understanding the crisis of that year.

Other scholarly books on the period, recreating parts of the atmosphere of the times, are Howard R. Floan, *The South in Northern Eyes, 1831 to 1861* (Austin, Texas, 1958); Larry Gara, *The Liberty Line: The Legend of the Underground Railroad* (Lexington, Ky., 1961); Louis Filler, *The Crusade against Slavery, 1830-1860* (New York, 1960); Russel B. Nye, *Fettered Freedom: Civil Liberties and the Slavery Controversy* (East Lansing, Mich., 1949); Philip S. Foner, *Business and Slavery: The New York Merchants and the Irrepressible Conflict* (Chapel Hill, N.C., 1941); and Alice Felt Tyler, *Freedom's Ferment: Phases of American Social History to 1860* (Minneapolis, 1944). Some of these have rarely been cited, and one has not been cited at all, but every study in the group has proven as useful in research as most of the exclusively political ones.

Valuable leads, especially in connection with illuminating source materials, have come from such old and newer volumes as Theodore C. Smith, *The Liberty and Free Soil Parties in the Northwest* (Cambridge, Mass., 1897); Milo M. Quaife, *The Doctrine of Non-Intervention with Slavery in the Territories* (Chicago, 1910); Arthur C. Cole, *The Whig Party in the South* (Washington, 1913) and *The Irrepressible Conflict, 1850-1865* (New York, 1934); George R. Poage, *Henry Clay and the Whig Party* (Chapel Hill, N.C., 1936); Avery Craven, *The Coming of the Civil War* (Chicago, 1957); and James C. Malin, *The Nebraska Question, 1852-1854* (Lawrence, Kans., 1953). Both synthesis and interpretation are present in Avery O. Craven, *Civil War in the Making, 1815-1860* (Baton Rouge, La., 1959); Glyndon G. Van Deusen, *The Jacksonian Era, 1828-1848* (New York, 1959); and Roy F. Nichols, *The Stakes of Power, 1845-1877* (New York, 1961). Richard H. Shryock, *Georgia and the Union in 1850* (Durham, N.C., 1926); Floyd B. Streeter, *Political Parties in Michigan, 1837-1860* (Lansing, Mich., 1918); and Henry T. Shanks, *The Seces-*

sion Movement in Virginia, 1847-1861 (Richmond, 1934)
have been the most rewarding analyses of pertinent limited
situations in individual states.

Much of the spadework resulting in the separation of
1850 fact from fancy has been performed by biographers,
particularly those doing their research during the second
and third quarters of the twentieth century. Among "standard" interpretations of major actors in the drama are
William N. Chambers, *Old Bullion Benton: Senator from
the New West* (Boston, 1956); Charles M. Wiltse, *John C.
Calhoun: Sectionalist, 1840-1850* (Indianapolis, 1951); Glyndon G. Van Deusen, *The Life of Henry Clay* (Boston,
1937); Gerald M. Capers, *Stephen A. Douglas: Defender of
the Union* (Boston, 1959); Robert J. Rayback, *Millard Fillmore: Biography of a President* (Buffalo, 1959); Holman
Hamilton, *Zachary Taylor: Soldier in the White House*
(Indianapolis, 1951); and Claude M. Fuess, *Daniel Webster*
(2 vols., Boston, 1930).

Supplementing these are books about less dominant but
important figures in the 1850 Senate and House—William
E. Parrish, *David Rice Atchison of Missouri: Border Politician* (Columbia, Mo., 1961); Joseph H. Parks, *John Bell
of Tennessee* (Baton Rouge, La., 1950); Frank B. Woodford,
Lewis Cass: The Last Jeffersonian (New Brunswick, N.J.,
1950); Hudson Strode, *Jefferson Davis: American Patriot,
1808-1861* (New York, 1955); Llerena Friend, *Sam Houston:
The Great Designer* (Austin, Texas, 1954); Richard N. Cur-
rent, *Old Thad Stevens: A Story of Ambition* (Madison,
Wis., 1942); and Don E. Fehrenbacher, *Chicago Giant: A
Biography of "Long John" Wentworth* (Madison, Wis.,
1957). There is also a wealth of detail in Glyndon G. Van
Deusen, *Horace Greeley: Nineteenth Century Crusader*
(Philadelphia, 1953) and *Thurlow Weed: Wizard of the
Lobby* (Boston, 1947); in Albert J. Beveridge, *Abraham
Lincoln, 1809-1858* (Boston, 1928); in Albert D. Kirwan, *John
J. Crittenden: The Struggle for the Union* (Lexington, Ky.,
1962); in Philip S. Klein, *President James Buchanan: A*

Biography (University Park, Pa., 1962); and in David Donald, *Charles Sumner and the Coming of the Civil War* (New York, 1960).

Articles having a direct bearing on the subject include Robert P. Brooks, "Howell Cobb and the Crisis of 1850," *Mississippi Valley Historical Review,* IV (Dec. 1917), 279-98; Herbert D. Foster, "Webster's Seventh of March Speech and the Secession Movement, 1850," *American Historical Review,* XXVII (Jan. 1922), 245-70; Holman Hamilton, "Democratic Senate Leadership and the Compromise of 1850," *Mississippi Valley Historical Review,* XLI (Dec. 1954), 403-418, and "'The Cave of the Winds' and the Compromise of 1850," *Journal of Southern History,* XXIII (Aug. 1957), 331-53; George D. Harmon, "Douglas and the Compromise of 1850," *Journal of the Illinois State Historical Society,* XXI (Jan. 1929), 453-99; Frank H. Hodder, "Stephen A. Douglas," *The Chautauquan,* XXIX (Aug. 1899), 432-37, "The Authorship of the Compromise of 1850," *Mississippi Valley Historical Review,* XXII (March 1936), 525-36; Robert R. Russel, "What Was the Compromise of 1850?" *Journal of Southern History,* XXII (Aug. 1956), 292-309; and St. George L. Sioussat, "Tennessee, the Compromise of 1850, and the Nashville Convention," *Mississippi Valley Historical Review,* II (Dec. 1915), 313-47. The Hodder and Russel contributions are particularly significant.

No list of books and periodical literature dealing with western and southwestern aspects of the 1850 crisis would be complete without Cardinal Goodwin, *The Establishment of State Government in California, 1846-1850* (New York, 1914) or Dale L. Morgan, "The State of Deseret," *Utah Historical Quarterly,* VIII (April-July-October 1940), 65-251. William C. Binkley broke ground with "The Question of Texan Jurisdiction in New Mexico under the United States, 1848-1850," *Southwestern Historical Quarterly,* XXIV (July 1920), 1-38. His treatment is still basic. It has been complemented by Loomis M. Ganaway, *New Mexico and the Sectional Controversy, 1846-1861* (Albuquerque, N.M.,

1944); by Kenneth F. Neighbours, "The Taylor-Neighbors
Struggle over the Upper Rio Grande Region of Texas in
1850," *Southwestern Historical Quarterly*, LXI (April 1958),
431-63; and by William A. Keleher, *Turmoil in New Mexico,
1846-1868* (Santa Fe, N.M., 1952). Cleo Hearon, "Mississippi and the Compromise of 1850," *Mississippi Historical
Society Publications*, XIV, 7-229, does justice to that topic
and covers some of the Nashville preliminaries not in Dallas
T. Herndon, "The Nashville Convention of 1850," *Alabama
Historical Society Transactions*, V, 227-37. Recommended
for insights and conclusions are Allen Johnson, "The Constitutionality of the Fugitive Slave Acts," *Yale Law Journal*,
XXXI (Dec. 1921), 161-82; Harold Schwartz, "Fugitive
Slave Days in Boston," *New England Quarterly*, XXVII
(June 1954), 191-212; and Charles H. Foster, *The Rungless
Ladder: Harriet Beecher Stowe and New England Puritan-
ism* (Durham, N.C., 1954).

Newspapers of 1850 are storehouses bulging with information. In Washington, the Democratic *Union* and the
Whig *National Intelligencer* were consistently procompromise, while the *Republic* was the "organ" of the Taylor
Administration and the *National Era* of the abolitionists.
They have been extremely useful, as have several Boston
dailies, the New York *Express*, the Philadelphia *Pennsylvanian*, the Cleveland *Plain Dealer*, the Springfield *Illinois
State Journal*, the Lexington (Ky.) *Observer & Reporter*,
the Richmond *Enquirer* and *Whig*, the Nashville *Republican
Banner*, the Charleston *Courier*, and the New Orleans *Picayune*. As satisfactory a journalistic coverage as any in the
country was that provided for residents of New York City in
James Gordon Bennett's *Herald*, Horace Greeley's *Tribune*,
and William Cullen Bryant's *Evening Post*. Contrasting editorial viewpoints were represented in the Charleston *Mercury* and the Albany *Evening Journal*. Accurate "inside"
information on forthcoming events was regularly offered
by the Washington correspondent, Francis J. Grund, in the
Philadelphia *Public Ledger* and the Baltimore *Sun*. Oc-

casionally, an unusual account in such an out-of-the-way
publication as the Liberty (Mo.) *Gazette* has shed brighter
light on congressional intricacies than entire files of better
known papers.

Valuable contemporary confidential reports and opinions
may be found in the James Buchanan MSS. at the Historical
Society of Pennsylvania, Philadelphia; in Howell Cobb's
letters at the University of Georgia, Athens; in the papers
and letterbooks of Edward Everett and Robert C. Winthrop
at the Massachusetts Historical Society, Boston; in Philip
Hone's diary at the New-York Historical Society, New
York City; in the correspondence of John P. Kennedy at
the Peabody Institute, Baltimore; in the David Outlaw
letters, which have the immediacy of a diary, in the Southern Historical Collection, University of North Carolina,
Chapel Hill; and in the voluminous William H. Seward
Papers and Thurlow Weed Papers at the University of
Rochester. Likewise, important sources are the Salmon P.
Chase, Henry Clay, Thomas J. Clay, John J. Crittenden,
James H. Hammond, George A. McCall, and Martin Van
Buren Papers at the Library of Congress. And sometimes
a single letter—one in Ann Arbor, one in Philadelphia, one
in the hands of an Illinois physician—has revealed much
about main currents of history.

Convenient but not wholly dependable from standpoints
of comprehensiveness and accuracy are published versions
of 1850 leaders' letters, speeches, and state papers. The
most vital of these are in J. Franklin Jameson (ed.), *Correspondence of John C. Calhoun*, American Historical Association *Annual Report . . . for the Year 1899* (Washington, 1900); Calvin Colton (ed.), *The Works of Henry Clay*
(10 vols., New York, 1904); Ulrich B. Phillips (ed.), *The
Correspondence of Robert Toombs, Alexander H. Stephens,
and Howell Cobb*, American Historical Association *Annual
Report . . . for the Year 1911* (Washington, 1913); *The
Writings and Speeches of Daniel Webster* (18 vols., Boston,
1903); and James D. Richardson (ed.), *A Compilation of*

the Messages and Papers of the Presidents, 1789-1897 (10 vols., Washington, 1901). The federal laws, which constituted the Compromise of 1850, are available in Volume IX of *The Public Statutes at Large and Treaties of the United States of America* (76 vols., Boston, 1845-1963). Relevant state legislative opinion may be sampled in Herman V. Ames (ed.), *State Documents on Federal Relations: The States and the United States* (Philadelphia, 1900-1906). The debates on Capitol Hill may be followed most closely in the *Congressional Globe* and its *Appendix,* which are the virtual bibles of persons investigating the politics of the period. These records, however, are not infallible. Variants of *Globe* reports can be found in the Washington newspapers, and votes must be checked against those given in the official House and Senate *Journals.*

Research on Texas bonds and bondholders illustrates, in miniature, the totality of sources consulted. In the National Archives, Washington, are ledgers of the United States Treasury Department; the claims file of the General Accounting Office, and an untitled Treasury workbook—all in Record Groups 217, 39, and 56 respectively. In the Texas State Archives, Austin, is the "Register of Public Debts on Claims, 1835-1842." At the University of Texas are the Thomas J. Rusk Papers; in the Library of Congress, the William W. Corcoran Papers and the Riggs Family Papers; in the Essex Institute at Salem, Massachusetts, the George Peabody Papers; in the Southern Historical Collection, University of North Carolina, the James Hamilton Papers. Supplementing the manuscripts are the files of the Austin *Texas State Gazette,* printed House and Senate documents, and an unpublished Radcliffe College doctoral dissertation by Muriel E. Hidy—"George Peabody: Merchant and Financier, 1829-1854." Gaps have been filled by three books: Edmund T. Miller, *A Financial History of Texas* (Austin, Texas, 1916); William M. Gouge, *The Fiscal History of Texas* (Philadelphia, 1852); and Elgin Williams, *The Animating Pursuits of Speculation: Land Traffic in the An-*

nexation of Texas (New York, 1949), the last of these provocative but of uneven merit. Holman Hamilton, "Texas
Bonds and Northern Profits," *Mississippi Valley Historical
Review*, XLIII (March 1957), 579-94, represented part of
the investigator's findings. As the research proceeded, there
emerged a conclusion unanticipated at the outset—a picture
of the financier Corcoran as a far more influential political
figure than had previously been realized.

In conclusion, a word of gratitude is in order for the
quality of such reference works as the *Biographical Direc-
tory of the American Congress, 1774-1961* (Washington,
1961); Oscar Handlin *et al.*, *Harvard Guide to American
History* (Cambridge, 1954); and Allen Johnson *et al.* (eds.),
Dictionary of American Biography (22 vols. and index, New
York, 1928-1958). Almost as valuable in this study were
Howard K. Beale, "What Historians Have Said about the
Causes of the Civil War," Social Science Research Council
Bulletin 54 (New York, 1946), and Thomas J. Pressly,
Americans Interpret Their Civil War (Princeton, N.J., 1954).

INDEX

Margaret Jarman Hagood   *Mothers of the South: Portraiture of the White Tenant Farm Woman*   N816

John S. Haller and Robin M. Haller   *The Physician and Sexuality in Victorian America*   N845

Holman Hamilton   *Prologue to Conflict: The Crisis and Compromise of 1850*   N345

Pendleton Herring   *The Politics of Democracy*   N306

Robert V. Hine   *California's Utopian Colonies*   N678

Preston J. Hubbard   *Origins of the TVA: The Muscle Shoals Controversy, 1920–1932*   N467

George F. Kennan   *Realities of American Foreign Policy*   N320

Gabriel Kolko   *Railroads and Regulations, 1877–1916*   N531

Howard Roberts Lamar   *The Far Southwest, 1846–1912: A Territorial History*   N522

Peggy Lamson   *The Glorious Failure: Black Congressman Robert Brown Elliott and the Reconstruction in South Carolina*   N733

William L. Langer   *Our Vichy Gamble*   N379

William Letwin, Ed.   *A Documentary History of American Economic Policy Since 1789* (Rev. Ed.)   N442

Richard P. McCormick   *The Second American Party System: Party Formation in the Jacksonian Era*   N680

William S. McFeely   *Yankee Stepfather: General O. O. Howard and the Freedmen*   N537

Robert C. McMath, Jr.   *Populist Vanguard: A History of the Southern Farmers' Alliance*   N869

C. Peter Magrath   *Yazoo: The Case of Fletcher v. Peck*   N418

Donald R. Matthews   *U.S. Senators and Their World* (Rev. Ed.)   N679

Burl Noggle   *Teapot Dome*   N297

Douglass C. North   *The Economic Growth of the United States, 1790–1860*   N346

Arnold A. Offner   *American Appeasement: United States Foreign Policy and Germany, 1933–1938*   N801

Robert E. Quirk   *An Affair of Honor: Woodrow Wilson and the Occupation of Veracruz*   N390

Robert E. Quirk   *The Mexican Revolution, 1914–1915*   N507

Robert V. Remini   *Martin Van Buren and the Making of the Democratic Party*   N527

Bernard W. Sheehan   *Seeds of Extinction: Jeffersonian Philanthropy and the American Indian*   N715

James W. Silver   *Confederate Morale and Church Propaganda*   N422

Kathryn Kish Sklar   *Catharine Beecher: A Study in American Domesticity*   N812